THE ACTUALLY AUTISTIC GUIDE

THE ACTUALLY AUTISTIC GUIDE

A HELPFUL, HILARIOUS, AND DEFINITELY NOT DEFINITIVE HANDBOOK FOR LIVING LIFE ON THE SPECTRUM

Elora Dodd and C. R. R. Hillin

Hardie Grant
BOOKS

Contents

A NOTE FROM THE AUTHORS

Autism is not a personality type, or a clique, or a race of people. It is an unfathomably vast sea of diversity, featuring every demographic you can imagine. While we have attempted to make the content in this book useful to as many autistics as possible, we know that ultimately our perspectives aren't universal and that our experiences with autism aren't representative of everyone else's experiences nor our advice universally beneficial. We are both low-support-needs white assigned female at birth (AFAB) southerners raised Christian, and that shows in our writing. And we are not mental health professionals or educational professionals, though we have learned from those fields in our independent study of autism. We suggest that if this book piques your interest in autism advocacy, you should seek out additional materials by people different from us. There are free resources like podcasts and blogs, as well as paid resources like online workshops and other books. If you need help getting started, you can try internet search terms such as:

- 'Black autistic joy'
- 'Autistic parents of autistic children'
- 'Autistic mental health professional explains'
- 'Neurodiversity-affirming therapy for autistic kids discussed'
- 'Non-speaking autistic writers'
- 'Racial divides in autism'
- 'Hispanic autism representation in media'

- 'Inter-abled autism relationships'
- 'International responses to autism'
- 'Racialised voices speaking on neurodiversity'
- 'Religious approaches to autism'
- 'Late-diagnosed elderly autistic'

While we hope to start you on your path to understanding your autism, we make a better starting point than a destination. Happy travels!

Love,
Cat and Elora

Throughout this book, you will find questions that invite you to explore your own perspectives, hopes, and experiences surrounding autism. You may want to keep a journal and write your thoughts down as you explore them. You may also use these questions as conversation starters with a trusted friend or therapist. You may even use these questions as prompts for artistic expression! However you use our questions, remember that your thoughts matter. You do not have to agree with us. Express yourself!

PART ONE

Autism – What It Is and Isn't

I am Different, not Less.

- Temple Grandin

WHAT DOES EVERYONE GET WRONG ABOUT AUTISM?

Elora: I think a lot of people view autism as a glitch in the system, a problem, a mistake. Religious people might see it as a test from God. Parents might see it as a terrifying enemy. Schools might see it as a threat to the delicate balance of their organisation. People seem to see autism as something that disrupts their status quo. But we autistics spend a lot of time wondering if people should be so committed to the status quo in the first place.

Cat: Yes, exactly! Autistics spend so much time asking why the rules are the way they are, because we keep breaking them by mistake. And there's no logic to so many of them. Everyone's just so hive-minded and decided that's how it would go. And it's our fault somehow for not getting the memo.

Elora: I think that normies' use of social expectations is pretty cool. They're shortcuts for when you don't know how to handle a situation or how to behave. Normies are polytropic, meaning their brains are designed to focus on several different things at once. Just a guess here, but I think the unspoken social 'rules' normies have developed serve as shortcuts so they don't get too caught up in any one thing. It helps keep them from having to focus too much on any one issue when their brain is meant to expend its energy on a lot of different things at once.

Cat: It would really be a huge help to know all these annoying shortcuts.

Maybe make a Wiki or something. I think you're right; there are rituals and shorthand that they use, like their own language.

Elora: 😂 Yeah. Just because the shortcuts help them doesn't mean they help everyone.

How would you describe autism?

WHAT IS AUTISM?

Did you know humans have operating systems, and that there are different types? These operating systems are called neurotypes and reflect our different categories of brain wiring. They seem to be genetic, and it's unclear exactly how many there are. While autism is officially known as a disorder (autism spectrum disorder or ASD), it can be more accurately described as a neurotype.

The neurotypical neurotype is most common (hence the name), but the autistic neurotype – shared by about 3 per cent of the population[1] – is what we're going to discuss in this book. And while a neurotypical human and an autistic human may look alike, do many of the same things, and function similarly, at the core they are fundamentally different – kind of like how Mac and PC computers are different, or how Xbox and PlayStation are different. To someone who doesn't know much about computers or video games, these systems may seem identical, but the deeper you dive, the more differences you find. And those differences govern everything about the machines, from what programs they can run to what tasks they can complete.

We can't really talk about the autistic neurotype itself. That's up to the scientists. We can only talk about the downstream effects. But it's important to understand that our individual neurotype shapes everything about how we interact with the world. It impacts how we think, socialise, and process information.

For example, many autistic traits stem from oversensitivity to stimuli. A simple increase in sensitivity leads to a lot of processing, sensory, and communication issues. This sensitivity is not the only trait that comes out of the autistic neurotype, but it's a major part of the network of traits that make this neurotype unique.

One way to understand the complex web of traits that make up the autistic mind is to think of it as an ecosystem.

How would you describe a rainforest to a friend who has never heard of such a place?

You might describe its weather, or its wildlife, or its plants. But a rainforest is so much more than those individual elements. The geography, geology, plants, animals, weather, and seasons all work together to make a rainforest a rainforest. Neurotypes are mental ecosystems, combinations of many specific characteristics that make one beautiful system. And as with an ecosystem, each individual characteristic affects the whole. You cannot transform a rainforest into an arctic tundra by killing all its animals – you'll just make an unhealthy and unbalanced rainforest. In the same way, you cannot turn an autistic person into a neurotypical person by killing some of their autistic traits. You will just create a traumatised autistic person. This is what so much of the discussion of autism misses. Autism is not an amalgamation of negative traits. It is a vibrant, deeply interconnected way of being human. Yes, living with autism comes with challenges and dangers, like living in a rainforest does. You might even argue that a rainforest is one of the most challenging environments for a human to live in. But the solution is not to burn down the rainforest and build a gated community. Work with the rainforest, build infrastructure in the rainforest, learn the secrets of the rainforest, but never destroy it. Autism may have its challenges, but its challenges don't invalidate its beauty or value.

How do people know what their neurotype is? Besides identifying it for yourself through a lot of study and self-reflection, you can turn to a health professional for guidance.

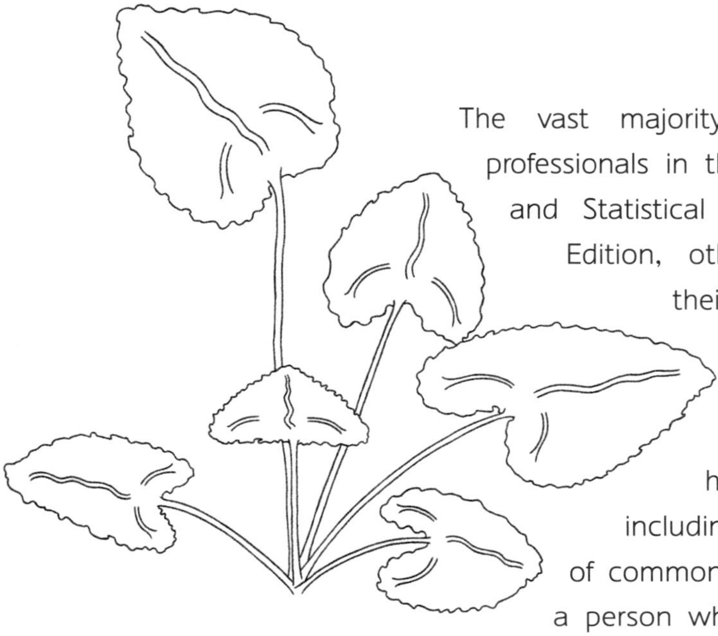

The vast majority of doctors and mental health professionals in the United States use The Diagnostic and Statistical Manual of Mental Disorders, Fifth Edition, otherwise known as the DSM-5, as their guide when helping someone understand how their brain works. The DSM-5 is a reference book that defines all kinds of mental health and brain-related conditions, including autism, according to various sets of common traits and experiences. For example, a person who struggles with changes in routine, experiences difficulties communicating with others, and exhibits 'restricted' or 'repetitive patterns of behavior, interest, or activities' might fit the definition of autism according to the DSM-5.

The three primary diagnostic criteria for autism laid out in the DSM-5 are the following:

1. Exhibiting poor social skills and/or difficulty in social interactions.
2. Stimming, needing predictability, hyperfocusing, or showing hypersensitivity to certain stimuli.
3. Showing these traits from an early age and eventually becoming impaired by them.

The DSM-5 also states that the traits attributed to autism must match with autism's diagnostic criteria better than the diagnostic criteria of an intellectual disability. Essentially it has to make more sense that the person has autism than that they have something else (some people do, however, have both).

You might think that these criteria are perfectly fine. But people – health professionals and others – often use confusing and ableist language that emphasises the negative aspects of autism while ignoring the positives. Remember that third criterion: struggling to the point of impairment.

If an autistic person's struggles aren't obvious, a lot of people simply don't know the autistic person is struggling at all.

A person who isn't outwardly struggling – perhaps because their routines are meeting their needs or because they have figured out how to fit into a group of people – might go undiagnosed because the person doing the evaluation looks at them and says, 'She's doing great!'

But autism isn't about struggling. It isn't a tumour or a disease. It's a neurotype. We autistics are disabled, but we wonder how much of that is because we are living in a world that wasn't built for us. We have to fit in with the dominant neurotype, oftentimes pretending our brains work differently than they really do, and that causes a lot of, well, struggle. Asking if autism would still be a disability if we lived in a world built for us is a bit like asking what the world would look like if most people were gay and straight people were the outliers, or what the world would look like if matriarchy replaced patriarchy. It is impossible to know. All we know for sure is that it would look radically different.

Regardless of how things would work out in an impossible-to-test thought experiment, we believe that autistics deserve to be seen and considered by our society as more than just a list of struggles, but as full people with a wealth of experience and depth to offer.

Autistics who are diagnosed as adults know that the DSM-5 casts a net with a lot of holes in it. They were autistic all along, so why wasn't their autism recognised during childhood? Children may go undiagnosed because they don't have any conspicuous impairments to their daily lives. Their grades are good, they don't have many meltdowns or tantrums, and anything abnormal is shrugged off as being tied to the standard difficulties of childhood. You can dismiss a lot of things with children as 'kids being kids' or a kid being 'weird', and if a kid is any good at masking, most people will never assume they are autistic. The DSM-5 criteria are also a bit rigid to apply to children. Is a six-year-old 'hyperfixating' on dogs, or are they a normal six-year-old who is passionate about their interests (as most six-year-olds are)? It is often impossible to tell.

There are many other reasons autistic children may not be diagnosed. Among them:

- They may grow up in a community that frowns on mental healthcare and sees autistic traits as 'being weird' or as committing 'sins' to be corrected. An autistic child might have their need to stim labelled 'temptation to be immature' and their burnout as 'laziness'.
- They may be born to undiagnosed autistic parents who struggle to see anything unusual about their child because they share the same behaviours. 'Abnormal' in one family is another family's 'normal'. (Fun fact, autism is highly genetic!)
- They may be part of an appearance-focused family that refuses to consider that their child is 'different' because they are embarrassed by disability. This family might demand that their child 'try harder' to fit in despite seemingly obvious difficulties the child is having.
- They may not have adults who know them well enough to notice their autistic traits. Perhaps the child is one of many siblings, poverty is forcing their parents to stay out of the house working multiple jobs, or they are growing up in the foster care system.
- They may be diagnosed with other conditions that explain away some of their autistic traits, so their parents and doctors miss that there's autism as well.
- Mental healthcare is often prohibitively expensive and has long waitlists, so some autistic kids don't have the option of receiving professional care.
- Or maybe the autistic child simply doesn't live in a community or a family where autism is well understood. You can't notice what you don't know exists.

On top of all this, autism looks different in every person. It's entirely possible that one autistic person can be diagnosed while another in the same family is not.

Elora: Many of these factors contributed to my experience. I was homeschooled, so I had a lot more flexibility in my behaviour (I could stim *a lot*) and was able to avoid many of the stressors that other young autistics had to face in over-stimulating schools full of hundreds of other children. I also grew up in a religious family and sometimes faced backlash when my autistic traits were interpreted as moral failings. My parents knew more about autism than most people (my father is a psychologist!), but they had only been exposed to the stereotypical presentation of autism. As a chatty extrovert who got good grades, I was misdiagnosed as having 'anxiety, depression, and panic disorders'. And while I *do* have those disorders, they're more of a by-product of years of undiagnosed autism. For all of these reasons and more, I wasn't diagnosed by any of the doctors and therapists who treated me for years. And even though my father is a mental health professional, he works in a different field from childhood disabilities. These things happen. Sometimes you slip through the cracks.

Cat: I wasn't diagnosed until I was twenty-six for the simple reason that I was doing 'well'. My grades were excellent, I got into a good university, and my potential was, apparently, limitless. Every time I failed a test it was seen as a fluke, or an instance of not trying hard enough, or a result of depression. I thought being 'normal' was a skill I had to learn, just like everything else I was learning in college, and I couldn't figure out why it was so hard for me. Nobody around me knew what autism looked like, let alone in a girl. When I finally figured it out, it made perfect sense, both to me and my family, but it took someone close to me being diagnosed before I made the connection. I technically 'slipped through the cracks' too, but I'm glad I did. I think I was better off being a 'gifted kid/crazy weirdo' than labelled as autistic under the

limited understanding of the people around me. I was already bored and unchallenged; if my teachers and family got it into their heads that I was deficient in some way, things would have only gotten worse.

As hard as it may be to believe, a lot of autistic kids may actually be better off not being diagnosed. School systems are often not adequately equipped to deal with the stigmas attached to autism. If a person manages to pass as neurotypical until their twenties, they may not have needed specialised care or attention the way another autistic person would have. In fact, an outsized amount of attention could have created more problems than it solved. They may have needed a little more patience and understanding, but it could be argued that this is true of all children.

A one-size-fits-all approach to treating autism is never going to work.

This said, we do not recommend hiding your child's autism diagnosis from them, nor are we suggesting that autistic children do not need additional support because they 'seem fine'. We are referring to the widespread bullying, stereotyping, and disrespect that come with being 'outed' as autistic.

Even under the official diagnostic criteria, there are a lot of holes that can come from human error and biases. Cat was taught about autism in nursing school, in a master's program, and when training to be a teacher, and each time she encountered the same narrow portrayal of what autism looks like. Many people are still convinced that girls can't be autistic, so girls with autism are often misdiagnosed with conditions like bipolar disorder, social anxiety, general anxiety, or major depression.[2] [3] Children of colour are also far less likely to be diagnosed,[4] which means the image of autism most people have in mind is of a white boy.[5]

Additionally, the experiences of autistic people don't always agree with the narrowest interpretations of the diagnostic criteria, especially as people learn more about autism. Autism is something that you think you understand from reading books, but many folks can't spot it even when it's staring them in the face. In our various educational experiences, few of the descriptions given came close to capturing the nuances and complexity of autism.

We have a long way to go in how we diagnose and study autism, and how we help people with it. Most people simply don't know enough about the brain, the science of which is constantly evolving. Even the most educated geneticist on the planet couldn't give you a complete picture of the role of genetics or specific genes in autism. There is a lot we *do* know though, and every licensed doctor *should* be able to tell you what does *not* cause autism, like vaccines, poor diet, or radioactive spiders – but unfortunately disinformation and bad science have misled many people, including professionals. Thankfully, though, we've come a long way from thinking of autistic children as demonic changelings, as they used to – so at least there are signs of progress!

If this multifaceted look at autism is already blowing your mind, buckle up. There's still a long way to go and we're just getting started.

WHAT ABOUT ADHD?

Attention Deficit Hyperactivity Disorder (ADHD) is classified in the DSM-5 as a separate disorder from autism. These disorders seem to be connected in some way, but science has yet to determine how or to what extent, which makes discussing both disorders difficult. They aren't the same, but they have a lot in common, and plenty of people (Cat included) have both. This is not a book on the overlap between autism and ADHD or their differences; however, it may be a useful resource for people with ADHD. So to any ADHD-er reading this book, we just want to say, welcome. We're glad you're here.

TERMS TO KNOW

Able-bodied: Not disabled. We know this can sound a bit lacking as a term, because many disabilities, including autism, are psychological. You can be disabled and still have an 'able body'. At the moment, though, this is the most common term for 'non-disabled', so we still use it.

Ableism: The discrimination of or prejudice against disabled people in favour of able-bodied people. An example is building an office that can only be accessed by stairs, with no wheelchair ramp nearby.

Allistic: Not autistic.

Autistic: An adjective used to signify 'having autism' or a noun used in reference to a person who has it.

Crazy, insane, etc.: As people with mental disorders, we use these words not to describe the mentally ill but as slang to describe a thing or behaviour that is extreme or strange with no logical explanation, like eating tomato sauce on pasta.

***Diagnostic and Statistical Manual of Mental Disorders, Fifth Edition* (DSM-5):** A book of mental disorders created and distributed by the American Psychiatric Association, which is considered the highest authority in diagnostic criteria. You can think of the DSM as the dictionary of mental disorders. It is updated every fifteen years or so. The fifth version came out in 2013.

Discrimination: The unjust or prejudicial treatment of different categories of people based on a particular trait, such as sex, race, or disability.

Eugenics: The ideology supporting, and the pursuit of, the perceived 'improvement' of the human race through controlled breeding. Throughout history it has been enacted through extreme measures like genocide (to wipe out an entire race) and subtler measures like 'Better Baby' contests (to inspire white couples to have more children).

While most people may not use the word 'eugenics', the ideology is still alive today, and disabled people face it often. We use the term to reference any belief that people with disabilities are inferior and should be removed from the population by preventing our births, accelerating our deaths, neglecting our care, and demanding 'cures' regardless of whether we need them or not.[6]

Neurodivergent: Having a different neurotype than the average person or having mental illnesses, disorders, or conditions that affect the brain; the opposite of neurotypical. In essence, someone is neurodivergent if their brain does not follow the pattern expected by society, through inborn or developed differences.

Neurotype: A particular pattern of processing information in the brain; the brain's preset. Some neurodivergent neurotypes include people with autism, ADHD, Tourette's, and dyslexia. There is no official list of neurotypes, nor a hierarchy of which neurotypes are 'better' than others. All neurotypes are equally beautiful, and everyone, regardless of neurotype, deserves respect.

Neurotypical: Someone who has the average neurotype; the opposite of neurodivergent.

Normies: Slang term by which we mean people whose brains function 'typically', that is, differently from autistic brains. We use 'normie' a lot in this book because the word 'neurotypical' can be a bit narrow and 'allistic' can be a bit broad. For example, a 'normie' in the context of communication means 'anyone who communicates in the most common way'.

Retarded, spastic, etc.: These words are considered slurs by us and the disabled community and should be retired from everyone's vocabulary. These slurs are used against us but actually do the most harm to people who are physically or mentally disabled and cannot speak up for themselves. So when it comes to using them, just don't. It's not that hard.

Weird, odd, strange, bizarre, etc.: All of these words have different connotations and some are considered offensive by some disabled people. In this book, however, we do not treat them as such. We like being weird; we don't find the characterisation insulting.

WHAT DO YOU WISH EVERYONE KNEW ABOUT HOW YOUR AUTISTIC BRAIN WORKS?

Cat: Honestly? The biggest problem is that *I* don't really know how my brain is different. I've never experienced any other kind of brain. The only clues I have are when someone who's not autistic does something that seems weird to me and I realise our brains are working differently. I think I'd start with just helping people understand that brains work differently. Not everyone thinks the same way you do. That's totally okay, and it doesn't merit a huge freak-out when someone isn't getting your point. People get so upset when they expect you to act one way and you don't. If you don't want an authentic response, just tell me what you want me to say!

Elora: Mostly I wish that society at large, autistics and everyone else too, understood that brains aren't 'good' or 'bad' based on how easily they fit into the systems chosen for them. A metaphor I use a lot when describing disability to kids is 'Imagine that you're a mermaid who lives in a world of fairies. How would you survive out of the water? How would you get around without wings? How would you get anything done without a magic wand? Would you be excluded? In pain? Embarrassed? Would you need extra help from the fairies? Does all that struggle mean that being a mermaid is bad? No! Mermaids are supercool! But a mermaid in a world of fairies would seem "broken" all day, every day.'

That's how I feel as an autistic person: I'm a mermaid in a world of fairies. And it's really hard, but I'm not someone to look down on. I'm supercool the way I am, even if it's not easy.

Cat: It's not easy because people aren't accepting. Being a misunderstood minority sucks no matter what minority group you are in. A lot of people treat me differently when I mention I'm autistic, even after knowing me for months. It's not something to pity or look down on. It's who I am. But there's a big difference between what people think autism is and what it actually is, so I guess it's not surprising. Just really, really annoying.

Elora: For me the hardest part of conversations like this is trying to hold space for people who disagree. Lots of autistics don't like being autistic and would change it if they could, and that's okay. People are allowed to feel however they want to feel about their own challenges. I just don't feel that way myself.

Cat: I don't blame those people. It is hard being autistic. But I still adamantly believe that the hardest part is people refusing to make room for us. It's weird how differently you learn about autism in different professions. I've studied autism from a few different perspectives – nursing, social work, and education – and I found that the way autism was talked about always felt incomplete or too shallow. It always seemed to come back to this idea of the eight-year-old autistic boy in special education or whatever. It's why I took so long to get diagnosed. I didn't see myself in those studies. Yeah, all of my own stuff was there, but it was not described in a way that *really* looked like me. I knew, for example, that I had had some issues with social situations, but I didn't recognise that I was having meltdowns, because they were all on the inside. They didn't look like the meltdowns you might see in a clinical setting. So I didn't know my brain worked differently, because I didn't know what the default was. And there aren't a lot of visibly autistic women out there to see and think, *Oh hey, that's me!*

Elora: I feel similarly. It really hurts to be so different and not know how or why. Sometimes the best cure for a problem is to give the problem a name. Maybe once you learn more about it, it won't seem so bad anymore.

Cat: It was such a relief putting a name to what made me different. At first I panicked, but then it was euphoria. I'm autistic – nothing is wrong with me! Even when I thought autism was a problem, it was still a relief to know that there was a reason I struggled so much. It wasn't just that I wasn't trying hard enough. I think when people see an autistic person they think that person isn't trying hard enough.

But they don't know that person is trying so hard.

If they knew what to do, they'd do it – they're using all their strength just trying to figure it out. But it shouldn't have to be so hard. What's the end goal anyway? To be like everyone else? What's the fun in that? Every once in a while you meet people who are completely off the wall and they're the most fun people in the world.

Elora: I completely agree. Autism is amazing. I wish the world could see that.

My dog, Panda, is so loud and barks constantly, all day. She's stinky and noisy and steals shoes and sometimes pees on the floor, but she's also my best friend and has made my life so much better. She sleeps next to me, which makes me less afraid of nightmares, and because she barks at everything and seems scary, I know I'm safe from burglars. They won't mess with her. Because she's so high-energy, she pushes me to run around and have fun too! When she steals my shoes, sometimes it's kind of funny and I laugh at how silly she seems. My autism is a lot like Panda; it's annoying and hard to deal with sometimes, but I wouldn't trade it for the world. It makes my life better, even though it also makes my life harder. And I love it, just like I love Panda.

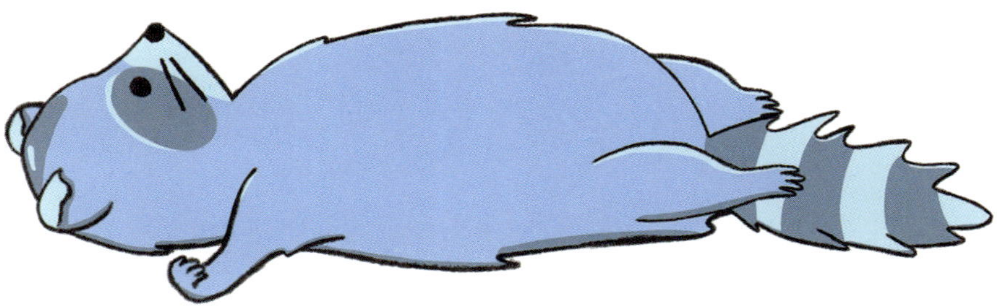

MONOTROPISM BY ELORA

The more I get to know other autistic people and the more I study my own brain, the more apparent it seems to me that autistic brains work in *chunks*. Imagine that focusing on something is like swimming in the ocean. The deeper you go, the longer it takes to get there and the longer it takes to get back to the surface. On an average day normies are like snorkellers who swim around right under the surface and don't go very deep. Autistics are like scuba divers who go deep into the ocean, far below the surface.

While normies can swim from reef to reef pretty easily, autistics are down in the shipwrecks, caves, and trenches and can't get out so easily. If someone is exploring a sunken ship, they can't simply move to a different part of the ocean. They have to manoeuver through the maze of the wreckage, swim out from the giant pit the ship landed in, navigate around an underwater heat vent that could be dangerous to swim through, detour to avoid a barracuda, adjust course for ocean currents, and pause at different heights to avoid getting 'the bends'.

Normies can swim from idea to idea easily but they aren't completely surrounded by the subject in the same way autistics often are. This doesn't mean that normies or autistics are smarter than the other. It means that we operate differently in how we approach whatever we are facing in the world. Sometimes autistics find that being too intensely focused is not a good thing. This is particularly true if you can't control what you're focusing on. It can feel like your body's refusal to do what you ask it to is slowly ruining your life – that it is entirely preoccupied no matter how much you beg it to please just do the one thing you have to do.

So often in my life I find myself getting the mental bends. It can take forever to sink down to that quiet depth: I have to get settled, get comfy, get quiet, realise that something's making a noise and get up to stop it, get up again to pee, get up again to grab a sip of water because I know I might be here awhile, get a sweater . . . And then, at last, focus.

Then it happens. I'm in my groove, I've found my rhythm, I'm cruising right along. I'm following a delicate thread of ideas to see where they go, when suddenly something breaks me out of it. Maybe I'm startled by Panda barking. Maybe plans change without warning. Maybe someone tries to talk to me when I was not previously socialising. Maybe I have to stop what I'm doing when I only just got into the groove! Maybe someone needs me to do 'just one thing' that takes a different mental energy from what I'm doing. And the next thing I know, I'm mentally reeling. I might get

snappy or yell at the person who interrupted me, even if I know that's not a nice thing to do and they don't deserve it. I might feel an overwhelming urge to cry, even if it doesn't seem like I have a good reason to. I might struggle to do the new task, even if it's simple. I might stare at the new task for five or ten minutes and then simply forget to do it, lost somewhere between the old task and the new one. If I'm already on edge, I might have a meltdown. It seems like I am overreacting, but it feels like someone dragged me out of the depths of the ocean and expects me not to feel sick.

The idea that autistics deep-focus on one or two things while normies gentle-focus on many things has a name: monotropism. This theory was developed by Dinah Murray, Wenn Lawson, and Mike Lesser (all three of whom were autistic) in the 1990s and early 2000s as a way to explain how the autistic brain works.[7] It conveys the idea that monotropic thinkers are better able to focus on a single thing at a time (*mono* means 'one') than polytropic thinkers (*poly* means 'multiple'), or neurotypicals, who can switch focus more easily. The monotropism theory is one of many theories of how autism works, but for us it's a useful way to think about our brains and experiences.[8] [9] So many autistic traits can be understood more fully if we look at autism through this 'deep-dive' lens. Here are just a few.

'Autistics love routines.' Trying to sink into a deep focus only to pause every few minutes to do something else is incredibly frustrating. It feels like someone is talking to you right as you are about to fall asleep and then you have to start all over again. Routines help us avoid getting sidetracked and instead stay in the zone. Hours of uninterrupted hyperfocus? *Swoon*.

'Autistics are bad at transitions.' Yes, if you compare us to normies. Normies expect autistics to shift focus without accounting for the fact that we are deeply engaged in a subject and mentally get the bends when we are forced to change focus too quickly. This can look like:

- Feeling reluctance about or difficulty breaking away from the previous task
- Experiencing anxiety about upcoming plans
- Refusing to make plans without proper warning
- Feeling stress instead of joy when pleasantly surprised

- Fixating on a previous task while moving on to the next one
- Becoming easily distracted between tasks

'Autistics obsess over their special interests.' When we like something, we dive deep into it. We are less likely to like things on a surface level the way that normies do. If we look at special interests through the monotropism theory, we can see that our brains are focusing on one thing at the expense of others. Our brains go deep and relate everything back to that singular interest.

'Autistics have a poor awareness of what's happening around them.' Our brains naturally focus on one thing and tune out everything around us. If an autistic person is diving deep into a subject, everything else fades away. Even if that diving deep is just thinking about something, we can get lost in it, like we are underwater, and the rest of the world doesn't necessarily register.

'Autistics are obsessed with doing things in certain ways.' Our commitment to a specific way of doing something helps us dive deep into other things. Doing something in a new way takes mental energy, and that can keep us on the surface. If you always make grilled cheese for lunch, you don't have to go back to the surface to decide what to eat, check if you have special ingredients, and make sure you're cooking it correctly. You don't have to worry that it will taste odd and break your focus. All those choices and potential distractions can be skipped because you already planned for the grilled cheese and know what to expect. You may even be able to make the grilled cheese without breaking your focus on whatever else you're doing because it's so routine. If what's happening on the surface of the water is always the same, it's easier to dive deep under the water because you don't have to worry about checking on the surface.

'Autistics are extra-sensitive to sensory input.' Every day your brain has to process a million things – people talking around you, strange smells, moving bodies, itchy clothes, music somewhere in the distance, a thousand footsteps, the feeling of the hair on your neck, and the sound of your heartbeat in your ears, to name just a few. That can be hard for a neurotypical brain to process, so what about ours? The monotropic brain fixates on single things, and not only the things we like! We might fixate on a scratchy tag on a shirt and because of monotropism find it nearly impossible to ignore.

Diving deep can be incredibly useful. Autistics may be experts in specific fields because they found something they loved and went deeper than other people. It's also helpful in everyday life. Sometimes when we need to get a job done, autistics can focus with laser-like precision on the goal, even forgetting to eat, sleep, or use the restroom. This can be handy in urgent situations. It is less useful when you're busy living your life and realise it's evening and you haven't drunk a single glass of water that day.

Staying on the surface can also be incredibly useful for normies. Many normies can elegantly glide from focus to focus, accomplishing one task after another. There are countless benefits to having a brain like this. But I imagine it can get frustrating too, when a deep-dive is required and your brain struggles to focus as much as you want it to.

I have thought for some time that I would be terrific at planning a last-minute wedding in four hours, or throwing together a variety show in one evening, or delivering a stranger's baby while locked in a gondola lift. While sudden transitions can be hard for me, in a crisis I find them easier. The adrenaline hits and I leave the world behind, eagerly diving into whatever problem I'm faced with and knowing that for a few hours nothing can touch me but this one issue. The surface fades away in a rush of bubbles, and I dive.

Another way to understand monotropism, other than our 'diving deep' metaphor, is to think of your brain as an octopus. You have a bunch of different tentacles that can do different things. According to monotropism, autistic people use all their brain tentacles to do one thing, while normies (polytropic brains) use each of their tentacles to do a different thing. Autistics are using all their

power for one task, while normies are splitting their power among different tasks. This means that the autistic octopus is getting that one task done better and faster and in more detail than any of the tasks that the normie octopus is doing, but on the other hand, the normie octopus is getting a lot done at once. People might expect that autistics use their brains for lots of tasks at once, not realising that the autistic brain can really only do one thing at a time.

Imagine that filtering out uncomfortable stimuli takes up one octopus arm. Keeping track of your schedule takes another octopus arm. Registering your physical needs, like hunger, thirst, and the need to go to the restroom, takes yet another. Normies don't even realise that their octopus arms are doing these background tasks. To a normie these tasks are super easy. But our octopus arms have to be working on the same thing. It doesn't matter that they're easy; they're still different and our octopus arms can't do different tasks at once.

Elora: One way that I've used monotropism to improve my life is by scheduling my days in chunks. Rather than trying to do a little bit of everything every day, I do a couple of big tasks every day. One day I might really focus on cleaning and spend hours on it. Another day I might really focus on writing this book. Another day I might be outside the house and focused on running errands. Another day might be more business-focused, with tasks like paying taxes and answering emails. By organising my life in chunks rather than in tiny pieces that I always have to shift between, I'm allowing my brain to dive deep as much as possible, and it's wonderful.

THE ROOT OF AUTISM

Autism is complex. With the scientific community's constant efforts to group individuals by 'level', 'functionality', or 'severity', it is important to recognise that these divisions are simply an acknowledgement of the diversity of autism's expression, not necessarily differences in the root causes. Our knowledge of what causes autism is limited. Scientists are exploring the roles of genetic influences as well as maternal infections or environmental exposures in utero, but all we really know is that we don't know enough.

One thing that seems apparent is that autism involves the interplay of multiple genes and other factors. Experts estimate that between two hundred and one thousand genes could be involved. Each gene has a different level of expression based on the individual, as well as environmental factors that change from person to person, such as the level of methylation in certain genes. This leads to even the same genetic code resulting in different traits in different people, and ultimately those traits determine our impulses, our sensitivities, and our biology.

When we discuss the psychology of autism, making broad generalities is the only way to approach such a complicated subject. We simply do not have the knowledge to talk about it in a different way, nor the vocabulary to differentiate among different autistics with different traits. Autistics may share a similar genetic makeup, but the ways their autism is expressed and how it affects their lives can be vastly different.

So yes, we deep-dive, but that is an action that feels more natural to us because of a blend of traits. Yes, we are hypersensitive, but that is an internal process driven by multiple factors. These are intermediary 'causes' with downstream effects that change our behaviours accordingly so that we act differently than our neurotypical counterparts, but they are not the origin. A complex constellation of different genes, each expressed in a different way according to the individual, creates the traits that lead to behaviours that feel natural to us.

What we claim to know now about autism, what we theorise, the connections we try to make, all might be modified tomorrow as new information is discovered, such as when autism and Asperger's were finally recategorised as a single spectrum disorder in the DSM-5. As our understanding changes, we reevaluate. With our current understanding of autism, it is far easier to discuss actions, feelings, and thoughts downstream than it is to discuss the imperceptible coding that might be influencing our behaviours. It is easier to draw connections between the common experiences of autistic people than their common genes. And ultimately that might prove to be all that we are: a group bonded by the way we move through the world, regardless of the genes that cause it. Humans cannot see their genes. To us they are far less relevant than the urges, drives, and impulses that those genes ultimately lead to. And if something changes in that pathway, it feels just as real to us and has the same effect as if our genes had programmed us that way in the first place.[10] [11] [12]

A BRIEF HISTORY OF AUTISM

Premodern: Evidence of autism shows up across all of written history even if it isn't specifically named as such. Many historical figures show strong signs of autism. Myths about djinni and fae changelings mirror the sudden onset of autism symptoms around the age of two that some children experience.[13]

Late 1800s: As psychology moves towards more analytical labelling and diagnosis, several (now offensive) umbrella terms likely describe autistic patients as well as other neurodivergent individuals.

1911: Eugen Bleuler, a Swiss psychiatrist, coins the term 'autism' to describe symptoms present in some cases of schizophrenia.* He based the term on the Greek word *autos*, meaning 'self', because he believed autistic children were drawn deep inside themselves, rather than living in the real world with the rest of us.

1921: Grunya Sukhareva, a Soviet child psychologist, founds a school for children with psychological problems in Moscow and publishes a paper that includes a detailed description of what she refers to as 'schizoid psychopathy', which mirrors the modern DSM-5's description of autism astonishingly well.

Early twentieth century: Austria becomes a centre of psychological research, including some of the first studies of autism. With the rise of the Nazi Party, many doctors and researchers flee, including Jewish researchers George Frankl and Anni Weiss, who had both written papers on autism. Austrian doctor Hans Asperger is appointed head of mental health treatment at the University of Vienna's Children's Clinic.

---

* The term schizophrenia, like many other mental health terms, has evolved over time. Someone diagnosed with schizophrenia in the past might be given a completely different diagnosis today.

1939 through the end of WWII: Asperger cooperates with the Nazi Party's program to euthanise children with physical or mental 'defects'. Aktion T4, the euthanasia program that followed the earlier child euthanasia program, is expanded to justify the murder of a quarter of a million disabled people, thousands of whom are children, as well as the forced sterilisation of, experimentation on, and abuse of countless more.[14] Many of these victims were likely autistic, though it is hard to determine exactly which ones.

1940s to 1960s: Autism gradually becomes better known among medical professionals and the general public. A long parade of organisations, papers, theories, and definitions of autism emerge, many of them ableist and later disproven. Parents of autistic children begin to work together to support each other and their children.

1943: Donald Triplett receives the first official diagnosis of autism as its own condition. Triplett was an American banker from Mississippi who had been temporarily institutionalised at about the age of three and diagnosed at about age eleven. He died in June 2023.

1952: The first DSM is published, with autism mentioned in connection with schizophrenia.

1960s: What is now called sensory processing disorder is discovered and studied by the American occupational therapist and clinical psychologist Anna Jean Ayres.

1960s to 1970s: Multiple researchers build on each other's work to create what is now known as Applied Behavioural Analysis (ABA). ABA uses rewards and punishments to train autistics to act 'normal' and achieve tasks. In its early years ABA could be particularly brutal, crossing the line into torture. Additionally, the social model of disability, which proposes that society causes a disability, not the physical or mental impairment, is introduced and developed by disability advocates. Disabled people, it argues, are unnecessarily isolated and excluded and deserve accommodations that allow them to participate fully in society at the same level as people without impairments.

1962: Rosemary Kennedy, sister of President John F. Kennedy, is the feature of an article in the *Saturday Evening Post* by her sister Eunice, which reveals Rosemary's struggles with intellectual disability for the first time. In the following years the Kennedy family goes on to champion the rights of disabled people in many ways, such as founding the Special Olympics. The story of Rosemary's forced lobotomy in 1941, which led to her inability to speak or walk, will not become public knowledge until 1987. Rosemary Kennedy's story, though tragic, sparked changes in the way the American people treat those with intellectual disabilities.

1963: A UK organisation called the Society for Autistic Children (now called the National Autistic Society) introduces the puzzle piece symbol to show autism as a 'puzzling condition'.

1972: The TEACCH autism program is founded by German-American psychologist Eric Schopler and recognises autism as an innate and unique way of experiencing the world. The program pushed back against the inhumane ways that some researchers treated autistics and the once-common perception that autism was caused by cold and distant parents. The program continues to this day and many organisations around the world have followed in its footsteps.

1973: The Rehabilitation Act bans discrimination based on handicap by the federal government and its contractors in the United States.

1975: The Education for All Handicapped Children Act guarantees disabled children a free public education in the United States. The act will be renamed the Individuals with Disabilities Education Act in 1990.

1980: The DSM-III formally recognises autism as a distinct disorder from schizophrenia.

1988: *Rain Man*, starring Dustin Hoffman as an autistic savant, becomes the highest-grossing film of the year, winning four Academy Awards, including Best Actor for Hoffman and Best Picture. The movie becomes the picture of autism in the public consciousness.

1990: The Americans with Disabilities Act makes it illegal to discriminate against people with disabilities in a number of categories and requires employers to provide reasonable accommodations. This makes some difference in disabled people's everyday lives but fails to address our problems fully.

1990s to 2000s: Autobiographies by autistics begin to receive widespread attention. Two of the earliest and most influential, *Nobody Nowhere: The Remarkable Autobiography of an Autistic Girl* by Donna Williams (1992) and *Thinking in Pictures: My Life with Autism* by Temple Grandin (1995), bring autism to the public eye, and the authors' experiences give readers insight into what autism looks like in a way that had never been done before.

1993: Jim Sinclair becomes a leading voice of the 'anti-cure' autism rights movement when he gives a speech titled 'Don't Mourn for Us' at the International Conference on Autism, which he later publishes as an essay. 'Don't Mourn for Us' challenges parents of autistic kids to see autism as a core part of their children's identities.

Late 1990s: The term 'neurodiversity' is coined by the Australian sociologist Judy Singer.

1998: Andrew Wakefield and a group of colleagues publish a paper in the medical journal *The Lancet* that links the MMR (measles, mumps, and rubella) vaccine to autism. Though the work is later retracted and exposed as fraudulent, leading to the revocation of Wakefield's medical licence, the idea that vaccines cause autism becomes an insidious and persistent conspiracy theory among parents.

2005: Autism Speaks is founded by the grandparents of an autistic child. The organisation has been involved in many controversies over the years, most notably shameless fearmongering that portrays autism as a monster. Many autistics label Autism Speaks as a hate group, and we strongly discourage any autistic from associating with the organisation or its members.*

2013: Asperger's syndrome is removed from the DSM-5 as its own diagnosis and combined with autism to form autism spectrum disorder.

2014: Autism Speaks, Google, and Toronto's Hospital for Sick Children's Centre for Applied Genomics begin the Autism Speaks Ten Thousand Genomes Program, or AUT10K, which collects the genetic material of autistic people and their families for the purpose of research. This program, which would become known as the MSSNG project, has received backlash due to concerns over privacy, consent, and potential ways the databases may be abused by bad actors once data are compiled.

2020: The FDA bans a tool called the 'graduated electronic decelerator', which administers electric shocks and was used on residents at the Judge Rotenberg Educational Center, a residential care facility for people with mental health problems,

* Better alternatives include the Autistic Self Advocacy Network, the Autistic Women and Nonbinary Network, Academic Autism Spectrum Partnership in Research and Education, and Self-Advocates Becoming Empowered.

intellectual disabilities, or behavioural problems. The Judge Rotenberg Center appeals the ruling and wins, arguing that the FDA does not have jurisdiction over the device. The device is still used today, though the FDA proposed a new ban on it in 2024.

2022: The Association for Behavior Analysis International, a leading professional organisation in the field of behaviour analysis, finally condemns the use of electric shock.

Present day: Autism awareness has skyrocketed in the public consciousness and is no longer possible to ignore or avoid. Some people see this as an omen of a failing society and seek to return to a time when, in their minds, autism did not exist. Others have embraced autism as a part of humanity and are fighting to make sure no attempt is ever again made to erase it.

In summation: we have a long way to go.

AUTISM AND DAILY LIFE

How does autism affect your day-to-day functioning? What are some things you struggle with because of autism that others don't? What are the ways you manage your sensory issues, processing issues, miscommunications, etc.? How can you work with your autistic traits and sensitivities instead of against them? What are the ways autism makes your daily life better?

THE SPECTRUM, REMIXED

Many people see autism as a scale, where you are more or less autistic. Really, autism is more like a big jumble of different traits that show up differently in different people. But we are all 100 per cent autistic.

It can be difficult for an autistic person to explain how they are different or even know that they are different. We don't know what would happen if an allistic person and an autistic person switched bodies. All we know for sure is that some people are different, and when people are different, they sometimes struggle. Those struggles manifest as feelings and physical reactions.

Autism presents differently in different people. While all autistics are 100 per cent autistic, specific autism traits are stronger in some people than others. Autistic traits are not a package deal where if one is strong, all the others are just as strong.

Autism is more like a board that a DJ might use to edit and mix sound.

A DJ will turn up and down different sound effects and audio tracks to create the perfect mix. In the same way, every autistic has their own perfect mix of autistic traits that makes them who they are. Here's an example of what an autistic's autism might look like on a mixer board.

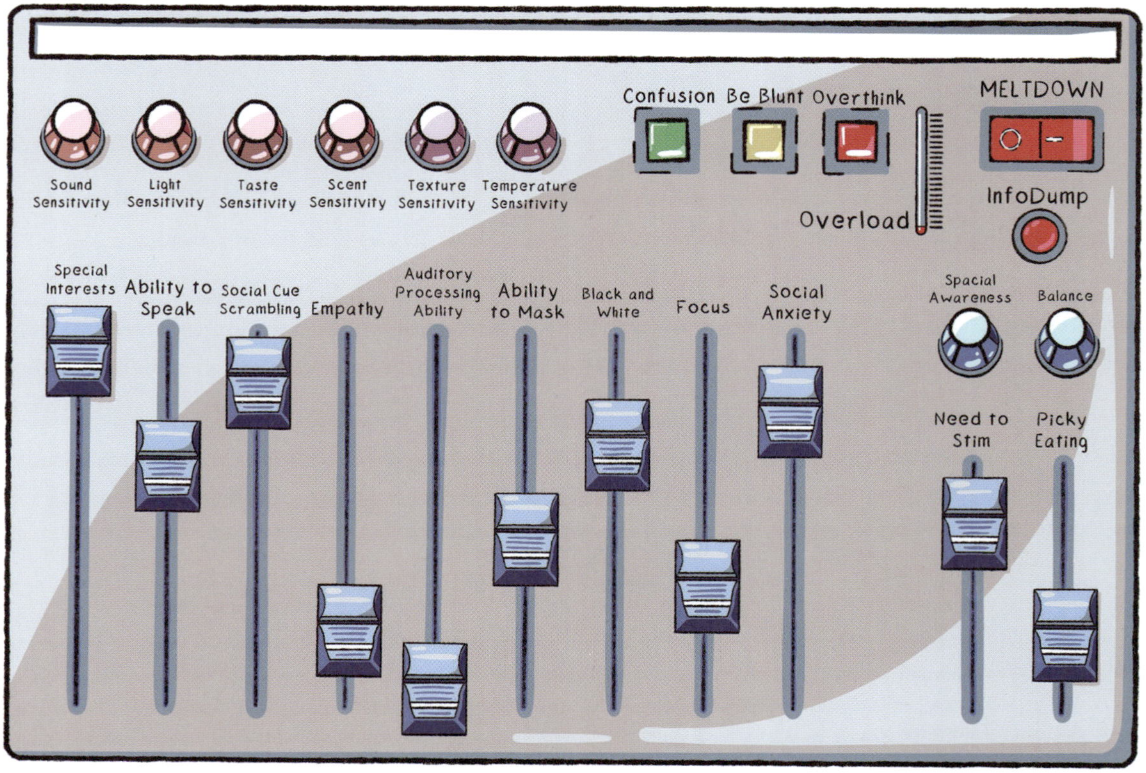

On the next page is your own autism mixer board.

It's blank – no intensities or labels – you get to fill those in yourself. Choose some of your autistic qualities (you can look at our sample mixer board for inspiration) and add them onto this mixer board. You can make it as detailed or simple as you like. Share the completed board with someone else to help them understand what it's like inside your brain!

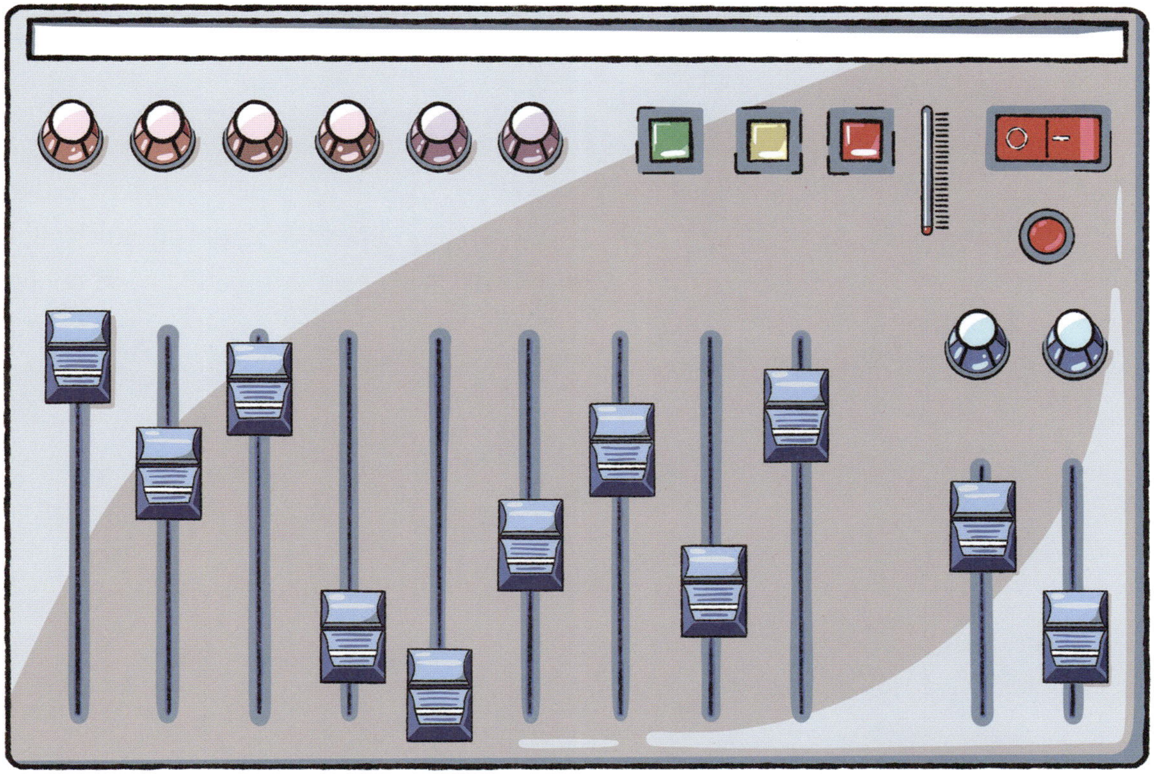

Not sure which qualities are autistic? Here's an incomplete list to get you going!

- Sound Sensitivity
- Light Sensitivity
- Taste Sensitivity
- Scent Sensitivity
- Texture Sensitivity
- Temperature Sensitivity
- Confusion
- Bluntness
- Overthinking
- Infodumping
- Meltdown
- Special Interests
- Ability to Speak
- Social Cue Scrambling
- Empathy
- Auditory Processing Ability
- Ability to Mask
- Black-and-White Thinking
- Focus
- Social Anxiety
- Need to Stim
- Picky Eating
- Spatial Awareness
- Balance

THE B-SIDE

Neurotypicals might look at a lot of autistic traits and see them as purely negative. But we know that they all have a B-side. Each of the traits below has a positive and a negative. Colour in the coins and identify how your life is affected by the pluses and minuses.

1. PATTERN RECOGNITION Humans look for patterns to help a chaotic world make sense. Autistics tend to excel at this. This is a form of creativity that is born from a completely different way of seeing the world, and without it we might not have things like calculus, astronomy, electricity, or cheese. We all know which of those is the most important.

B-SIDE: BLACK-AND-WHITE THINKING The downside of a brain that tries to organise everything into categories and patterns is that sometimes things don't fit into a set category or pattern, and forcing them into one can limit your thinking. A common trait in autistic people is thinking that there's an answer to every problem and that there are clear categories to sort things into. But black-and-white thinking can be limiting. Putting labels onto anything is limiting. Some things don't fit nicely into a little box.

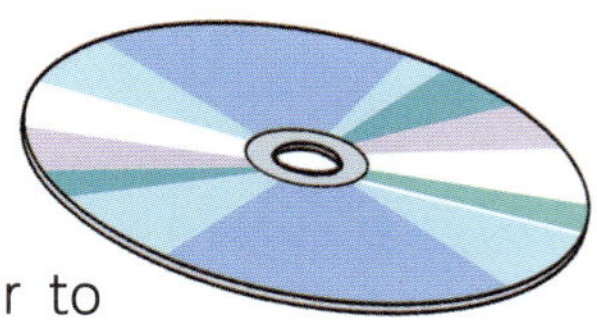

2. LOGICAL REASONING The stereotype of the hyper-logical robotic autistic man does have a grain of truth to it: autistics excel at solving problems in logical ways that might never occur to allistic people. Neurodivergent people are commonly teased for having completely random responses to a question or comment, but in reality our brains are working quickly and in a different direction from the neurotypical brain, so everything is linked. This thought process might seem utterly ridiculous to an allistic person, but to an autistic person it makes perfect sense.

B-SIDE: TROUBLE WITH IMPRECISE FORMS OF REASONING Certain kinds of reasoning, like interpreting social cues and facial expressions, are imprecise and can't be broken down into specific rules. Autistic people often struggle with these more intuitive kinds of intelligence. Making logical connections no one else sees is a strength only when people don't assume you will make the same connections as everyone else.

3. SENSITIVITY In today's world, where food is regulated and therefore unlikely to kill you, having a super-sensitive palate makes you seem like a picky eater and nothing more. Fifty thousand years ago, however, having a super-sensitive palate might have saved you from being poisoned. Being super irritated by a loose thread on your shirt is an inconvenience now, but back then the little sensation could have been a tick or a leech that someone else may not have noticed. Even today these sensitivities aren't always bad. Sensitive taste buds can make someone an excellent cook. Catching a sensation while it's tiny and should perhaps be ignorable early on might help predict something major later, like noticing the tiny changes in the body in the first weeks of pregnancy before it will show on a test.

B-SIDE: OVERSENSITIVITY Our sensitivities are survival skills that we never learned to turn off. Nothing more, nothing less. The difference between allistics and autistics is that allistics either can't feel the loose thread or the weird sock lump or the slight crunch in something that should have been smooth, or they can ignore it. We often can't. Everything in us is screaming that this stimulus needs our immediate attention and signifies danger. This can make it hard to focus on more important things.

4. HYPERFOCUS Have you ever experienced a state of mind in which all your concentration was focused on one task or item and the rest of the world was shut out? For people with ADHD and autism, this is a normal occurrence. Hyperfocus is the state of obsessing over something so that your mind is tuned in to that and only that. While obsessively focusing on one problem may not be convenient when you have many different problems that need attention, it is incredibly useful when one problem is urgent. The autistic ability to tune the world out and dedicate yourself to one cause is useful for inventing, creating works of art, and making scientific discoveries. Many famous figures in these fields exhibited strong autistic traits and many of humanity's most celebrated accomplishments were the result.

B-SIDE: INABILITY TO UNFOCUS Hyperfocus can be great! Hyperfocusing on the wrong thing, though, is not. If we could choose what to hyperfocus on, this book would have been finished a solid six months earlier. Anyone who's ever taken ADHD meds to study for a test only to be completely absorbed by *The Sims* for twelve straight hours knows the danger of hyperfocusing on the wrong thing. We assume. We've certainly never spent the night before an important exam writing angsty teen fantasies instead of studying. Of course not. But someone probably has.

5. HONESTY Autistics have a truly beautiful way of communicating when unmasked and unconcerned with social protocols. It is direct, sincere, and peppered with special layers of knowledge and insight. We see truths as inarguable facts and say so. You never have to wonder what an autistic thinks of you or a situation.

B-SIDE: BLUNTNESS Neurotypicals often find us too blunt or think we bring ourselves or our special interests up too much, or find our sincerity off-putting. They sometimes feel uncomfortable when we are direct about our feelings. To allistics, autistic people may seem to always say the wrong thing, say it the wrong way, or use the wrong tone or body language. To autistics it feels as if our English and Neurotypical English are two different languages and we're constantly translating. While this is not entirely our fault, it is a part of autism that makes life difficult.

What parts of your autism do other people see? What parts do they not see? What parts of your autism do you see in yourself the most? What autistic traits do you think are less prominent in you?

AUTISTIC MYTHS AND WHERE TO SHOVE THEM (HINT: THE TRASH)

MYTH: Vaccines cause autism.
FACT: **Vaccines do not cause autism.**[15] [16] An infamous study that showed a link between the two was riddled with errors, the results of the study could not be replicated, and the unethical doctor responsible for the study lost his licence. The anti-vaccination trend is just another conspiracy theory that people have been swept up into. There is no evidence that vaccines cause autism. In fact, vaccines are great and almost always cause only mild, infrequent problems while providing absolutely outstanding benefits to humanity as a whole.

'The most dangerous part of getting your kid vaccinated is driving them to the doctor's to do it.' —John Oliver[17]

MYTH: Autism can and should be cured.
FACT: **Autism isn't a disease.** It's a neurotype. To fix it you'd have to change the brain's wiring and the entire personality with it. If you think that a good cure for something is to erase all that makes a person who they are, then feel free to cure your headaches with a lobotomy.

MYTH: Autism must be diagnosed in childhood to be real.
FACT: **Autism can exist without ever being diagnosed and certainly doesn't have to be diagnosed in childhood.** Autistic adults don't get a lot of attention – mostly

because people would rather listen to the parents of autistic children than the actual autistic community. But that doesn't mean we don't exist and that autism is only present in children or that it has to have been diagnosed when a person was a child. Autistics with less 'severe' autistic traits often get through childhood without anyone realising they were autistic all along. So while many autistic adults were not diagnosed as children, they still had certain struggles that went unaddressed. Autistic kids have to grow up eventually, and they become us, and we are still autistic.

MYTH: Autism is caused by bad parenting

FACT: **Autism is a neurotype. It's genetic and not caused be external factors like parenting.** This actually ties into a common problem with autism: we are identified and diagnosed by how we affect the lives of neurotypicals, or how we respond to stress in a neurotypical world, not by how we actually are. If children are happy and supported properly, it may be hard for the casual observer to tell they're autistic. Parents can't, and shouldn't, be blamed for their kids' autism. Where autism is present, bad parenting won't make the autism stronger, worse, or different in any way. It just produces an unhappy kid who will have an even harder time coping.

MYTH: Autism mostly affects white male children.

FACT: **People of colour, females, and adults can all be autistic (and are).** Because of the barriers to getting a diagnosis that we discussed earlier, some demographics have historically been underrepresented, but the gap is lessening. It is still too early to know exact numbers, but autism is certainly prominent across racial, gender, and age groups.

MYTH: All autistics are savants.

FACT: **Only a third or less of autistics show signs of savantism.**[18] But more importantly, autistics don't have to have some kind of spectacular talent to be valid, which is a good thing because plenty of us don't. Savants used to be called 'idiot savants' because it was believed that they were utterly helpless except for the one cool thing that they could do that allistics found 'useful'. 'Bradley can't feed himself or talk or communicate at all, but he's a piano genius, so that makes up for it!'

Our lives aren't transactional. We are valuable even if we have no abilities that allistics find 'useful' or 'interesting', or any abilities at all. We're people. You wouldn't assume every allistic has some sort of special genius talent, so don't assume that for autistics either.

MYTH: Autistic people are violent, throw frequent tantrums, or are likely to have screaming, thrashing meltdowns.
FACT: **Autistic people are more prone to having meltdowns when they are overwhelmed or are having difficulty communicating, but autistics are not inherently violent and not all autistics react in these ways.** Some autistic children have frequent meltdowns because they lack the communication skills to say what they are feeling, and their parents don't realise that their child doesn't have the same threshold for stimuli that they or other children might have. Autistic adults have meltdowns too, but they don't necessarily look like a child's meltdown. Sure, if every sense were being attacked and nobody seemed to care and there was no end in sight, any adult might lose their mind and start screaming, but often the meltdown is more subtle. It can look like snapping at someone for no apparent reason, crying, shutting down, not focusing, or going to bed early.

For Elora, meltdowns often involve crying and hyperventilating, but they can also involve shutting down, disassociating, and experiencing physical symptoms like pain, hot and cold flashes, tingling all over her body, nausea, and a squeezing sensation in her chest. For Cat, a meltdown looks like straight-up dissociation, a brain vacation, but being overstimulated will turn her cartoonishly evil. Many people differentiate between a meltdown (an explosion of stress outward) and a shutdown (an implosion of stress inward). Because our experiences of the two seem so similar and overlap with each other, when discussing our own experiences we interpret them as different expressions of the same event.

MYTH: Autism is an excuse for bad behaviour.
FACT: **Define bad behaviour. If you mean being weird, having breakdowns and lashing out, saying inappropriate things at parties, or generally not trying hard enough, then no, autistics are not making up excuses.** Having meltdowns, experiencing social differences, missing context, refusing to play by social rules that

don't benefit them, and struggling to meet normie's expectations in general are all common experiences of people with autism. That doesn't mean that frustrating behaviour cannot be adjusted – for example, if someone regularly has meltdowns and lashes out in a certain circumstance, you can work with them to figure out what's causing the meltdowns and make changes to the situation so a breakdown is avoidable, and come up with a game plan for how to handle a meltdown if they feel one coming on.

But expecting someone who is having a fight-or-flight response to simply act calm is not reasonable. You aren't asking them to 'behave' better; you are asking them to override their entire sympathetic nervous system. Also, sometimes people explain their bad behaviour by giving context for it, such as, 'Sorry I snapped at you; I'm really tired.' This might help you to forgive them, or it might not. It's not an excuse; it's an explanation. If you don't find it sufficient, that's your right, but it's not a reason to resort to ableist insults.

Unfortunately, we need to point out that some people *do* use autism as an excuse for truly bad behaviour. Autism does not excuse assault, sexual harassment, prejudice, or other evils. Autism affects how we communicate our beliefs and show respect to others, and some level of conflict around difficult subjects is natural because of that. But we still need to take accountability for our beliefs and actions.

THE AUTISTIC AGENDA

1. Don't get discriminated against.
2. Don't get talked to like a kid.
3. Go home and put on pyjamas.

MYTH: Self-diagnosed autistics are faking.
FACT: **Self-diagnosis is completely valid.** We'll go into more detail on why some people choose to self-diagnose and the advantages and disadvantages of formal diagnosis and self-diagnosis. Even in the autistic community there are some who believe that a self-diagnosis isn't valid, but we believe that formal diagnosis for adults isn't always worth it, sufficient, or necessary.[19] Autistic people are autistic, and if a person says they're autistic, we believe them. There's room for all of us.

MYTH: People are faking autism for attention.
FACT: **People who say they are autistic deserve to be believed and respected.** There are a lot of reasons why someone might be accused of faking autism. Perhaps they're self-diagnosed and not diagnosed by a doctor. Perhaps they're a teenager and prone to trying on different identities that they then discard. Perhaps they're saying they are autistic when you've never noticed autistic traits in them. Perhaps they are going on social media and sharing they're autistic for what you perceive as sympathy points when it doesn't appear to you that they've ever struggled with anything closely related to the difficulties autistics often face. That last scenario is 'faking it for attention', and it's certainly possible that someone could do it. There are eight billion people on the planet. However, the other scenarios are far more likely and none of these deserve any hate. Plus, unless you are someone's doctor, it's not your place to judge whether they have autism. It's best to err on the side of believing people.

Autism is an invisible disability that is difficult to define and understand, even by other autistics. Nobody owes anyone autistic behaviour or outwardly autistic signs. Someone may mistake themselves as autistic, but they aren't exploiting us or hurting anyone by calling themselves autistic. They're trying to learn if it works for them. Autism comes with way too much annoyance, baggage, and hassle to use the label if it doesn't fit. Plus with how much autism is demonised, nobody actually *wants* to be autistic unless they understand at least a little about it. There's no real advantage to being one of us, unfortunately. We don't throw any fun parties or have our own Secret Santa. Although, maybe we should.

9 STIM CLASS

'Stimming' is short for 'self-stimulating behaviour'. That's a fancy way of saying 'anything you do to add sensory input'. You know how you feel when you're so happy you could burst and you have to dance, or clap your hands, or do *something*? Whatever you do, it's stimming. You know when you're so bored and restless that you can't sit still and you have to get a pen just so you have something to click and tap? That's stimming.

Stimming can be a conscious action or an unconscious one. You can choose to do it, or find yourself doing it, or not even notice that you're doing it. What defines the behaviour is that it's repetitive and done in the interest of self-regulation.

Some of the strongest autistic stereotypes involve stims: hand-flapping and rocking back and forth are two of the most recognisably autistic stims. But stimming isn't just for autistics. Stimming is natural human behaviour. When you're so happy you could sing, or when it's too quiet so you whistle, or when you like a word and you repeat it a few times for the fun of it, all of that is stimming. Singing is a vocal stim, like chewing gum is an oral-motor stim. There are tons of stims, so if one doesn't help you, try another! Follow your instincts and do whatever feels right.

You may have heard of fidget toys. These are toys made to give satisfying avenues of stimulation. There are a wide range of them. Cat also likes chewy candy and keeps it around as an oral stim (this book would not exist without strawberry straws and sour gummy worms). Elora likes to stim by pacing and playing simple app games on her phone. Both of us like to sing as a vocal stim.

If you don't stim, try it out. Even allistics benefit from stimming every once in a while. When you have a lot of emotion, just let it out in whatever way you want – use your voice, your hands, your feet, anything and everything. You might be surprised how *right* it can feel!

Stimming may seem like something that only kids do, but there is some real wisdom in stuff that kids do. The majority of people have a 'kids just being kids' attitude with children that allows kids to do weird, gross, off-the-wall stuff all day long without anyone batting an eye. Pretending to be a dog, playing in mud, pretending to be a beached whale, making their Barbies twice-divorced war refugees about to cross a minefield – whatever it is, if the kid's young enough, most people shrug it off. This also goes for being accidentally offensive: you correct the kid, but you don't hold it against them because they didn't mean to be insulting. This is an attitude that we believe should carry over to everyone. Being weird isn't harmful or dangerous. If people were more tolerant of people's idiosyncrasies or more understanding of people's difficulties communicating, then autistics (and everyone else who's different) wouldn't have such a hard time fitting in. We try hard to act 'normal', but we often can't. Instead of shaping a child to fit the world, we could shape the world to fit everyone.

Try some different stims. What are your favourites?
How do they make you feel?

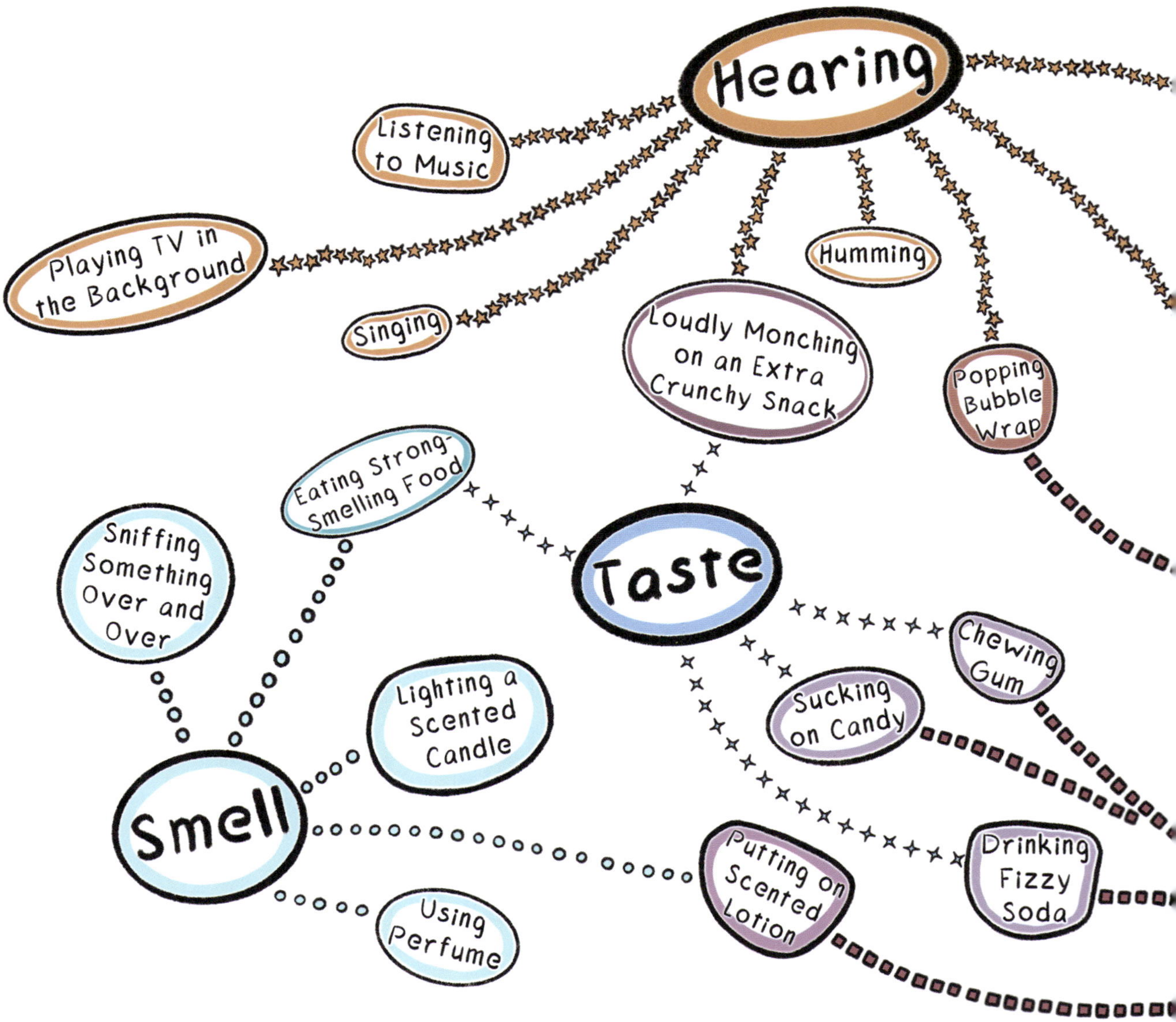

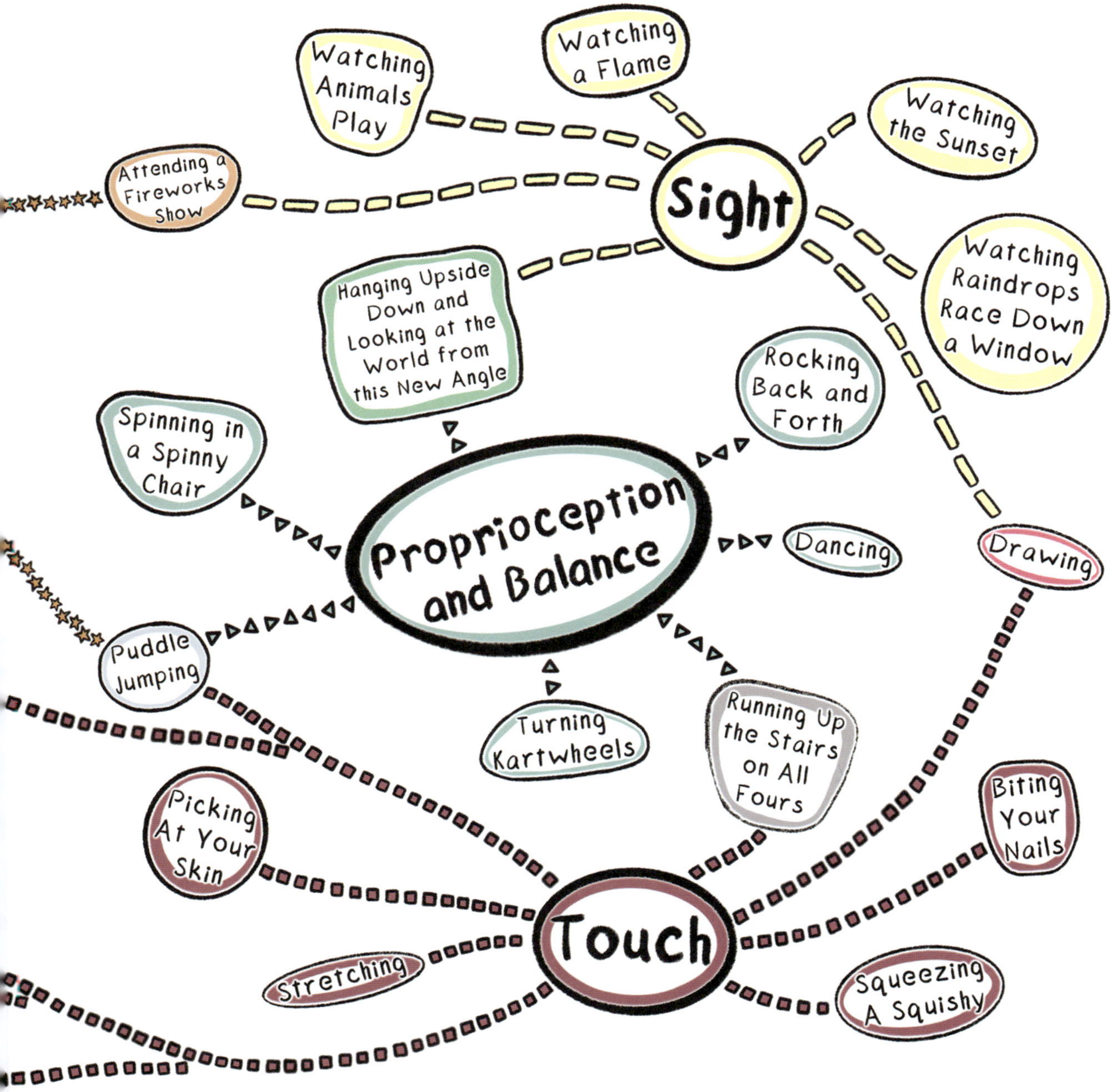
Sight
Watching Animals Play
Watching a Flame
Watching the Sunset
Attending a Fireworks Show
Watching Raindrops Race Down a Window
Hanging Upside Down and Looking at the World from this New Angle
Drawing
Proprioception and Balance
Spinning in a Spinny Chair
Rocking Back and Forth
Dancing
Puddle Jumping
Turning Kartwheels
Running Up the Stairs on All Fours
Touch
Picking At Your Skin
Biting Your Nails
Stretching
Squeezing A Squishy

MASKING 101: THE BASICS

Masking is . . . exactly what it sounds like.

Fun fact: All Hallows' Eve, or Samhain as it was originally called by the Celts, had a tradition of wearing masks. Celts believed that on that day the gods appeared to play tricks on mortals and that only by hiding your true face could you protect yourself. This is where modern-day Halloween costumes come from.[20] Sometimes the Halloweener is an autistic person. And instead of a monster mask, it's the facade of being neurotypical.

Since autistics look like everyone else, we don't need a physical mask. The mask is for our behaviour. We put it on metaphorically and change our behaviour to fit the situation. Everybody does this in some areas of their life. It's sometimes called code-switching. You don't talk the same way around your grandparents as you do around your friends. You might show a different version of yourself to a police officer than you show to your doctor, which is different from what you show a romantic partner, which is different from what you show your parents. Different attitudes and speech patterns fit different situations.

For autistics it's kind of like the difference between Halloween now and All Hallows Eve or Samhain back in the day. There is an element of danger, of fear. We feel we *have* to mask. In fact it's so vital that most of us don't even realise we're doing it.

Should autistic people mask? We're not here to say 'yes' or 'no', because it's not always a choice. Some people cannot stop masking – they've done it for so long that they don't know how to stop. Other people cannot mask at all and are punished by society for it. Some of us can choose to turn it on or off, but even then it can be hard to switch, or know when to switch, or know whom it is safe to switch around. We may mask when we are alone, or around a few chosen people. As we get older and more experienced, we may learn to be more intentional with our masking and become aware of what we are doing and why. Other times we don't even realise we are masking.

Masking is like any other habit. While learning to drive, Cat built into her starting-the-car routine the act of putting on the seatbelt, so now she feels naked if she's in a car and not wearing one. She would have to consciously choose to not put one on and catch herself if she started to put it on mindfully. Just like a seatbelt, a mask is a safety feature. The whole world can't always know, all the time, that you're autistic.

> Anybody who's ever been different knows that it's a privilege to have the ability to hide difference because it can make life easier in a world that is often judgemental, even cruel.

Playing 'dress-up like a normie' is one way we get by.

Most of us autistics learn how to mask at least a little bit. Some of us are better at it than others. But if you never take the mask off, even you might not know who you are underneath. The person under the mask is beautiful and amazing, and no matter how often you hide that person, you should never forget who you are. Remember:

1. You, as you are underneath the mask, are perfect the way you are.
2. The traits being hidden underneath aren't bad.
3. Even if masking is your 'normal' doesn't mean it has to be. You have a right to unmask at any time. Even if you don't know what that looks like, it's completely up to you when and where you unmask.

Some types of masking cause more harm than others. If you find yourself in a situation where you feel you need to mask, here are a few of our favourite ways to mask that are fairly low effort. You might call them 'tricks'.

Instead of forcing yourself to make eye contact with someone else, try one of these:

- Look at their eyebrows, glasses, nose, forehead, or some other feature close to their eyes. They won't notice the difference.
- Bounce your eyes. Look at the other person's eyes, then look away, then look again, then look away. Think of it like a game of 'tag'. Instead of staring right into their eyes, you need to 'tag' them enough.
- Unfocus your eyes so it looks like you're looking at someone's eyes but actually their face is a little bit blurry.
- Come up with a task that shows you're paying attention but doesn't require eye contact. For example, if you're in a meeting, you could volunteer to be the one taking notes. You'll be looking at the paper or computer – no eye contact necessary!

Instead of forcing yourself to stop stimming, try these socially acceptable stims:

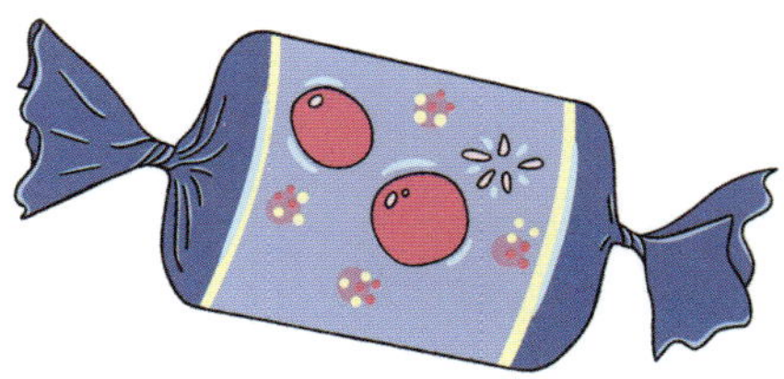

- Chewing gum
- Sipping water from a water bottle
- Fiddling with your jewellery or keys
- Listening to music
- Carrying a sketchbook around and drawing
- Rubbing lotion into your hands
- Playing with your fingernails
- Placing your hand on your heart or wrist to feel your heartbeat
- Using a phone app – whether it's social media or a bubble-wrap popping app, it'll give you something to do.

Instead of forcing yourself to either act normal or expose yourself as autistic, find alternative ways to explain your needs:

- A lot of people attribute personality traits to zodiac signs. If someone's giving you a hard time for your autistic traits and you don't want to tell them you're autistic, you can always say, 'I'm sorry I can't help it; I'm a Gemini,' or whatever your sign is. They may not buy it, but hey, it's worth a shot!
- Try explaining the specific trait, rather than bringing up autism as a whole. For example, 'Thanks for being so patient with me. I have sensory issues.'
- If you're in a foreign country, you can always attribute problems (especially social problems) to cultural differences or a language barrier.
- Instead of explaining auditory processing disorders, tell people you have 'hearing issues'. People with auditory processing issues have a lot of the same needs as someone who is hard of hearing. You need things repeated or written down, and you might have trouble understanding speech or even need to read lips.
- Try thanking the person you're clashing with for being 'patient' or 'understanding' rather than apologising. Apologising makes it seem like you're a problem. Thanking them makes them seem like a good person. This approach can simultaneously diffuse tension, encourage future patience and understanding, improve your self-image, and make you seem like less of a pushover. This strategy is often recommended to women in business, especially in traditionally male environments.

Cat: I use the language excuse a lot, and people are usually quite nice about it.

Instead of forcing yourself to engage in every social situation, try these ways to avoid interacting with people when you've reached your limit:

- Interact with people with simpler social expectations, like kids, pets, and (some) elderly people.
- Bring some work you enjoy to social occasions. When you're done with the social situation, excuse yourself with 'I'm sorry, but I have something I need to work on.'
- Wearing headphones signals that you don't want people to talk to you. It doesn't matter if you're listening to music or not, just that you're wearing them.
- Have a prepared excuse to leave. You can text someone to call you with a reason to go, tell the person you're out with in advance that you might have to go, or suddenly 'remember' something you need to do. Say you have to get home to your dog – we've all been ditched for a dog before; we get it.
- If you are feeling overwhelmed and need to go home, you can always say, 'I have somewhere else I need to be.' The same goes for scheduling. Try saying, 'I have plans.' It doesn't matter if the plan is to stay home. That counts.
- If you have a friend who doesn't mind getting unexpected phone calls, you can get out of a lot of situations by saying, 'Sorry, I need to make a call.' Then you're free to step out of the room and talk on the phone to your friend until you calm down. You can arrange to be called at a certain time.

People don't know enough about autism to call you on it when you don't mask. So the simplest way to mask is this: if you want to hide your autism, don't say you're autistic. People will assume that you're odd, having a bad day, or (if they're generous) that you're nervous. Autism will be way down their list of reasons a person is acting slightly off. And if they decide that your autistic traits make you a 'bad' person, that's their problem.

We know that masking is vital. We are not trying to say that unmasking is the best choice for you in every situation. We know that it's especially hard for people who are discriminated against for other reasons as well – like Black autistics, who might get labelled 'troublemakers' for behaviour that would get a white autistic labelled as

'quirky'. But we also know from experience that living a lie every day of your life can be devastating and even life-threatening. Masking – or camouflaging, as it is called in some scientific literature – can be associated with increased levels of anxiety, depression, and social anxiety among autistic adults.[21] Other studies have shown that when masking is accompanied by increased levels of 'thwarted belongingness' and 'defeat and entrapment', it is in turn accompanied by an increased risk of suicidality.[22] More research is needed in this area, however, to determine whether or not one *causes* the other.

We are not saying that unmasking is easy or always safe. We are saying that 'just try to be normal' is not a healthy or realistic way to live your life forever. We are saying that you deserve to unmask, and you have lots of options to make masking less difficult. Unmasking can be dangerous, but so can masking for too long. So try to find times and places where you can unmask, even a little bit, and work from there to decide how to move forward.

The real you is beautiful. When you finally feel safe to show that person to the world, know that we are cheering for you.

AUTISM AND SCHOOL

How was your school experience affected by autism and how did it differ from those of your peers? What were the early signs that you were autistic? Were your teachers and classmates understanding or did you feel you were treated unfairly? How did your autistic traits affect your school performance, especially in upper levels of schooling? Do you think they affected your choice to pursue higher education and your experience if you did?

SPECIAL INTERESTS

If there's one thing autistics are known for, it might be our special interests. In the stereotypical vision of autism, a brilliant white man is hyperfocused on a maths problem of some sort. *Maybe* theoretical physics, which is just maths with extra steps (don't come at us, physicists – you know we're right).

As the term 'special interest' becomes more common, autistics might be asked by allistics or each other, 'What's your special interest?' A better question might be, 'What's your special interest *right now*?' Because we all know they can change.

Some special interests do last a lifetime. They're the hobbies or interests that define a major part of your personality. They're what you think about when you're not thinking about anything else. Other special interests, however, are temporary. Maybe you spend a couple of days learning origami or you crochet your own Christmas ornaments one year, and then you never touch those skills again. Sure, maybe you'll use those skills again someday, but also maybe you won't. On to the next thing!

You can take a special interest in anything, and it doesn't matter what. If it's trains or planets or the digits of pi, cool! If it's a more tactile skill, like writing or acting or making art,

"Were you happy when you painted these pictures?" asked Mr. Rochester presently.

"I was absorbed, sir, yes, and I was happy," Jane replied. "To paint them, in short, was to enjoy one of the keenest pleasures I have ever known."

From *Jane Eyre*, by Charlotte Brontë

awesome! If it's stereotypically autistic, like maths or science, great! If it's considered silly or childish or not 'suited' to your gender, who cares? Not us!

> No moment on this earth is wasted if it brings you joy, contentment, peace, or mental stimulation.

If you're like us, you can't just 'like' something. You either have no interest in it or it sets up shop in your brain and rotates in there like a rotisserie chicken for months, consuming your entire soul and becoming a core part of your personality. If one of these things has consumed your entire soul at one point, then you're in good company because many autistics share a special interest in it!

1. *Hello Kitty*
2. Studio Ghibli movies
3. All things Disney
4. Trains
5. Dinosaurs
6. *Doctor Who*, *Star Wars*, *Star Trek*, and other space adventure shows and films
7. Superheroes, such as those in Marvel movies (having an obsession with their various series is kind of required to purchase a ticket at this point because nobody else understands what's going on),
8. DC movies, and comics
9. A specific colour
10. LEGO
11. Video games
12. Maths or science, including specific sub-types like computer coding
13. True crime
14. Specific animals (horses, dolphins, dogs, and cats are all popular)
15. Books and reading
16. Arts and crafts

Elora: Some of my biggest special interests are all forms of performing arts (especially ballet and comedy), Christian disability theology, and dogs!

Cat: I love to cycle through anything related to art – different media including physical and digital but also graphic design, music, writing, movies, video games, and books. I have collected so many utterly useless skills. Lately I've explored papercraft, foil hardcovers, *Horizon: Zero Dawn*, and movies with huge budgets that were box office flops. (I must understand why!)

AUTISTIC CULTURE

Pop culture is full of autistic icons. Most of them are not canonically autistic, but the autistic community holds them dear all the same. Here, 'canon' means 'confirmed by the creators or explicitly stated in the media itself'. When we say that some characters are 'canonically autistic', we mean that they are officially confirmed to be autistic. When we say that a character is 'non-canonically autistic', we are saying that they are autistic in our personal interpretation, or headcanon, of the character. Characters can also be 'autism-coded'. A character who is 'coded' as something is portrayed as a member of that demographic but is not explicitly labelled as such. An autistic-coded character is one who seems to have been written as autistic, even though it is not stated. Saying that you have a 'headcanon' that a character is autistic puts the emphasis on your interpretation of the character, while saying that a character is 'autism-coded' puts the emphasis on the details of the writing.

CANONICAL REPRESENTATION

These characters are confirmed as autistic and are, according to autistics, good representations of autistics (if not necessarily good people). Based on our research, there are only about a hundred canonically autistic characters in major media, but that number is growing. Some you might recognise:

- Abed Nadir (*Community*)
- Entrapta (*She-Ra 2018* reboot)
- Renarin Kholin (*The Stormlight Archive* series)

- Tiberius 'Ty' Blackthorn (*The Dark Artifices* series)
- Rick Sanchez (*Rick and Morty*)
- Julia (*Sesame Street*)
- Woo Young-Woo (*Extraordinary Attorney Woo*)
- Dr. Brigid Tenenbaum (*BioShock*)
- Symmetra (*Overwatch*)
- Twyla Boogeyman (*Monster High*)
- Asteria (*Dungeons & Dragons: The Book of Many Things*)
- Kayo and Rose (*The Orphan's King*, Cat's fantasy debut)

NON-CANONICAL REPRESENTATION

These characters are not labelled as autistic by the creators, but many fans view them as autistic (which means we can't be convinced otherwise). All jokes aside, these characters are open to interpretation because they aren't real people. If you don't agree with us that these characters are autistic, that's fine! But looking at characters in a new way might help you start seeing yourself in places you hadn't expected before, and that's part of the point of art – we get to project our own experiences onto it and see it through our own lens.

If a character's autistic traits are more likely due to some kind of extreme isolation or other trauma, we excluded them. Also keep in mind that these may not come from good shows or be good characters. A lot of characters on this list have committed crimes. But they are a good or okay representation of autism. If a character on this list has multiple incarnations, we specify which version or versions of this character are, in our opinion, autistic, not that all of them are. Except for our beloved Sherlock Holmes. He's always autistic.

- Lilo (*Lilo & Stitch*)
- Spock and Data (*Star Trek*)
- Spongebob Squarepants (*Spongebob Squarepants*)
- Every member of the Belcher family (*Bob's Burgers*)
- Abby Sciuto (*NCIS*)
- Hermione Granger and Luna Lovegood (*Harry Potter*)

- Beth Harmon (*The Queen's Gambit*)
- Buddy (*Elf*)
- Kronk (*The Emperor's New Groove*)
- Newt Scamander (*Fantastic Beasts and Where to Find Them*)
- Elizabeth (*BioShock Infinite*)
- Charlie Bradbury (*Supernatural*)
- L (*Death Note*)
- Link (*The Legend of Zelda*)
- Flint Lockwood (*Cloudy with a Chance of Meatballs*)
- Ferb Fletcher (*Phineas and Ferb*)
- Elizabeth Bennet and Mr. Darcy (*Pride and Prejudice*)
- The Doctor (*Doctor Who*)
- Leslie Knope (*Parks and Recreation*)
- Michael Scott (*The Office*)
- Geralt of Rivia (*The Witcher*)
- Pinkie Pie (*My Little Pony*)
- Raymond Holt and Amy Santiago (*Brooklyn Nine-Nine*)
- Dr. Gregory House (*House, M.D.*)
- Matilda Wormwood (*Matilda*)
- Belle (Disney's *Beauty and the Beast*)
- Elsa (*Frozen*)
- Marshall Eriksen (*How I Met Your Mother*)
- Chihiro Ogino (*Spirited Away*)
- Eleanor Crain Vance (*The Haunting of Hill House*)
- Bruno and Mirabel Madrigal (*Encanto*)
- Many characters from *Pokemon*
- Ford Prefect (*The Hitchhiker's Guide to the Galaxy*)
- Allison Reynolds (*The Breakfast Club*)
- Lydia Deetz (*Beetlejuice*)
- Wednesday Addams (*The Addams Family* and *Wednesday*)
- Norman Babcock (*ParaNorman*)
- Dr. Hannibal Lecter (*The Silence of the Lambs*)
- Ben Hanscom (*It*)
- Harlan Cooper (*Umbrella Academy*)
- Sterling Archer (*Archer*)

Who are some of your favourite autistic characters, canonical or not?

THERE'S SOMETHING ABOUT SHELDON

The Big Bang Theory's Sheldon Cooper is the bane of the autistic community and weirdly helpful to it at the same time. In short, he's bad representation – but is bad representation better than no representation at all?

The Big Bang Theory, for those unfamiliar, aired on CBS from 2007 to 2019 for twelve seasons and a total of 279 episodes. According to the Nielsen data, almost eighteen million people[23] tuned in to watch the finale. The show was wildly successful with millions of viewers and reached a cross section of Americans who wouldn't otherwise seek out shows about anything related to science. The sitcom aspect made it more accessible to viewers, and the show often delivered scientific information through a joke so as not to alienate anyone who didn't understand the science. The show has some flaws and has received valid criticism – it follows a lot of tired eighties 'bully versus nerd' tropes and started out extremely misogynistic – but it can't be denied that it was popular. Sheldon, who was the most popular character, got his own spin-off series, called *Young Sheldon*, and it ran for seven seasons.

Sheldon is absolutely coded as autistic, though the show's creators have specifically dodged the issue by never labelling him as such on the show or off. On the show it's said multiple times that he's 'not crazy; [his] mother had him tested'.

Which brings us to the real problem about the show: it's ableist. Sheldon is called 'crazy,' made fun of to his face and behind his back, and his traits that resemble common autism ones are the butt of many jokes even among his friends, who are arguably autism-coded as well.

There is a big difference between having ableist writers and having ableist characters. Ableist characters in a show can be depicted as wrong, like a hurdle to overcome. Unfortunately, in this case, it's the writers who are the problem. The show depicts Sheldon as an often over-the-top character who should be laughed at for his quirks, especially in early seasons. Still, he's only laughed at. He's not forced to change who he is, or abused, dismissed, or made into inspiration porn.

Sheldon can also be a bit of a jerk. He certainly isn't the most likeable of characters, and he tends to demand that everyone around him bend to his wishes. Some people feel that Sheldon is an amalgamation of all the worst stereotypes of autism wrapped into one annoying man. However, he's a rounded character who has moments when he is selfish or cruel but also moments when he is generous and loyal. He seems unfeeling at first glance, but has moments where he feels deeply. He is in the category of characters written by a large team of writers over several years, which can sometimes result in personality discrepancies or inconsistent arcs. Viewed holistically, he might be over the top, but he's not one-dimensional. He's complicated, just like real people are. And though some people hated him, got so annoyed by him that they quit watching the show, or pitied his friends and family for having to deal with him, others loved him and found a way to connect with the autistic people in their lives through him.

A lot of the main characters in *The Big Bang Theory* are autistic-coded. They can also be misogynistic, condescending, creepy, racist, and pathetic. They reinforce the jock–nerd binary, even though that binary doesn't really represent the world today. Sheldon may be blunt and rude but he treats everyone the same way and you could argue that he is the only one of the men in his group to give women the same amount of respect as men. This is likely by accident because he's coded as asexual and so views men and women roughly the same, without any bias due to sexual attraction. But the writers never go into that or take that seriously, so it's left up to interpretation.

So Sheldon is a white asexual male savant, which is a stereotype of autism that needs to be dispelled. But he's also complicated and real.

The fact of the matter is that there really aren't that many autistic people, white and male or otherwise, to point to in pop culture. So while in many respects he's bad representation, it can be argued that he's better than no representation. And it can be argued further that bad representation opens doors to good representation – and that we might even have Sheldon to thank in part for the slow but steady increase in autism representation in today's media.

Elora: I personally don't think that Sheldon is that bad of a character, but not because he would actually be a good person in real life. *The Big Bang Theory* is a sitcom, a genre that always exaggerates character traits to play into comedy. If you took any sitcom character and put them in the real world, they would probably be difficult to deal with because the genre only works if the characters have exaggerated personalities. Sitcoms have to fit a lot of goofy moments and wild hijinks into short, typically twenty-two minute episodes, and they accomplish that by adding 'very' to every character. In a sitcom extroverts become very extroverted – extroverted enough to constantly befriend new people, which leads to fun new side characters for episodes. Dramatic characters are very dramatic, which leads to big performances. Sassy characters are very sassy, which leads to iconic lines. As the protagonist of a sitcom, Sheldon has to be 'very' something. The show wouldn't work otherwise. For some reason the character traits that the writers exaggerated for Sheldon are some of his least likeable traits, which also happen to be bad stereotypes of autism. With little autistic representation in the media, though he didn't come across as a traditional sitcom protagonist to everyone but rather as an overwhelming and mean person. Personally, I think he's just the autistic stereotype version of Raymond from *Everybody Loves Raymond*.

Cat: I used to be really annoyed that Sheldon had become the unofficial face of autism, but I think seeing him on TV really helped my parents understand autism better. Before *The Big Bang Theory* there was basically only *Rain Man*. But Sheldon depicted a different kind of autistic character. He lives on his own, can speak and go outside, has a job, etc. He's not 'normal' by any means, but he's able to engage in normal activities and live a normal life. Instead of thinking of autism as a non-verbal screaming child who would have to stay at home forever, my parents could picture Sheldon. And they were like, 'Okay, yeah, that makes sense. My child is definitely like that.' Which . . . sure, that's fair.

#ACTUALLYAUTISTIC

The hashtag #autism has always been common, covering as it does many subjects, from health care to parenting to education to lived autistic experiences. However, for a long time it was used less by people who actually had autism and more often by relatives of people with autism and charitable or research organisations. Too often it was used by fearmongering groups who wanted to 'cure' autistics, parents of autistic children exploiting their children for sympathy likes, people making jokes at the expense of those with autism, and many other people portraying autism as a terrifying illness that turns children into robots.

In an effort to create their own online space, autistic teenagers and adults came up with a new hashtag, #ActuallyAutistic, to enable people who are actually autistic to connect with one another. Using that hashtag, someone can jump from one post by a person with autism to another, and another, and so on.

We each learned about autism through grassroots online advocacy using this hashtag. We explored where it led and found ourselves. It's how we found each other too! Community is important, and forming new communities across a distance (like the vast, uncrossable wasteland between Texas and Oklahoma) is exactly what the internet is supposed to be for.

While hashtags on social media have their limits, a discerning mind is able to learn quite a bit from #ActuallyAutistic posts – not only those about autism but also ones about how autistic people see themselves, how they are treated, and how broad the array of our experiences really is. In short: no information is 'useless', having a wealth of data is helpful, and with proper distillation, we can find something approximating the truth.

THE ACTUALLY AUTISTIC GUIDE PERSONALITY QUIZ

Personality tests can be useful in describing how we feel and understanding ourselves. That's why we made one! Throughout this book, you'll notice eight different animals. Each animal represents a way someone can identify with their autism. You might identify with one, several, or all of the animals, or with none. The point of the personality test is to give you some new tools to understand and explain yourself to other people. Personality tests can do a lot of harm if they're taken too seriously, so remember, this is just a fun game.

If a personality test is something you'd like to try, move to the next page and start reading the statements and deciding if they are true for you. If a statement reflects the way you feel, check the box next to it. If a statement isn't true for you, leave the box blank. The statements are colour coded. Each colour represents one of the animals. Once you've gone through and checked all the boxes that apply to you, tally up how many boxes you checked of each colour. Whichever colour has the most checks indicates which animal you might have the most in common with! Remember, there is no right or wrong answer. This is only a tool to help you contextualise your experiences, not a diagnosis of an autism subtype.

- [ ] If people dislike me because of my autism, that's their problem, not mine.
- [ ] If people dislike me because of my autism, I'm going to make my autism even more obvious to annoy them.
- [ ] If people dislike me because of my autism, I get angry.
- [ ] If people dislike me because of my autism, I feel sad and tired.
- [ ] If people dislike me because of my autism, I feel anxious, like I'm taking a test and doing poorly.
- [ ] If people dislike me because of my autism, I feel like a failure.
- [ ] If people dislike me because of my autism, I'm not quite sure how to feel about it.
- [ ] If people dislike me because of my autism, I need to know why. I need to understand what made them feel this way.
- [ ] If people dislike me because of my autism, I'll just avoid them.
- [ ] I like who I am, so what other people think doesn't matter.
- [ ] I like who I am, so I'm going to be who I am as forcefully as possible.
- [ ] I like who I am, and I'm angry that people expect me to be anyone else.
- [ ] I like who I am. That doesn't change the fact that being me is exhausting.
- [ ] I like who I am. That doesn't change the fact that I'm stressed about who I am.
- [ ] I like who I am, but that's irrelevant. I still need to try to become someone else instead.
- [ ] I don't know if I like who I am. I don't know who I am in the first place!
- [ ] I like who I am more and more as I learn about the psychology that makes me who I am.
- [ ] I like who I am, so why would I need other people in my life? I'm good enough for me.
- [ ] I try to mask my autism sometimes, but I don't usually go out of my way to do it. I might make a little effort to make the normies comfortable, but I won't strain myself by putting on a complicated performance.
- [ ] I might hide my autism in special circumstances or if I think I'm in real danger, but most of the time I unmask as much as possible. If that makes someone angry? Too bad.

- ☐ I try to mask my autism sometimes, but it makes me angry. It's like the anger is growing inside me the whole time I have to fake being someone else until I want to explode.
- ☐ I try to mask my autism sometimes, but I end up feeling empty, like I don't have any energy left to be myself.
- ☐ If I mask my autism, I feel stressed because I'm not being myself. If I am my authentic self, I feel stressed because I'm not masking. I can't win!
- ☐ I've masked my autism so much and for so long, trying to be who everyone else wants me to be, that I don't think I even know who I am.
- ☐ I might mask my autism. I'm not sure.
- ☐ When I mask my autism, I do it intellectually, relying on advice I've learned online and in books. It's a challenge and I feel like a spy, undercover as a normie.
- ☐ My favourite way to mask is to simply not be around people in the first place. Then they don't know I'm autistic because they don't know I exist. Problem solved!
- ☐ My autism (or people's judgement of my autism) has gotten me into so many awkward situations, but there's not much I can do about that. I'll keep doing my best. That's all I can do.
- ☐ My autism (or people's judgement of my autism) has gotten me into so many awkward situations that I've given up trying to avoid them. Bring on the awkward! I'm ready!
- ☐ My autism (or people's judgement of my autism) has gotten me into so many awkward situations that I get mad at people before I even meet them. If they're going to end up disliking me anyway, I'll save us both some time and dislike them first.
- ☐ My autism (or people's judgement of my autism) has gotten me into so many awkward situations that I feel doomed to bad interactions, like it's a waste of energy to try making allistic friends.
- ☐ My autism (or people's judgement of my autism) has gotten me into so many awkward situations that I feel panicked in social settings, like one misstep will create a humiliating experience.
- ☐ My autism (or people's judgement of my autism) has gotten me into so many awkward situations, but I keep promising myself that I'll work harder to get things right the next time.

- [ ] My autism (or people's judgement of my autism) has gotten me into so many awkward situations. I like to analyse my memories of them and try to figure out where it all went wrong.
- [ ] My life has been full of awkward situations, but I'm not sure how much they have to do with my autism.
- [ ] My autism (or people's judgement of my autism) has gotten me into so many awkward situations that I avoid social settings altogether.
- [ ] I feel like a weirdo, but I'm getting comfortable with that.
- [ ] I feel like a circus animal, so I might as well give people something wild to look at.
- [ ] I feel like a ticking time bomb of emotions, always about to explode.
- [ ] I feel like a big disappointment.
- [ ] I feel like I'm on trial all the time.
- [ ] I feel like a puppet for what everyone else wants.
- [ ] I feel a lot of things, but they're hard to understand.
- [ ] I feel like a detective and my whole life is a mystery I get to solve.
- [ ] I feel alone and that feels really good sometimes.
- [ ] I think as time goes on and I get more and more used to being my self, I'll get happier.
- [ ] I think that if I could find friends who are as weird as I am, I'd be happier.
- [ ] It's hard to be happy with so much frustration inside me all the time, but I'm not sure if there's anything I can do about it.
- [ ] I'd like to be happier, but sometimes that doesn't feel possible.
- [ ] I think that if I could just relax, I'd be happier.
- [ ] I think that if I could just be liked by the people around me, I'd be happier.
- [ ] I think that if I could come to some kind of conclusion about who I'm supposed to be, I'd be happier.
- [ ] I think that if I could learn more about what makes people think the way they do, I'd be happier.
- [ ] I think that if I didn't have to rely on other people so much, I'd be happier.
- [ ] It's hard for me to pay attention to the people who try to make me fit in. It's usually a boring conversation.

- [ ] It's hard for me to not purposefully annoy the people who try to make me fit in.
- [ ] It's hard for me to not hate the people who try to make me fit in. They've hurt me so much.
- [ ] I feel drained when people point out that I don't fit in, even if I wasn't trying to fit in in the first place.
- [ ] I panic when people point out that I don't fit in, even if I wasn't trying to fit in in the first place.
- [ ] It's hard for me to not do what people tell me to do. I'll do what they say I should, so I can fit in.
- [ ] It's hard for me to understand whether or not I'm fitting in at all. I usually don't have a clue.
- [ ] I sometimes find myself psychoanalysing the people who try to make me fit in. I want to understand why it's so important to them.
- [ ] I try to avoid the people who try to make me fit in. I don't understand why I have to fit in with people in the first place.
- [ ] People tell me a lot of things about myself, but often I just don't listen.
- [ ] People tell me I'm really weird and I like that. Freaking people out is my specialty.
- [ ] People tell me I have anger issues, but I think anger is the right response to a world that tries to change you.
- [ ] People tell me I need to think more positively, but I'm so exhausted inside that it's hard to have the energy to think at all.
- [ ] People tell me I worry too much, but I think being on guard is the right response when the whole world is judging you.
- [ ] People tell me I'm a pushover.
- [ ] People tell me I'm really weird and I don't know if they're right or not. Sometimes I think I'm weird. Sometimes I think I'm the only one who makes sense.
- [ ] People tell me I'm obsessed with my autism, but I think learning everything I can about autism is the rational response to being autistic.
- [ ] People tell me I'm too isolated, but I think being alone is what's best for me.

IF YOU CHECKED MOSTLY ORANGE STATEMENTS, YOU'RE A . . .

PLATYPUS AUTISTIC

Unbothered

The defining characteristic of platypus autistics is their assurance of their unique self. Platypus autistics know they're different and are okay with that. They see their uniqueness as a simple fact of life and accept their autism as a part of who they are without feeling a need to change it. They are autistic and don't see a need to be ashamed of that. Platypus autistics do not fight their autism. They vibe with it.

Key words: ambivalent, detached, content

IF YOU CHECKED MOSTLY RED STATEMENTS, YOU'RE A . . .

BEARDED DRAGON AUTISTIC

Purposefully Wild

The defining characteristic of bearded dragon autistics is the way they chaotically embrace their autism. These autistics do not fight their autism. In fact, they enjoy it like a sweet treat! Bearded dragon autistics indulge their autistic needs as a form of rebellion.

Bearded dragon autistics purposefully fight societal expectations. They might wear clothes that they know people will hate just because they think dress codes don't make sense. They might purposefully unmask around people who really hate autistic traits. They might bring up their autism the moment someone says something mean about autism, just to make the situation uncomfortable. To a bearded dragon autistic, being autistic is a form of resistance.

Key words: rebellious, chaotic, independent

IF YOU CHECKED MOSTLY GREEN STATEMENTS, YOU'RE A . . .

CROCODILE AUTISTIC

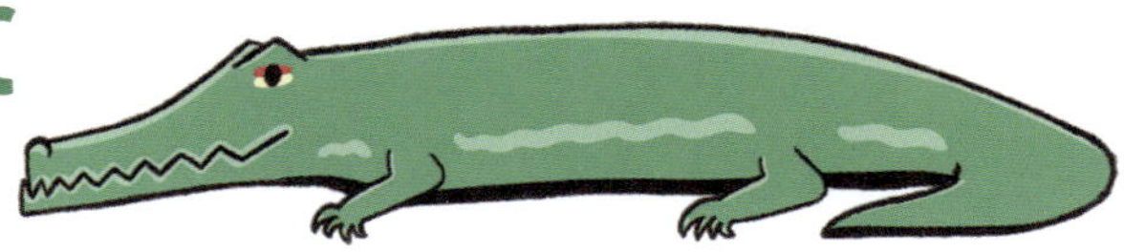

Angry

The defining characteristic of crocodile autistics is their rage. Crocodile autistics are frustrated with the challenges they face, both from autism and from society. Crocodile autistics may openly show their rage or they may hide it. They may channel their rage into socially acceptable activities, like sports, or they may participate in social activism, allowing their fury to motivate them to fight for justice. When pushed, they might snap and unleash a catastrophic meltdown. They also might keep it all inside, causing them to be tense and on edge. What makes someone a crocodile autistic is not how or when their anger escapes but rather how much anger they have inside in the first place.

Key words: frustrated, protective, defensive

IF YOU CHECKED MOSTLY PURPLE STATEMENTS, YOU'RE A . . .

HEDGEHOG AUTISTIC

Exhausted

The defining characteristic of hedgehog autistics is exhaustion – physical, emotional, and mental. Hedgehog autistics have been trying for a long time to control their autism and it's taken a steep toll. Still, just because someone is a hedgehog autistic doesn't mean that their exhaustion keeps them from living. What it means is that it's an extra obstacle for them to face, and doing so can feel like trudging through mud. If your sense of exhaustion is preventing you from living a healthy life, you may need to seek help. There are plenty of medications and therapies that mental health professionals can provide if your exhaustion has become debilitating.

Key words: drained, burned out, weary

IF YOU CHECKED MOSTLY YELLOW STATEMENTS, YOU'RE A . . .

LEOPARD AUTISTIC

Stressed

The defining characteristic of leopard autistics is stress. This is not just a temporary feeling but a long-term, overwhelming restlessness. Leopard autistics have spent so much time being criticised and micromanaged for their autism that they don't know how to stop feeling tense, as though at any moment someone will jump out at them and yell, 'You messed up again!' Leopard autistics aren't only stressed, but stress is a constant challenge for them, even in situations when they think they should feel relaxed. If your sense of stress is preventing you from living a healthy life, you may need to seek medical attention. There are plenty of medications and therapies that mental health professionals can provide to treat clinical anxiety.

Key words: anxious, vigilant, afraid, tense

IF YOU CHECKED MOSTLY PINK STATEMENTS, YOU'RE A . . .

JACKALOPE AUTISTIC

People-Pleasing

The defining characteristic of jackalope autistics is their commitment to being the person society wants them to be, even if they suspect it's impossible. Jackalope autistics try to satisfy everyone around them and are desperate to fit in. Jackalope autistics feel like they need to be respected as part of a group to have value. They change the way they talk, move, dress, and interact with the world in order to satisfy their family and peers. Jackalope autistics may not even be sure who they really are because they've spent so long trying to be who they feel they are 'supposed' to be instead.

Key words: conciliatory, fawning, obsequious

IF YOU CHECKED MOSTLY LIGHT BLUE STATEMENTS, YOU'RE A . . .

RACCOON AUTISTIC

Curious

The defining characteristic of raccoon autistics is their ongoing exploration of their autism. Raccoon autistics are curious, open to new ideas, and in a state of mental change. They are in the process of discovering what autism means to them. Raccoon autistics share a lot with raven autistics but are distinguished by their lack of stability. A raven autistic is intellectually delving into autism, trying to find as much clarity as possible. A raccoon autistic, on the other hand, is still struggling to see the big picture and may not even be sure they are autistic. A raven autistic (see below) is a scholar of autism. A raccoon autistic is a new discoverer of it.

Key words: curious, uncertain, explorative

IF YOU CHECKED MOSTLY DARK BLUE STATEMENTS, YOU'RE A . . .

RAVEN AUTISTIC

Intellectual

The defining characteristic of raven autistics is their scholarship of autism. Raven autistics analyse their experiences and the experiences of other autistics to learn as much as they can about autism. They pursue the study of autism as a science, whether in an official capacity (as a scientist, journalist, doctor, therapist, etc.) or as a hobby. For raven autistics, autism itself is a special interest. They ask tough questions about what makes autism autism. You can be a raven autistic without having access to a lab, scientific studies, or a fancy degree. Being a raven autistic is a state of mind. It is about what you do with the information you have. It is about having a dedication to understanding autism better and enjoying the discovery.

Key words: scholarly, analytical, scientific

IF YOU CHECKED MOSTLY GRAY STATEMENTS, YOU'RE A . . .

BAT AUTISTIC

Isolated

The defining characteristic of bat autistics is their self-enforced solitude. Bat autistics choose to be alone. This may be because they feel like being with other people is too difficult. It may also be because they simply love to be alone. Either way, bat autistics find happiness in their privacy.

Bat autistics isolate themselves from society in some way. For some bat autistics, this means leaving parties as soon as possible and doing the minimum in social situations. Other bat autistics literally leave society and live their lives completely alone most of the time. Regardless of how alone bat autistics are, the solitude feels safe to them. Bat autistics find peace in a life other people would find far too lonely.

Key words: self-sufficient, introverted, loner

AUTISM AND IDENTITY

How much of who you are has been shaped by autism? What are some of the core lessons you have learned about how to be and act as an autistic person? What role does autism play in your life and identity? When someone asks about you, do you tell them about your autism? What behaviours have you changed in your life to accommodate your autism? What core beliefs of yours have been shaped by your experiences with autism?

PART TWO

What Autistics Should Know

My intensity does not discredit me.
My self-acceptance does not limit me.
My fear does not shame me.
My anger does not disgrace me.
My uncertainty does not undo me.
My intellect does not determine my value.
My popularity does not define me.
My grief does not shrink me.
My isolation does not erase me.

WHY DO WE NEED THIS BOOK RIGHT NOW?

Cat: So my original idea for this book was really simple. I wanted to put everything I'd learned in my studies inspired by the #ActuallyAutistic hashtag in one place. I'd learned about autism from a bunch of different sources before being diagnosed, but I only ever really related to what I found online in the autistic community. It's weird how incomplete a picture is painted in medicine and pedagogy about autism.

Elora: So true. I think one of the biggest problems with the way autism is taught is that it's so clinical that it's hard to see yourself in it. We need to remember that for autistics, they've never known any different. They may not realise how different they are in the ways they speak, move, think, and socialise. I learned about autism in a high school psychology class and felt sorry for people with autism. I did not make the connection that I was one of them, because how could I? One of the most valuable aspects of the #ActuallyAutistic hashtag is how it presents information in an accessible, relatable, easy-to-comprehend way. It's not sterile anymore. It's close, it's human, it's more than statistics on a page.

Cat: For sure. Especially when you're assigned female at birth and doctors will bend over backward to diagnose you with anything *but* autism. Bipolar, social anxiety, the list goes on. So you look at autism symptoms and think, *No, I'm not like that! There are other explanations!* And the real killer here is that the other explanation is usually *I just need to work harder. I just need to learn how to be better.* But you're just holding yourself to an impossible standard if you don't know why you're struggling in the first place. I thought I was a broken neurotypical for half my life instead of a perfectly normal autistic!

Elora: In college I would start to black out around the edges of my vision from stress when I was walking to class. I would bite my pillow at night so my roommate wouldn't hear me cry myself to sleep. I would pace for hours, unable to break out of the cycle even though I knew I was supposed to be doing something else. It was like my willpower would turn off, and even though I had other things to do, I'd be unable to do them. I learned to check to see that the bathroom was empty before I had a meltdown in it, swallowing the sobs a few seconds longer. I heard my own voice screaming in my head so strongly during class that I struggled to hear my teacher. And you know what? I still thought I just needed to try harder. Yeah, I looked for solutions, medications, therapies, but really I constantly worried that I was just weak. How could everyone else handle the stress but not me?

When I finally began to wonder if I was autistic, I decided to give myself a 'free trial' of autism and use autism-specific coping skills I'd learned from the #ActuallyAutistic community to see if they'd help. Standing alone in my kitchen, overwhelmed with stress as usual, I decided to try flapping my hands as a stim. And just like that, my brain quieted. I'd thought I'd have to live with gruesome intrusive thoughts my whole life, but they left like magic. My eating disorder left immediately too – turns out it was a coping mechanism to make up for suppressing my autistic traits. The community behind the #ActuallyAutistic hashtag gave me understanding, hope, and clarity after decades of me blaming myself for my struggles.

Cat: I've never been much for stimming, but I've always known there was something 'off' about me. I didn't learn about #ActuallyAutistic until after my therapist and I talked about it and decided I was autistic. But then when I read things posted by community members, I saw myself everywhere. I never related to the symptoms list given out by doctors, and when I took the official test I felt like I knew what the right answers were supposed to be and not what *my* answers were. But posts from other autistics were like, yes! That!

And the relief. To know I wasn't just not trying hard enough. I could finally give myself a little grace and be weird. I think I didn't have enough influences in my life telling me that it was okay not to be like everyone else, but mostly I needed to let myself off the hook. I needed something, anything, that took some of the blame and pressure off of me. And once I realised that it might not be my fault, so much relief came.

Ironically I am more socially skilled now than I ever was. I struggled for years to learn how to talk to people and suddenly, overnight, way after learning I had autism, it clicked. I think it's confidence. And I never would've had that if I didn't know who I was.

Elora: What people don't seem to understand about those of us who are just discovering our autism as adults is that when you're a kid you don't know that people's brains are working differently than yours and that the categories that seem self-evident to everyone else are going over your head. And no one knows that they need to teach you that there are different categories of social convention. If, for example, growing up you're taught that stimming is inappropriate and touching people without their consent is inappropriate and screaming inside is inappropriate and not looking people in the eyes is inappropriate, you don't know that these are different categories of rules. You just think that stimming, touching people without consent, screaming inside, and not looking people in the eyes are all terrible, and so you spend your life terrified that you're doing everything wrong. But the 'stimming is inappropriate' rule should be completely thrown out. The 'no touching people without consent' rule should stay. 'No screaming inside' depends on the event and context. 'Look people in the eyes' doesn't matter, but the *goal* of the rule, which is to let people know you're listening to them, is still a good idea.

When autistics connect with other autistics, we can help each other work through those rules we've internalised. But doctors, strangers on the street, and the media don't understand that our brains have to sort through years of blurred lines and contradictions. They expect us to know what the categories are, turn them on and off at command, and make them conveniently visible to the world around us. But that's not how it works. Our autism, our masking, our social conditioning, our culture, our religion, and more all create this big rule soup in our heads of how we are 'supposed' to be.

Cat: As I always say, unlearning is the hard part. After that, learning the new thing is easy. When you're diagnosed late, you have to unlearn and relearn so much. I think it would be fine if everyone around you was busy unlearning and relearning too. But so many people are stuck where they are while you're re-organising your entire life.

DIAGNOSIS VS. REALITY

There is a world of difference between the way autism is depicted in medicine and how it affects different people. This is often the case with mental disorders. Take something like depression. When you look up what depression is, you find a list of symptoms: fatigue, anhedonia, low appetite, feelings of sadness or emptiness. But does that really paint a full picture of what depression feels like? Does this dry summation really capture its depth and pain and loneliness? Say you had a friend who seemed suddenly distracted and unable to focus and then gave you a possession you knew she really valued. Based on this list, is that enough to decide she's depressed? Real life is messy. People are messy. And breaking something down into a technical one-page description is rarely enough to capture the full picture of what's going on in someone's head.

If a mood disorder like depression is hard to pin down and explain, even with its clear list of symptoms, then we can understand why something as varied and complex as autism is hard to talk about, much less diagnose. Because autism isn't an illness with a list of symptoms. It's a neurotype that is identified by the rest of the world through certain characteristics. Everything in our brains is coded differently because of our autism. It's more than just social anxiety or hyperfocus or any of the other characteristics we share. In our case it's actually a lifestyle.

So the DSM-5's list of symptoms doesn't paint a complete picture. It may be a starting point, but ultimately it tends to reinforce a stereotype of an autistic person: a white man who's good at maths but has bad social skills; a child who throws tantrums for no reason and can't communicate; an alien or a robot. But an autistic person who is struggling and doesn't know why may well look at those stereotypes and think, *That's not me. I must not be autistic.*

Historically, these stereotypes have come from the specialists who diagnose autism.

The scientific community is not immune to bigotry, and prejudices from other areas of life can spill over into the mental health field.

Let's say you're a teacher and a child in your class is acting out. How do you decide if that child has a mental health concern and should be referred to a doctor, or if they are just being naughty and should be sent to the principal's office? Whether you like it or not, subconscious prejudices might influence which children you label as 'having a problem' and which children you label as 'being a problem'. And these prejudices compound over time. If white boys are more likely to be referred to clinics for any number of reasons, those white boys are more likely to be studied and thus white boys with autism will be what experts have data on, making doctors less likely to notice autism in people who aren't white boys. This is part of why females and people of colour have been diagnosed less often than white males. Many people say that certain groups of people, like boys, or children in general, or white people, are more likely to be autistic, but the diagnostic system is so intertwined with societal biases that there's no way to prove that! That's why we, the authors of this book, assume that autism is more or less equally distributed across groups until it can be proven otherwise.

What we'd like to see is an understanding of autism that is more inclusive of diverse presentations of autism and less dependent on stereotypes. Until then our society, as a whole, will continue thinking about autism the wrong way and teaching doctors, therapists, educators, and parents of autistic children the wrong way.

SELF-DIAGNOSIS

Self-diagnosis is an individual's determination, after some research, that they have a disease, condition, or neurotype. In the age of the internet, self-diagnosis has become a possibility for the average person because nearly everyone has access to professional knowledge and peer-reviewed scientific research. As we've learned from WebMD, self-diagnosis has its flaws, but it's also a valuable way of narrowing down possibilities. With something like autism, we can see if it's something that vibes with us, try it out a little, mull it over, and ultimately decide if it feels right. Without access to this information, many autistics would go through life never knowing why they're struggling and feeling completely alone in that.

Self-diagnosis is a heavily debated issue among autistics. Many autistic people insist that self-diagnosis is not valid. They insist that autism must be diagnosed by a mental health professional and that to claim to be autistic without official validation is disrespectful to autistics with diagnoses from medical professionals. They fear that people will diagnose themselves with autism as a way of seeking attention or feeling special and worry there is no way to separate fake autistics from real autistics.

Others, however, believe that self-diagnosis is valid. Autism is not a well-understood condition (which is why this book exists), and as we've pointed out before. Like any medical care, the results you get will depend entirely on the qualifications and opinions of your doctor, and professionals like doctors and psychiatrists don't always have the most up-to-date information or the lived experience to know what being autistic feels like. There is no blood test to take or genetic marker to find. Learning about autism from autistic people's firsthand experiences can provide a more comprehensive, in-depth depiction of what autism looks like than learning from a doctor who may have experience with autism only in a clinical setting. And doctors, unless they are autistic, can only understand autism from the outside in, while autistics can understand it from the inside out. The experiences of actual autistic people are far more valuable than current formal education about autism and will continue to be until our society better understands autism.

When you learn about autism from other autistics, you get a much better idea of what autism really feels like. That doesn't mean every autistic knows everything about autism – it means that their perspective is often more useful than that of a doctor. After all, if you want to know if you have autism, asking what it *feels* like to have autism will provide you with different insights from those of someone who has only ever seen autism from the outside. This is why if enough time is spent in the community, online or in person, a self-diagnosis can be incredibly meaningful. It can also be much faster than pursuing a formal diagnosis and even help someone decide if a formal diagnosis is the right course of action for them.

This is also a good time to point out a fun fact about autistic people: we are very queer. One 2017 study found that autistics were more than twice as likely to identify as 'non-heterosexual' than their allistic peers, and one 2014 study found that autistic children were 7.59 times more likely to show signs of 'gender variance' than the control group.[45] Autism and queerness are both believed to be genetic and defined in the womb, but there is no known link between the two. Our theory? Autistic people are more comfortable being 'othered' and are more likely to try on different identities and see which one fits. It is far easier for someone who is already a social outcast to admit all the ways they're different, instead of just the one. And when you've already struggled with and rejected many rules in society, what do you care if you break the 'rules' of traditional gender roles?

THE PROS AND CONS OF A FORMAL DIAGNOSIS

PROFESSIONAL KNOWLEDGE

PRO: If the medical professional assessing you is up-to-date on autism research and biases in the community, they can offer insight based on years of experience that you could not access on your own. This is particularly useful if you are unsure if you are autistic and need an outside opinion.

CON: Not all medical professionals are up-to-date on research and biases, and they may consciously or unconsciously refuse to diagnose you based on outdated information or stereotypes about your race, gender, or age.

EMOTIONAL TOLL

PRO: Receiving an official diagnosis can be validating, especially if you are prone to anxiety and impostor syndrome or don't trust your own judgement.

CON: Going through the diagnostic process can be emotionally taxing. It can feel high-stakes, feature degrading questions, and open you up to judgement by people who may have no interest in hearing what it feels like to be you. The assessor may make a snap judgement based on oversimplified criteria, like whether you can make eye contact, which can feel devastating. Plus, many of the personal benefits of knowing that you are autistic (like learning to take care of yourself better) don't need an official diagnosis in the first place.

FORMAL RECORD

PRO: Having a formal record of your autism enables you to receive certain accommodations like governmental disability benefits and special treatment in certain circumstances (for example, some theme parks may let you skip the lines, and you can apply for a special pass that lets you into all US national parks for free).

CON: If those records fall into the wrong hands, you may be discriminated against. How often autism diagnoses are used against people, and which autistics are targeted specifically, varies, but job opportunities, educational opportunities, custody of your children, the ability to control your own money, and the ability to move to certain countries can all be affected, at least in theory, by a formal diagnosis. It is difficult to make statements about how common these situations are, because they vary widely by country, institution, perceived 'severity' of the person's autism, and other individual factors, and there are no databases (that we know of) that track these situations. There have, however, been attempts to make a catalogue of individuals diagnosed with autism, and you have no way of preventing that information from falling into the wrong hands.

COST AND ACCESS

PRO: An autism diagnosis may allow you to receive certain financial benefits and support services from the government or other institutions, though it will probably not be much.

CON: Autism assessments are sometimes very expensive and difficult to access in the first place. Accessing assistance can also complicate things; for example, if you are on disability in the United States, it can be difficult to save money or get married without losing some or all of your benefits.

CHANGING TIMES

PRO: A law could pass tomorrow that expands support for autistics, and your formal diagnosis could help you receive that help without having to wait. Similarly, a new organisation could open in your area that offers help you need.

CON: Situations could also change for the worse. Getting a formal diagnosis doesn't just mean having a record of your disability in our current system. It means whatever our government and society evolve into in the future have those records too.

The treatment of autism and the understanding of it are rapidly improving. If you're reading this book ten years in the future, things may have drastically changed by then.

But no matter when you're reading it, know that whether or not you seek an 'official' diagnosis is up to you. There's no one right option.

We're self-diagnosis fans around here; we're both self-diagnosed, technically, although we got 'official' diagnoses later. We firmly believe that few people would fake being an oppressed minority for the attention. Sure, there are some, but they are a tiny percentage of a much larger whole that greatly benefits from self-diagnoses. Maybe there are a couple of teenagers faking autism on TikTok for likes. But that is difficult to prove and dangerous to accuse someone of. Compassion is usually a more appropriate response than frustration.

And the good news is other autistics don't ask to see your paperwork when you try to connect with them (well, not the ones we're friends with, anyway). In fact, nobody wants to see your diagnosis unless you're applying for special services like accommodations, disability payments, or student loan forgiveness. Outside of the official-versus-self-diagnosis arguments, no one asks what type of diagnosis you have.

We believe that if you examine information about autism to the best of your ability and think that it describes you, you're one of us. And if you're autistic, we welcome you. Proper autism education means that a lot more people will realise they're autistic, and we may come to find that tons of people are autistic. But as outsiders ourselves, we know not to ostracise, and a lot of autistics agree with us.

SO YOU'RE DIAGNOSED, NOW WHAT?

Being diagnosed with autism later in life is different from being diagnosed as a child. A school-age child may be placed in special classes or their teacher may modify an academic plan with the child's autism in mind. But adults with autism, especially those who were not diagnosed until adulthood, rarely get any kind of support, special treatment, special classes, jobs, or places to live. Typically you get diagnosed and then you go back to your regular life. Everything is different, but nothing has changed.

It is extremely common for an autistic person to struggle with a new diagnosis and panic, grieve, or feel lost. When you learn you're autistic, you reevaluate everything about yourself from a new perspective. You dig down into the core of who you are and recalibrate. You can't go on like everything is the same as it was. That would be like struggling with out-of-date software because you refuse to restart your computer. It's unsustainable and eventually something's going to crash.

The good news is that you're not alone. The autistic community is growing every day and is there to help people who have recently been diagnosed. We offer support, guidance, and education. We dispel misconceptions and outdated myths. We are on your side. The autistic community is not perfect – we have challenges and problems like any other group of people. However, in general, engaging with other autistics can go a long way towards helping you grow and heal.

The process of adjusting to a diagnosis takes time. There might be some grief over the person you were before, or what you wanted to be, or what you could have been if things were different. That's fine. It's a process you have to go through. But for a lot of us, something amazing happens. You finally understand that you were never broken, or wrong, or not trying hard enough. You were exactly who you were supposed to be. You're not a caterpillar with weird legs. You're a butterfly. And it's time to get your colourful little butterfly butt up so you can finally fly.

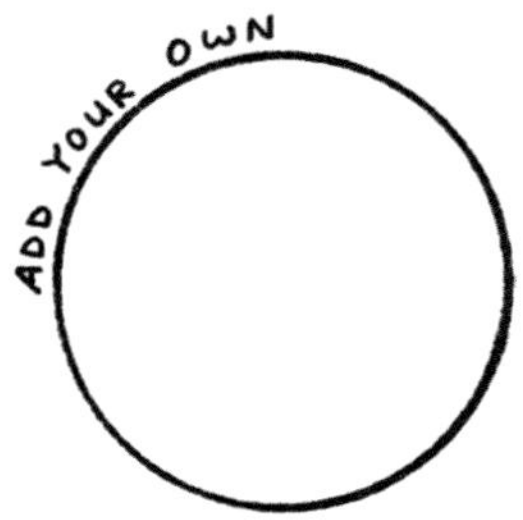

9

SKILLS AND STRENGTHS

Autistics are often judged by how 'normal' we seem. A lot of the time, we equate the value of a person with how well they can function in a 'normal' life with a home, job, and family, because people who cannot work are considered a burden in our competitive, money-focused society. And so as autistics we end up judging our own value by the things we can do, especially when our need for help annoys the people around us.

This is flawed logic. The skills a person needs vary depending on their culture, location, family situation, age, and finances. It is nearly impossible to be completely self-reliant in our current global economy. And besides, people have value beyond what they can do to serve others, especially governments or businesses that don't care about their well-being.

Our money-obsessed culture might tell you that you need to perform certain skills to contribute to society, but often the people who do the most for society are the ones who don't fit the mould. Many of the people throughout history who contributed the most to humankind were considered weirdos during their time – eccentric artists, big-dreaming revolutionaries, paradigm-defining scientists, and radical religious figures, to name a few. Extraordinary people often can't fit in, and it's a waste of their time and talents for them to try when that effort could be put towards creating something that an ordinary person could never imagine. Sometimes the best thing you can do to help society is to be different.

We firmly believe that no one's value is based on the work they can do for other people. People are important because they are people, and that is enough. Plus, people are different! Everyone has different skills because everyone is unique. And all of those skills matter – the hard work of all the physicists, coders, and engineers in the *Apollo*

STICKING TO A SCHEDULE
S M T W T F S
ADAPTING TO SURPRISES
PATTERN RECOGNITION
ADAPTING TO CHANGE
REMEMBERING FACTS
MULTITASKING
ADD YOUR OWN
BUSINESS SENSE
STRESS MANAGEMENT
PRIORITISING
1
2
3
4
WORKING WITH ANIMALS
NEGOTIATION
MAINTAINING HYGIENE
DRIVING
CLEANING
ADD YOUR OWN
LEARNING LANGUAGES
自闭症
COOKING
CHARISMA
REGULATING MY EMOTIONS
CONFLICT RESOLUTION
INTUITION
READING

program would have been for nothing if not for the equally hard work of plumbers, clothing designers, mechanics, accountants, janitorial staff, and everyone else who helped to keep the lights on.

If everyone had the same skill set we would still be living in caves and trying to figure out how fire works!

Everyone has different abilities, but no one person is big enough to have all of them, and we need all of them to thrive as a society.

LET'S PLAY A GAME. On this and the previous pages are thirty-three different skills someone can have. Colour in each skill you think you are good at. No one is going to be good at all of them, and many people will only be good at a few. But they are *all* important to the human race. Your value does not come from the skills you have – but your skills are still pretty impressive and you probably have more skills than you realise. We even left you some blank spaces so you can add your own!

MASLOW'S HIERARCHY OF NEEDS

Maslow's hierarchy of needs is a visual representation of the different needs we have as humans and how we spend energy to meet those needs. Often shown in the shape of a pyramid, the hierarchy demonstrates which needs support the others. Maslow's pyramid is not a hard and fast rule that governs every thought we think, and in fact in many ways it's too simplistic. Rather, Maslow's pyramid shows us how humans grow and meet their needs in broad strokes. It's about helping us understand our priorities, not about establishing strict uncrossable lines.

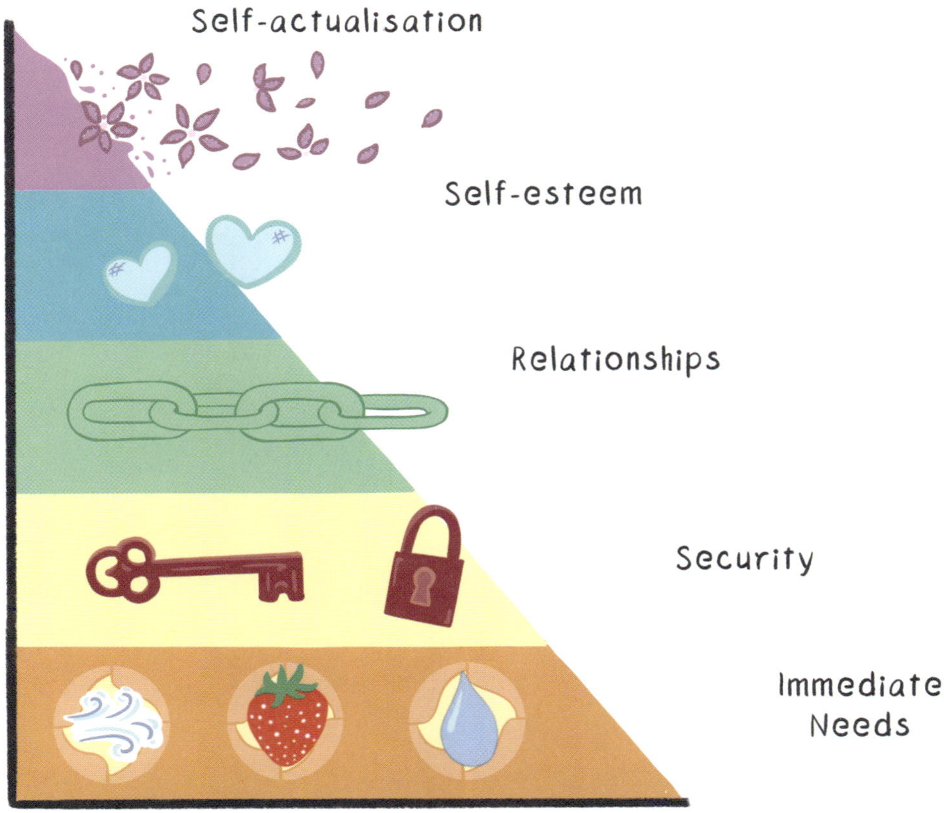

In order to meet one of the needs on the pyramid, you must first meet the needs below it. This makes sense – after all, you only have so much energy. It's hard to focus your energy on something lofty like 'developing self-confidence' when you are starving. Your energy will go towards meeting the most urgent need first. Yes, developing confidence is important, but it's of no use if you're dead.

The bottom tier of the pyramid represents our immediate survival needs: food, water, air, sleep, short-term shelter, and safety from immediate danger. If these foundational needs are not being met, our energy immediately goes towards meeting them. What if you were having a very deep think about the meaning of life and then you started choking? Would you say, 'I can deal with the choking later. I'll keep thinking for now.' No! You'd immediately focus on trying to breathe again and would probably forget you were thinking about the meaning of life at all. Our most basic needs always take priority.

The second tier on the pyramid is security: permanent shelter, resource and financial security (i.e. knowing you are in no immediate danger of starving or freezing or not paying rent), health, and the absence of violence. We need to know that we are not in immediate danger. If the first layer of the pyramid is made up of the things we immediately need for survival, then the second layer is made up of the assurances that our needs will continue to be met, at least for a little while. You might be able to meet all your immediate physical needs if you were stranded naked on a deserted island, but you would feel so much better if you had clothes, a reliable source of clean water, nets to fish with, and a shelter to live in. Sure, you're scared and stranded either way, but in the first scenario you're just alive for the day, while in the second scenario you know you'll probably be alive for a while.

The third tier is relationships. Humans aren't meant to be alone. We need connection. We can get this from groups we are a part of, both small (like a book club or gym class) and large (like a country or a religion). We can get this through individual friendships with humans and animals alike. We can also get this through romantic relationships or our family relationships, which are essentially a premade community for us to connect with so this need can be met.

Speaking of deserted islands, there's a famous movie called *Cast Away* about a man who is stranded on an island alone for years. He needs friendship so desperately that he paints a face on a volleyball and names it Wilson. The castaway has met his immediate needs, and at least some of his safety needs, but that isn't enough. Humans *need* connection, desperately, and if they can't find it they will make it.

The fourth layer of the pyramid is self-esteem. You need a reason, or many reasons, to like yourself. You need recognition for your accomplishments. You need to believe in yourself and be believed in by others. In the popular television series *Avatar: The Last Airbender*, Prince Zuko of the warmongering Fire Nation hunts the Avatar in a desperate attempt to regain his honour. But even though he is a villain, we care about him as a character because over time we come to understand that he needs a reason to like himself. He needs respect from his community. He needs to take pride in himself again. Throughout the show, Zuko shifts from finding his self-esteem in the approval of his community to finding his self-esteem through doing what he believes is right. Incidentally, this bleeds into the top layer of the pyramid – self-actualisation.

Self-actualisation essentially means 'becoming who you are meant to be'. It encompasses many aspects of life, like developing your own beliefs about what's right and wrong, solving problems in your life, expressing yourself creatively, and just plain having fun. How many times have you seen a movie about a character who 'has it all' but isn't happy because they aren't being true to themself? These characters are seeking self-actualisation. For example, in the movie *Moana*, Moana has plenty to eat and drink, she's safe and protected, loved and respected, and can take pride in her accomplishments. She seems to be thriving – but that isn't enough. It's not that Moana is ungrateful for what she has. She is being asked to accept her parents' understanding of the world as her own without figuring things out for herself. She is being asked to deny her passions, curiosity, and individual strengths to maintain a status quo. In the end Moana achieves self-actualisation by sailing the ocean, fulfilling her dreams, exploring her questions, indulging her passions, and choosing her own path in life, with her own sense of morality.

Self-actualisation is not a onetime accomplishment. It's an ongoing state of being.

You might describe it as 'being true to yourself' or 'living life to the fullest'. You never 'become' self-actualised. You keep growing and changing and learning and maturing.

A person's position on this chart is dynamic. You can't just decide to self-actualise and then be done with the whole pyramid. Many of us understand what it's like to live pay cheque to pay cheque, and if we are worried about making rent, we don't have as much energy to worry about our place in the universe. Autistic people often struggle to feed themselves, maintain hygiene, stay hydrated, and support our other physiological needs because of sensory sensitivities, time blindness, difficulty shifting focus, and overload. Someone who is sleep-deprived or food-deprived can't focus well on anything else. Even if an autistic person finds unique methods to meet their basic physiological needs, people around the person might consider those methods abnormal and try to force them to change.

For autistic people, second- and third-tier needs can be much more difficult to meet than they would be for allistics. On average, autistic people struggle with maintaining jobs and keeping up a household more than allistics, which puts our personal safety in jeopardy. And if we have trouble communicating and being understood, as we so often do, the third tier, love and belonging, might also be in jeopardy.

The third tier, however, is significant and not one to overlook. If you are struggling to be loved and feel a sense of belonging, you simply do not have the mental energy to live life to the fullest. You will have a hard time moving past the need for external validation. If a person never experiences unconditional love, how much more difficult is it for them to learn to provide love to others?

We do not want to perpetuate the myth that you have to earn other people's approval to be worthy of love. You deserve love, whether other people give it to you or not. We are simply pointing out that it is difficult to give energy to complex mental processes like evaluating your self-worth and your place in the world if you have to spend massive amounts of energy remembering to eat and trying to make friends. Your brain is not a source of infinite energy. You have limits, and if you reach that limit just trying to stay alive and calm, you won't have any energy left for personal growth.

> It is hard to cultivate self-respect
> if you are never respected.
>
> It is hard to build self-esteem
> if you are never held in esteem.
>
> It is hard to know who you want to be
> if you barely know who you are.

An autistic person who is diagnosed as an adult will often go through a period of reframing their life in such a way that their entire personality seems to revolve around autism. The person may use autism to explain seemingly unrelated things, bring it up often and unprompted, and even appear to become 'more' autistic. This is not someone who is revelling in a newfound diagnosis and trying to excuse themself from personal responsibilities. This is more like a drowning person grasping at a lifeline. When someone finally gets insight into who they are, they may realise they need to tear down the pyramid of their needs and rebuild it from scratch. They need to recalibrate everything they know about themself and reevaluate what they once took for granted. The person's former pyramid needs to come down and be reconstructed from the ground up with their autism taken into full account.

They will come out better for it on the other side. The mask they used to rely on may now be a tool they can use, taking it off and putting it on as they please instead of using it as a shield. They finally have the option of understanding their own quirks and habits well enough to have them work *with* them instead of *against* them. And instead of thinking they are broken, they can understand that they are simply different.

We've covered a lot in this section, so let's circle back. What can we learn from Maslow's hierarchy of needs?

1. When people demand that autistics deny their basic needs in order to seem normal, they are sabotaging that autistic person's life as a whole, not only in that one moment. We are all going to have times we have to push ourselves or step out of our comfort zone, but if an autistic person is always denied the opportunity to wear comfortable clothes, eat foods that are easy for them to handle, relax in ways that work for them, socialise with people who respect them and in quantities they can handle, and so on, they are being denied the opportunity to build the foundation of their pyramid of needs.

When have you been told you need to act 'normal?' How did it feel to be told this?

2. Unmasking is about more than being ourselves. When we unmask we are better able to take care of ourselves. When we stop forcing ourselves to be 'normal', we can better meet our basic needs. People may have sold you the lie that toughening up is a necessary step in thriving, but if you've tried to toughen up your entire life and it's still sapping all your energy, then maybe toughening up is actually the problem, not the solution. Normal is not the finish line of a race you are required to run. Normal is a place some people are meant to be and other people aren't. As one famous fictional outcast, Morticia Addams, once said, 'What is normal for the spider is a calamity for the fly.'

What do you think is a normal expectation or belief held by allistic people that seems like chaos to you?

3. Finally, Maslow's hierarchy reminds us to give ourselves grace. Sometimes you have learned to unmask and accept yourself as autistic, and the people around you are supportive, but autism still makes it hard for you to meet your needs. This is really difficult to go through, but you should know that you're not a horrible person because you struggle to self-actualise. It can be devastating to watch the people around you learn to find themselves while you're still struggling to meet your basic needs. But you are not alone and it's not your fault. No one is a mental superhero who can just decide, 'I'm going to become super emotionally healthy and fulfilled today'. You're not a failure for not reaching your full potential yet. You can still pursue happiness and try to take care of yourself even if you aren't feeling like 'self-actualisation' is an option right now. Do your best and know you're not alone.

What would it take for you to be able to move further along in this journey?

ELORA'S EMOTION BREAKDOWN

(Not to be confused with Elora's big emotional breakdown, which came in 2018.)

Autistics often struggle to identify their emotions. Just because you feel *something* does not mean you know what you are feeling or how to express it. This is called alexithymia.

I do not have this problem. Whether I was just born without alexithymia, grew out of it along the way, or beat it to death with years of therapy and theatre classes, I am actually pretty good at identifying my emotions.

Cat: I *do* have this problem. I will feel something and have no idea what it is. Sometimes I don't even know that I'm feeling anything; I just suddenly want to take a nap or bury myself in something and ignore the world.

I have broken down the way I understand emotions into individual elements, what you might call emotional building blocks. By explaining emotions in detail like this, hopefully I'll help you get more comfortable with describing them yourself. At the end, I explain my personal step-by-step process for identifying emotions. This is just my own method for explaining emotions that works for me. If it doesn't work for you, that's fine.

There are three core types of emotion: positive, neutral, and negative. Positive emotions feel good. Negative emotions feel bad. Neutral emotions feel neither good nor bad, or they feel good or bad depending on the situation but not others.

Each core type of emotion has two expressions of itself. These are the six subdivisions of emotions. The two positive emotions are happy and safe. The two negative emotions are sad and angry. The two neutral emotions are interest and disinterest. From there the emotions split into more specific versions. Emotions feel different based on their individual intensity or the amount of energy you have to spend on them. Emotional intensity affects what you feel a lot.

For example, low-energy happy is **content**. When you feel content, you're feeling happy, but you're not very focused on it. Medium-energy happy is **cheerful**. When you feel cheerful, you're in a good mood and aware of it. You might even feel a bit bouncy because you're so happy. High-energy happy is **thrilled**. This is an all-encompassing happiness, consuming you like a very pleasant fire.

Low-energy safe is **relaxed**. You feel safe but aren't thinking about it too much. You're enjoying how pleasant it is to not feel in danger at all. Medium-energy safe is **secure**. It's similar to relaxed, only you're more aware of it. High energy safe is **confident**. At this intensity, your safety has spilled over into the way you interact with the world. The sense of safety is strong inside you and you feel prepared and powerful. Even if you know something could go wrong, it doesn't feel like it will hurt you much. When we think of confidence, we think of people doing hard things without worrying about them. The key to this emotion is not the 'doing hard things' part; it's the 'without worrying about them' part. When you are confident you are feeling a sturdy mental safety, and that makes doing hard things easier.

Low-energy interest is **bored**. Interest can feel positive or negative depending on what you are interested in. When you want to do something but you don't have the motivation to figure out what to do, you feel bored. Medium-energy interest is **curious**. When you're curious, you're interested in something and are invested in that emotion. You want to learn more. Curiosity kills boredom because curiosity is the motivation to do something about boredom. High-energy interest is **obsessed**. Obsession is the emotion of interest, but so strong it starts to take over your brain. When you're obsessed, interest is using a lot of energy.

Low-energy disinterest is apathetic. Like interest, disinterest can feel positive or negative depending on the context. Apathy is the emotion of not really caring about something, but not particularly *not* caring about it either. You're neither here nor there.

Medium-energy disinterest is disturbed. When you are disturbed by something, it bothers you and with enough energy that you are definitely aware of it. High-energy disinterest is repulsed. When you are feeling repulsed by something, you have a great need to not be involved in the thing you are disinterested in.

The feeling of low-energy sad is **melancholy**. When you are melancholy, you feel sad, but it does not stop you from doing the things you love. This is different from clinical depression, which is a medical condition that involves the feeling of melancholy, along with other symptoms, such as persistent fatigue. Medium-energy sad is **distressed**. You're sad and there's some power to it. High-energy sad is **distraught**. When you're distraught, sadness has taken over your brain. You're overwhelmed with the intense power of the sadness you are feeling.

Low-energy angry is **miffed**. You're angry, but you can brush it off easily. Medium-energy angry is **annoyed**. You're more than a little angry at this point, and you're definitely aware of it. High-energy angry is **furious**. The anger is very strong at this point, and you feel unable to do any task that does not have to do with the anger. You have to let it out!

Some things we call emotions are actually natural signals that our body is sending us.

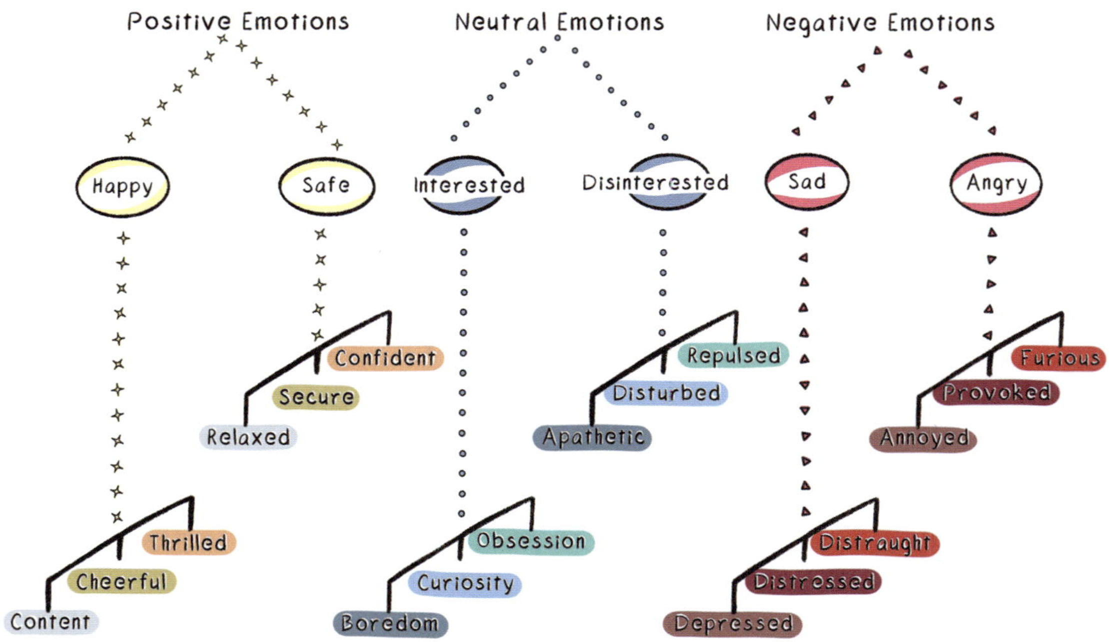

PHYSICAL ATTRACTION is an instinctual desire to enjoy someone's body, whether that's simply looking at them or touching, hugging, kissing, or being intimate with them. When you see someone and think, *Ooh, they're hot*, you're feeling physical attraction.

DISTRACTED is the condition of trying to focus on something and not being able to. If your focus were a train, distracted would be the feeling of the train derailing.

TIRED is your body telling you that you need rest. Tiredness can be physical, emotional, mental, and more. It's a signal that says, 'Hey, we don't have the energy to keep going like this.'

AFRAID is your body and mind telling you that you are in danger. Fear can be subconscious. You might not know *why* you are afraid but still feel fear. The things our bodies interpret as danger can be as obvious as a roaring tiger or as subtle as the voice of a person who sounds like someone who hurt us long ago.

HUNGRY is your body telling you that you need food.

THIRSTY is your body telling you that you need water.

SURPRISE is your body trying to quickly adapt to a new situation. Surprise can be paired with lots of other feelings, but surprise itself is your body going, 'Woah, there is so much happening. Let me catch up!'

DYSREGULATION is your mind telling you it's having trouble doing everything it should. For example, you can feel dysregulated because of sensory overload. Your brain can't do everything it needs to because it's busy processing too much.

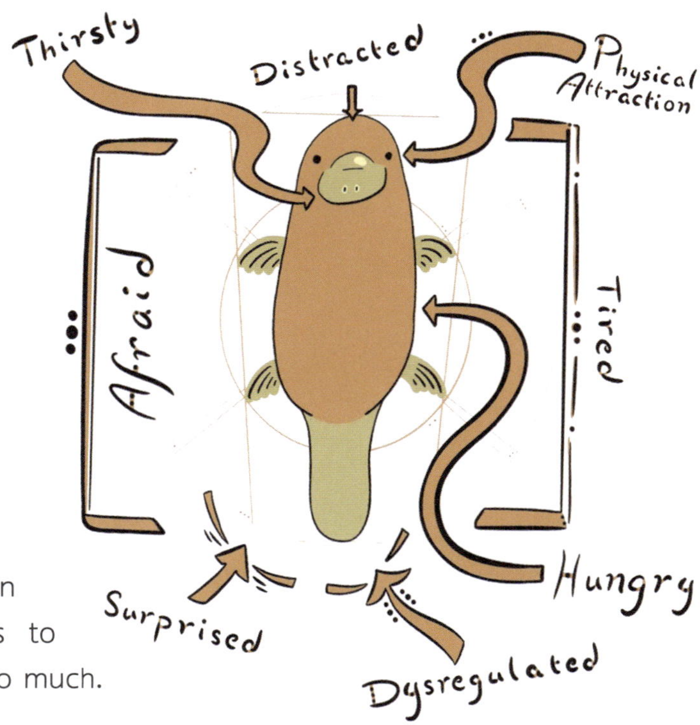

Some emotions have a direction. To better understand the emotions you're feeling, try asking, 'What caused this emotion?' or 'Where is it coming from?' Every emotion could probably have a direction if you spent enough time picking it apart, but for some emotions, directions are necessary to understand them. For example, if someone says that they are happy, you don't necessarily need to know *why* they are happy to understand how they feel. Where the happiness is coming from does not necessarily matter. You understand what happiness is. However, if someone says they are angry, understanding what they are angry at (the direction of their anger) gives important context. People are often happy because of many subtle factors – which I call the state of being content. They don't feel pressure to *do anything* with their happiness. They are just *being* happy. The happiness does not need to draw their attention to any specific action or situation. Anger, on the other hand, usually has a specific cause. Anger has direction. Anger focuses you on something specific.

For example, shame has direction. **SHAME** is sadness about yourself that comes from within. You're sad because of something you did, something that feels like your fault, or something about you that other people might look down on. This sadness can exist even if you know that the thing causing it isn't your fault.

PRIDE also comes from within. It is confidence in yourself because of your abilities, attributes, or accomplishments. When you feel proud you have a sense of admiration for yourself. You know you are someone worth celebrating because of what you have to offer the world.

FEAR always comes from something (like a roaring tiger or a voice that reminds us of someone who hurt us). If you don't know where the fear is coming from, you might describe it as being 'on edge' or 'jittery'.

ANXIETY is fear that comes from many directions. When fear seems to be coming at you from all sides or for several reasons, even if you're not entirely sure what those reasons are, that is anxiety.

TRUST is the feeling of safety that comes from a specific person, thing, or situation. If you feel that being with your dad or best friend is *safe*, you *trust* him.

You don't have to know the direction of an emotion to feel it. The direction is simply a way to describe emotions better. Knowing the direction of an unpleasant emotion can also help us learn how to fix the problems that caused the emotion. If you can pinpoint the source of your fears, for example, you might be able to come to terms with them and calm down, or make a plan to address the danger.

Combining two or more emotions, body signals, or specific situations makes more complex emotions.

ALARM is *surprise* plus *fear*.

BITTERNESS is *sadness* and *anger* aimed at a specific cause, such as an event or circumstance.

CRAVING is a *want* that is so strong it almost feels like an instinct. It motivates you to get the thing you are craving. For example, craving a specific food is a combination of interest (an emotion) and hunger (an instinct). It is a natural, human need, and a more intellectual experience.

DESIRE is *interest* plus a *want* for the thing you are interested in.

EXCITEMENT is *high-intensity happiness* coming from a specific experience that hasn't happened yet or is currently happening. For example, if you are excited for a party, you are intensely happy about it, even though it hasn't happened yet. Excitement often includes a bit of fear too, that things might not go the way you want them to, and a bit of uncertainty, which is what makes the happiness so intense. It feels like there's a risk that the happiness will evaporate, so while you are happily waiting for what's to come, there's a sense of urgency that it come as soon as possible.

FRUSTRATION is *unfulfilled desire* plus *anger* at whatever is keeping you from having the thing you desire. For example, if you are frustrated that the TV is not working, you are interested in what is on TV, you want to watch TV, and you are angry at whatever is preventing the TV from working, even (or especially) if you don't know what that is.

GREED is *desire* plus a *willingness* to take what you want, even if that causes problems for other people.

GRIEF is *loss* plus *sadness* about that loss.

HESITATION is desire, plus a *fear* that makes you stop and reconsider before acting on your desire or causes you to move slowly and cautiously while acting on your desire.
HOMESICKNESS is *loss* aimed at your home, even if you know you will return there eventually. It is often mixed with *loneliness*, *sadness*, and *discomfort* with the effort it takes to adapt to a new way of living.
JEALOUSY is *desire* for (aimed at) something that someone else has, plus *anger* at the person who has it when you don't.
LONELINESS is *desire* for (aimed at) companionship.
LOSS is sadness plus unfulfilled interest, for (aimed at) something you used to have.
PANIC is *fear* plus *dysregulation* at high-intensity.
RATTLED is *alarm* plus *dysregulation*.
REGRET is *sadness* plus a *desire to change* something that has already happened, when it cannot be changed.
TENSE is *fear*, plus *anger*, plus *dysregulation*, at low-intensity.

There are lots of different kinds of love. Let's break them down!
AFFECTION is *interest* in (aimed at) someone or something, plus *happiness* that comes to you from that person or thing.
DEVOTION is *interest* in someone or something, plus the decision to help, protect, or care for that person or thing.
FAMILIAL LOVE is *strong affection*, plus *devotion*. You can feel more than one kind of love. You can also feel an unexpected kinds of love, or no love, for someone. For example, you may not feel traditional family love for your family, and that's okay.
FRIENDSHIP LOVE is *affection* plus *trust*.
ROMANTIC LOVE is *affection* for someone plus a *desire* to have an intimate, special relationship with them that is closer and more committed than most relationships. It also includes a desire to be devoted to someone and receive devotion in return. We already talked about physical attraction, but to recap, physical

attraction is a natural instinct to enjoy someone's body, perhaps by kissing or hugging them. Physical attraction and romantic love often go together, but they don't always. You may desire physical affection from someone without desiring any kind of emotional intimacy, for example.

Sometimes our emotions involve our interpretation or perception of a situation.
AWE is *surprise* at a thing, plus a *perception* that the thing is impressive or amazing.
OFFENCE is *anger*, *sadness*, and *embarrassment* coming from a way that we have been treated, plus the **perception** that we did not deserve to be treated that way.
ABANDONMENT is *loneliness*, plus a *perception* that we are owed a certain level of care from other people that we are not getting.
PITY is *sadness* for someone or something. Sometimes pity is simple, like feeling badly for someone in pain. But sometimes pity is a sort of condescending sadness for someone perceived to be less important or weaker than the person feeling pity.
WONDER is *awe* plus *curiosity*.

You can feel more than one emotion at once. And your emotions can even contradict each other. For example, going into a contest, you might feel confident in your abilities but afraid that those abilities will not be enough to bring you through. Therefore your abilities may provide you with a sense of safety, but the situation might still feel dangerous. When our emotions are contradicting each other, we might call that feeling conflicted.

Feeling conflicted about your emotions can be an overwhelming experience, and that experience can create more emotions. For example, feeling conflicted may be uncomfortable and when paired with a high-pressure environment, it might make you feel anxious or panicky.

There are plenty of reasons that emotions can be hard to understand and communicate. Different people might use different words to describe the same emotion. It's not as if emotions stay in neat, labelled boxes. We are all just guessing the best ways to describe our emotions. You and your friend might be feeling the same emotion, but she calls it 'frustrated' and you call it 'annoyed'. This can lead to miscommunication. For example, you might use the word 'annoying' to describe things you see as childish and petty but the word 'frustrating' to describe situations which you think are serious and mature. This can subtly influence whether you view your friend's emotions as a 'big deal' or not. This is part of why having open conversations about our emotions is so important. One word can carry unseen baggage, but several words together are easier to understand.

Some emotions don't even have a name, at least not in English. One example is *schadenfreude*, which is a German word that describes the feeling of pleasure that comes from someone else's misfortune. If you saw a woman kick a puppy and then that woman slipped and fell into a puddle of mud and you felt happy that she fell, then you would be feeling *schadenfreude*.

The fact that the German language includes a word for this highly specific emotion and English does not brings us to another important fact: our culture affects how we approach emotions. It might be totally normal for men to talk about their emotions in one group. But in another, men might be bullied for talking about their feelings. So if a man from the 'don't talk about your feelings' group says, 'I'm sad', he might actually be feeling miserably sad and just not feeling as though he is allowed to say so until the sadness becomes overwhelming.

The context around an emotion can also tweak its meaning. For example, a use of the word 'thrilled' could either mean 'very happy' or 'scared in a good way'. If someone says they were thrilled to get their favourite book as a birthday present, they probably mean 'very happy'. If someone says the roller coaster they rode was thrilling, they probably mean that the way the ride scared them was exhilarating. If someone is thrilled to get married, they might mean the word in *both* ways at once! Marriage can be a wonderful thing that you're happy about, but it can also be an intimidating prospect that you're scared about in a good way.

You can even invent your own words for emotions! I have started calling the feeling I get when I had a lot of strong emotions the day before an 'emotional hangover'. Those earlier feelings may not still be in me, but my brain is a bit tired from feeling them and therefore I feel somewhat disoriented.

If you don't know what you're feeling, one way to find out is to pay attention to the signals your body is sending you. If you're overwhelmed and don't know what is going on inside you, but you notice that your stomach hurts and feels empty, that could be a clue that you're hungry. Trembling hands can be a sign of anxiety. Drooping eyes can indicate exhaustion. Stimming more than usual can be a sign that whatever is being felt is a high-intensity emotion.

Every person responds to their emotions in their own way. They might be difficult to discern at first, but over time you'll notice your body's response patterns. These clues come in handy in self-care.

Shaking hands means...

Blurred vision means...

Clenched jaw means...

Hot face means...

Pain behind my eyes means...

Lightheadedness means...

____________ means...

____________ means...

ELORA AND CAT TALK EXTERNAL INFLUENCES ON EMOTIONS

Cat: Our emotions can be affected by external sources too. Your hormones, physical health, and even the weather can affect how you feel. As autistic people, we are hypersensitive to the world around us. If we feel, hear, smell, taste, and see things that other people aren't sensitive enough to notice, is it really that unlikely that our emotions are being affected by some sensory experience that might not affect others or might not affect them as strongly?

Elora: The three typical external affecters of emotions for me personally are hormones, weather, and stomach and digestive issues.

I suffer from premenstrual dysphoric disorder (PMDD), a health condition that makes a person's hormones around their period much, much worse. Ninety-two per cent of autistic people who menstruate had PMDD in one 2008 study,[24] though more research is needed to confirm those numbers in the general population.

For many years my premenstrual symptoms were so extreme that I struggled to think straight. I felt like I was going insane. People would tell me my symptoms were not a big deal, but my body would bother me so much that I didn't want to live anymore – yes, really. Then, like a switch had flipped, it would turn off. Instead of realising that something wasn't right in my body, I got mad at myself for 'being dramatic' and 'not having self-control'. Eventually I remembered the stories of other women with PMDD that I had read about online and asked my gynaecologist about it. She prescribed me some hormonal birth control that would essentially replace my body's natural hormones so I could have a more manageable cycle. And it worked!

Since PMDD is so common in autistic people, I wanted to mention it here. Feeling so distraught that you want to die during PMS is not normal, and it's not something you should have to just 'tough out'. If you're experiencing this, ask your doctor for help. And if your doctor tells you 'that's just womanhood', *find another doctor!* If you are suffering horribly every month and your doctor says you just have to deal with it because that's 'girl stuff', then that doctor is either uneducated or a sexist jerk. There is a better life out there.

I still have some significant mood swings during my cycle, and those are worth noting if I'm feeling strong emotions. I know that if I'm feeling wild, overwhelming emotions at that time of the month, they will go away (or at least become manageable) on their own in a few days. It's a relief to know that some problems will go away on their own!

Cat: I too had PMDD for many years! I didn't even realise this until you described it to me. People told me that was normal. I also had that thing where periods basically leave you bedridden for years [dysmenorrhoea] to the point where I didn't even notice I had appendicitis for three days because I thought it was cramps.

Elora: Another factor that affects my emotions a lot is the weather. I don't know why, but when the weather changes suddenly, it *really* affects me. Often I'll toss and turn all night if a weather front is moving in.

Cat: The weather will also mess me up. Can't focus, can't function in the winter, it's just a mess. The weather recently turned cold for a bit and it's been impossible to do anything since then.

Elora: Sometimes I get brain fog for a day or two. As a child I'd often end up throwing up for a few hours when the weather changed. It was rough. This connects to the last big unusual factor in my emotions: my gastric issues. If my stomach is irritated, or I'm constipated, or I ate too much spicy food, my emotions can really be affected. I've gotten in the habit of taking an antacid whenever I'm feeling anxious for no apparent reason. A lot of the time the antacid helps calm me down.

Cat: The biggest shift in my emotions comes from changes in blood sugar. If I'm feeling overwhelmed or anxious or angry or if I hate the world and everyone in it, it's usually because I forgot to eat or I didn't eat when I took my medications that morning. It'll mess up my whole day. I can't always shake myself out of it, but most of the time getting something solid to eat helps a lot. My go-to has always been ice cream. I craved it all the time before I knew why, but it's dairy (settles the stomach) and sugary (restores low blood sugar). I've switched to yoghurt now. I don't have the digestive issues that are common with other autistics, but that's likely because I'm from Cajun country and we basically eat garbage.

Elora: Whenever I'm feeling strong emotions that feel out of control, I check in with myself about these three different forces that affect my mood. Is it that time of the month? Did I miss my hormonal medications? Did the weather just change? I also ask is my stomach okay, and am I having digestion issues? If the answer to any of these questions is 'yes', then I make sure to address the issue. With PMDD and weather issues I can wait it out. With stomach issues I can take antacids and be gentle on my stomach. These aren't necessarily instant fixes, but knowing that I'll feel better soon is a relief in itself.

FEELING TRIGGERED

Another important emotional experience is the phenomenon of being 'triggered'. This use of this word originated in the vocabulary of psychotherapy but has migrated into everyday slang – people will say they are 'triggered' as a joke, or to express irritation. But what does it really mean?

Sometimes in life we encounter strong, difficult emotions due to deeply painful experiences. These experiences leave us vulnerable, and the emotions that come with them can come up at unexpected times. Have you ever injured a part of your body, and after it wasn't ever quite the same? Maybe you hurt your knee years ago, and now if you're going for a run you have to wear a brace. The knee has healed, but it will never feel quite the same.

Just as our bodies can become sensitive from past hurts, so can our minds. Being 'triggered' is the experience of something hitting that emotionally sensitive area. It's more than feeling irritable, peeved, or offended. When you are triggered, your body thinks it's in danger, even if it's not.

Your mind and body can react to something instinctively without your conscious permission. If you accidentally stabbed a sensitive place in your mouth with a corn chip and it started to bleed, you would open your mouth automatically, not bite down more. You don't even have to think about it. Your mouth is bleeding, so you release your jaw and tend to the open wound.

Something can be a sensitive emotional area for you even if you can't describe why. For example, an autistic child might be traumatised by going to school, perhaps because of the sensory overload of dozens of screaming classmates or because of bullying. It doesn't matter if their parents and teachers say that the bullying 'isn't too bad' or the sensory issues are 'just something they have to learn to deal with'. If school is a constant, sustained source of stress, it's not unreasonable to expect someone to be traumatised by the experience of getting ready for school. But that child may grow up feeling ashamed of their 'over-dramatic' meltdowns before school. They might become angry with themself for 'being so weak'. Whether they recognise it or not, thinking about school, spending time in school-like environments, or even smelling school supplies might be enough to freak their body out, like a corn chip to a gum.

One big incident can also cause trauma. If you were walking your dog one day and the animal was hit by a bus, that would be traumatic. Even if your dog was not seriously injured, you might feel scared to walk them again. You might get nervous hearing the jangle of the dog leash or cry if you see a bus while driving. There's that corn chip again.

Trauma is immense and complicated, and there's no way we can describe it fully here. But there are three things you should really know about it:

1. Trauma isn't necessarily one specific thing that happens to you. Trauma can come in many shapes and intensities, from many different experiences, and affect you in any number of ways.
2. You might have trauma you haven't identified yet. Trying to identify it isn't you 'trying to be a victim' or 'looking for problems that aren't there'. You're just trying to see if you've got a big sensitive spot, so you don't get hurt again.
3. Trauma can trigger you when you don't expect it, even when you don't realise it.[25]

We wish we had a foolproof magic solution for making trauma go away, but that's not how it works. Thousands of people much smarter and more educated than us have been working on that problem for decades, and they don't have a cure-all answer. But there are two big pieces of good news: simply knowing that you are triggered can help you handle the emotions in tough situations, and triggers can be addressed and bother you less and less over time.

If you're really mad at someone you're arguing with and you realise that the fight has triggered a memory of someone else who hurt you, pinpointing that trigger can help you pause, reset, and be kinder to the person in front of you and finish the conversation amicably. If you can't control your emotions right away, you can always pause the conversation and tell the person that you need to calm down before you continue talking. A simple 'Give me a minute' will work, and if you don't want to admit you're upset, you can say you don't feel well and give yourself some time to straighten out your thoughts and feelings.

If you identify things that trigger you, you can even tell the people you love and trust what they are, so they can help you manage them. If going to the doctor triggers you because you've had bad experiences with doctors in the past, you could ask a friend or family member to go to the appointment with you. You could even make a day out of it and get ice cream or see a movie afterward if you aren't too drained. Managing your triggers doesn't have to be an embarrassing thing. Sometimes it's as simple as avoiding certain genres of media or having a backup plan to work through a conversation.

When someone invents a button to stop people from being triggered, we'll be the first in line to use it. But going to therapy, getting rest, and avoiding triggers all help. In the meantime, try to see if you have unidentified triggers. If something brings up a lot of emotions and is paired with painful memories, that's a good clue that you might have been triggered.

Readers may be familiar with Post-Traumatic Stress Disorder (PTSD), which is a reaction to an intense trauma. However, autistic people should also be aware of Complex PTSD (CPTSD), which is a form of PTSD that emerges from sustained traumas experienced over longer periods of time. There may be many issues that contribute to a person's CPTSD, and some of those may seem small compared to more clear-cut traumas that other people experience. But the aftershocks of these traumas are just as real and intense because the body has endured stress for long periods of time. Autistic people are already more likely to have PTSD than neurotypical people, and for many of us it will be CPTSD due to hundreds of microaggressions, years of forced masking, denial of bodily autonomy, and numerous other occasions where our authentic selves were repressed or condemned.

SO HOW DO WE HANDLE TRAUMA IN THE GRANDER SCHEME OF UNDERSTANDING OUR EMOTIONS?

Elora: What's worked well for me personally is learning to recognise when I'm triggered. For me there's one giant sign that I'm triggered: memories replaying in my mind. Sometimes I'll be really stressed and realise that I've been replaying a huge friendship-ending argument from years ago in my mind all day. Without even realising it my day has been filled with the strong emotions from an incident that occurred a long time ago. Other times I'll feel a burst of panic, and when I stop what I'm doing and investigate the emotion, I realise that I had been reminded of a bad situation I used to be in.

Cat: For me being triggered feels like a pit in my stomach or gut. Just a horrible sinking feeling of dread. I can't shake it, and I can't stop myself thinking about the sort of horrible stuff that triggered me in the first place.

Elora: Thankfully triggers can become less and less of a problem as years go on. Something that used to make you cry might bring you joy in the future. As I write this I'm getting ready to go to college again. I had a horrible time when I went to college when I was eighteen. There were specific incidents of trauma and long periods of stress. Two years of constant tension interspersed with traumatic encounters made college a nightmare, and I eventually dropped out. Even seeing the campus on the horizon would make my heart race and I would feel unsafe and unworthy, like I didn't deserve to be loved. I had horrible memories that my brain would go over again and again. I swore I'd never attend college again. But I've spent a long time healing. I've gone to therapy, taken care of myself, rested, talked with friends, and even publicly criticised the school's ableist environment. Now I'm ready to try again with a disability-friendly college. No one is pressuring me into it – I am just excited to learn more! Healing is possible.

AUTISM AND TRAUMA

Has autism been the root (or suspected root) of any traumatic experiences in your life? Do you think that struggling with autism (or others' struggling with your autism) has caused emotional wounds? What are these wounds and how do they affect you now? How are you trying to heal?

ELORA'S SEVEN-STEP PROCESS

As promised, here's my personal step-by-step process I use for identifying my emotions. Feel free to use it in your own life too!

You can remember this system with this acronym:

NECTEPA is not a real word. Unfortunately, I couldn't find a real word that fit this system, so we are stuck with NECTEPA.

N stands for 'Notice the feeling'. I can't do anything about an emotion if I haven't realised I'm feeling it!
E stands for 'Estimate what the feeling might be'. I don't have to know right away what I'm experiencing, but trying to get a rough idea of what it is will help me a lot. For example, I might not know all of what I'm feeling, but I know that sadness is part of it. Or I might not be able to name the feeling, but I know it feels positive.
C stands for 'Check in with my body'. Are my hands shaking? Is my chest tight? Are my eyes tired? Identifying physical clues can help me figure out what emotion I'm feeling.
T stands for 'Think about the memories that are coming up'. Sometimes I'll

have been playing a memory in the back of my mind for a while and didn't really notice it. By evaluating what memories, if any, are playing in my brain, I can help figure out what the emotion is connected to.

E stands for 'Evaluate outside factors'. At this point, I try to figure out if there are any unusual circumstances that might be affecting my body. Have I been sick lately? Am I dealing with difficult hormones right now? Did the weather just change? Did I have a lot of caffeine this morning? This will help me home in on whether the emotions I'm feeling are something I need to address or something I should ignore because they will go away on their own soon. It also helps me know if there's anything I need to do to get my body back to normal. For example, if I've had more caffeine than usual, I might try to avoid caffeine for the rest of the day and drink lots of water instead.

P stands for 'Plan how to handle the emotion'. Now that I have an idea of what I'm feeling, what might be causing that feeling, and whether there are complicating factors like trauma and hormones, I can make a plan to help myself feel better. There are many plans you can make to deal with emotions, but these are a few I use most often:

- Talking about my feelings with someone else to help me process them and begin to address them. Sometimes feeling like I'm doing something about a difficult emotion is all it takes to calm it.
- Journalling about my feelings to help me make sense of them.
- Avoiding difficult conversations and intense entertainment for the day so I have time to calm down.
- Distracting myself with something I love and waiting for the emotion to settle down.

A stands for 'Act on that plan'. Now that I have a plan for handling the emotion, I execute the plan! Not every plan will work, but with practice I've gotten pretty good at handling difficult feelings.

If we've learned nothing else from the *Inside Out* movies and sharing our therapists' advice with each other online, we should learn this:

Our emotions are not good or bad. They are simply trying to tell us something.

That is their job. The thing causing them is the reason we feel a certain way in a certain situation, not the emotions themselves. Maybe they're indicative of a problem to be solved, maybe not. Fear may seem like the enemy in the case of PTSD, trauma, or anxiety, but your body evolved to watch out for tigers when it's time to sleep – and today your body really thinks that tomorrow's quiz is a threat to your safety. Maybe it's reliving the same moment over and over again because it's trying to figure out a way to prevent a stressful situation. It loves you and wants to protect you. Give your body the same compassion that you'd give a friend, and realise that every once in a while you have to sit down with yourself like a toddler and say, 'Yes, we're having big feelings about this small thing and it may even be very silly, but those feelings are okay and we're going to process them and work through them together.'

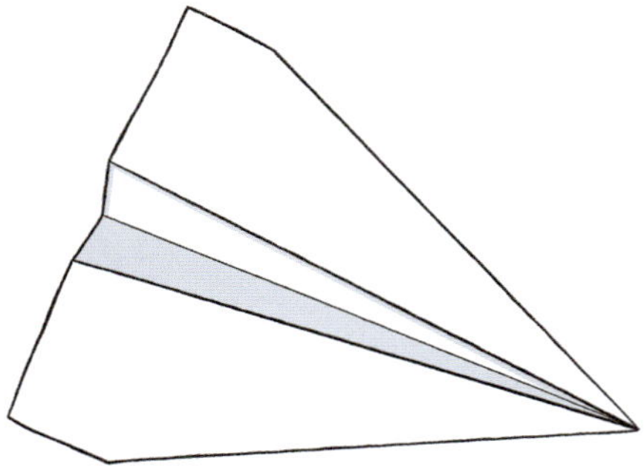

AUTISM AND COMMUNICATION

One of the biggest differences between neurotypicals and autistics is how we communicate. Our contrasting methods can be amusing at best but life-destroying at worst. There's no hard-and-fast way to bridge this gap, but by understanding where other people are coming from, we can avoid some issues.

Autistic communication is direct. It's blunt, straightforward, and usually not full of subtext. Autistic communication is often interpreted by normies as harsh, cruel, mean, or confrontational, even if the autistic person did not intend it as such. It can be easy for normies to assume that autistics are, in their directness, being purposefully nasty. It can also be easy for autistics to assume normies are looking for subtext in their messages as a trap. But what's actually happening is a fundamental difference in communication. Neither side is wrong or flawed; they're simply different and the meaning is getting lost in translation.[26]

One way to understand the difference between neurotypical communication and autistic communication is to view neurotypical communication as following an established path, while autistic communication is more like blazing your own trail. All those assumptions neurotypicals make in their communication have a useful function – they save time. How many times have you tried to explain exactly what you meant to a normie, only for them to get frustrated with you for taking too long? They might even say, 'Yes, yes, I get the idea', when you don't know if they've gotten the idea yet! Neurotypical communication sacrifices specificity for speed. When neurotypicals use their preprogrammed assumptions about the meanings of your words, it's like they're following a path in the woods. It's easier and quicker for them to continue down a path that's been prepared for them by society and assume you're on the path with them. The tone someone uses, their facial expressions, their body language, cultural expectations, and past experiences all create the trail that normies follow while communicating.

Have you ever watched a movie and felt like you were missing something, only for a friend to explain what was *really* going on? Maybe a character said something that seemed innocent, but it was actually a veiled threat. Or perhaps a character used an unusual phrasing to let an ally know they were in danger. Subtlety is a massive advantage of neurotypical communication. You can layer multiple messages into one sentence. But it's also terrible to live in a world where everyone expects you to understand these layered messages – and create them yourself – when you don't know how it works. When normies expect autistics to understand subtext, they're demanding that autistics follow a path they sometimes can't see.

Nobody is born knowing these things. When neurotypicals start to learn how to talk, they learn to pick up factors beyond the words: gestures, expressions, shortcuts, nuances. Their brains are wired to do that. Autistic brains are not.

Understanding communication as an autistic is like hacking through the jungle with a machete in the general direction you're trying to go. You aren't following the footsteps of the people who came before you. You aren't keeping to the patterns that neurotypicals know instinctually. You're going exactly where you intend, in a straight line. The benefit of this is that you're getting straight to the point. The downside is that it can take more time to explain what you're saying and, since you're deviating from the norm, you're more likely to be misunderstood.

Another way to understand the difference between neurotypical communication and autistic communication is to imagine whether you're leaving blanks in your communication for the other to fill in. Neurotypical communication relies a lot on someone's ability to correctly fill in the blanks in communication based on body language, facial expressions, and tone of voice. Normies expect you to fill in the blanks they are leaving based on the subtext. But if you can't follow clues like body language or vocal tone to fill in the blanks, you're left with a vague, confusing, half-finished communication. And filling in the blanks on your own can be disastrous! It doesn't matter if the normie who's speaking to you *thinks* it will be easy for you to guess what's supposed to fill in those blanks. If you don't have the skill set to figure it out, then you're just taking shots in the dark and communication will break down for sure!

> Autistics, on the other hand, typically don't leave blanks in their conversation, at least not as many as normies do.

But if a normie expects there to be blanks in the communication to fill in, they'll try to fill them in, whether or not there are any blanks at all! It doesn't matter if you said exactly what you meant and nothing more. They expect there to be blanks, so they're going to try to find extra meaning in your words.

Thankfully real life isn't like an action-adventure movie. We don't have to hide secret messages in our everyday conversation *too* much. But sometimes it can be helpful. The point here is that neurotypical communication and autistic communication both have unique advantages to them.

Yet another way to understand the difference between neurotypical communication and autistic communication is to consider the difference between poetry and technical writing. Poetry communicates more than bare bones concepts. Poetry is specifically designed to add extra meaning through devices like word association, rhyming, and metaphor. While typical neurotypical communication is not necessarily as layered as poetry, and not always as intentional, it nevertheless shares some similarities. There's a beauty to the way neurotypicals weave extra meaning into words, like magical messages you have to decipher, but it can also be exhausting.

On the other hand, autistic communication is blunt and direct, like the writing you'd find in an instruction manual or a textbook. It's much more practical and effective for getting a lot of everyday work done, but it doesn't always have the same layered meanings or shortcuts of neurotypical communication.

The clash of these different communication styles can result in terrible challenges. Neurotypicals may find meaning in autistics' words that isn't there, assuming that we are hiding messages in our words just like they do. Even when autistics explain exactly what they mean and promise there are no hidden meanings, neurotypicals often insist

that there's a second interpretation of the autistics' words. Furthermore, the blunt nature of autistic communication can seem aggressive to neurotypicals. When you're used to people always softening 'negative' statements, someone saying exactly what they mean can feel like a personal attack.

Let's use an example. Imagine that one neurotypical asks another neurotypical, 'Does this dress make me look fat?' That second neurotypical might respond, 'It's not flattering'. The assumption is that what they actually said ('It's not flattering') will start them down the path that leads to 'Yes, it makes you look fat'. They didn't need to go all the way to the final destination; they just needed to put the conversation on the right path. They know the first person will fill in the blanks. But the first person can also interpret it in a way that doesn't hurt their own feelings, because it's the dress's fault, not theirs. In this way neurotypicals avoid hurting each other's feelings.

Now imagine asking an autistic person the same question. The neurotypical asks, 'Does this dress make me look fat?' The autistic person, just like the second neurotypical in the previous example, wants to end up at 'Yes, it makes you look fat'. But instead of saying just enough to start someone down the path to get there, the autistic person takes them straight there. 'Yes,' they respond. 'That dress makes you look fat.' They left no blanks to be filled in.

The neurotypical who asked if the dress made them look fat in the first place might be super offended now. Why? Because they assume there's a path to follow, blanks to fill in. If the path starts with 'Yes, you look fat in that dress', then maybe the person asking thinks you want them to reach one of these, purposely hurtful, conclusions: 'And you're ugly', or 'You'd look fat in every dress', or even 'You're so fat I'm embarrassed by you'. The thing is, there was never a path to follow in the first place! The autistic person never said anything about being ugly or embarrassing. They didn't say that the person was fat at all, just that they looked fat in that particular dress. But the neurotypical is used to following a path from what is said to what is 'really' meant, and filling in the blanks along the way. If you say what you mean from the beginning, that can confuse them.

This is why communication is so difficult for autistics: we don't speak neurotypical fluently. We have to learn how to say things in a neurotypical fashion because neurotypicals don't know how to properly interpret what we say. So if we don't phrase something correctly, we're punished for it. In this way we learn to say that the dress isn't flattering or that another dress would look better instead of saying the truth flat out. Even then, the neurotypical person might still get offended. The obvious solution would be for one party to try to phrase things better and the other party to try to realise that not everything is a personal attack, but it doesn't usually work out that way.

Normies are used to speaking and being spoken to in a more or less poetic way. Blunt communication can sound jarring. Imagine if you were listening to a song and suddenly a robotic voice said, 'We've been trying to reach you about your car's extended warranty.' It might take you out of the moment and make it hard for you to enjoy the song. To normies, when autistics communicate it's like they take normies' favourite sad song and replace all the lines with 'I am very sad and everything sucks'. They expected subtext, and so bluntness would throw them off and ruin the fun.

HOW TO BRIDGE THE GAP

If autistics and normies struggle to understand each other so much, how can we fix this problem? Here are some strategies.

> **Strategy one** is to acknowledge how different your communication styles are. If we don't realise that the people around us communicate so differently from us, it's easy to assume that they are evil, manipulative, or overly aggressive. Whether you're autistic or not, long-term communication breakdowns can cause a lot of hurt. If you can acknowledge from the beginning that communication problems are likely to occur, you might have more faith in the other person and know to ask clarifying questions, avoiding a lot of painful assumptions along the way.

> **Strategy two** is to adapt your communication to match the person you're talking to as best you can. Whether you're autistic or not, recognising how the person you're talking to processes information can help you communicate better. You can try to be more or less blunt depending on

who you're talking to. It's not a magical solution. We can't snap our fingers and suddenly understand a whole new way to communicate, let alone do it flawlessly. But we can try to take the edge off in our conversations with people we *know* communicate differently from us.

Strategy three is to be honest about your needs. It's not always safe to disclose that you're autistic, but if it is, then you can tell people that you are autistic and work from there. People can't communicate with you the way that works best for you if they don't even know what works. You can also say you struggle with communication without revealing that you're autistic. The same goes for neurotypicals. If you're not autistic and you're trying to communicate with someone who is, explaining that you struggle to understand whether or not they're upset with you when they use blunt communication might help.

Strategy four is to get some help with communication. If you're autistic and have a normie friend, you can ask your normie friend for help with writing emails and other communication. They might know how to say what you can't. This goes both ways. You can help your normie friends with social situations where people use 'politeness' as a shield and assume you won't be blunt in response. Some normies could really use an autistic friend

Cat: A key phrase I use in everyday life now is something to the effect of 'This conversation has become difficult for me to understand.' Instead of interpreting what someone's trying to say incorrectly, I'm direct about feeling out of my element. I sometimes phrase this as, 'I have become too autistic to understand this conversation', 'I don't know how to interpret that', or, simply, 'I'm too autistic for this'. It puts any blame for miscommunication on me, which makes slowing down the conversation easier for the other person to stomach. At the same time, it pretty clearly lets my conversation partner know that if there is hidden meaning to be found, or a certain response is expected, I do not know what it is, and I don't know how to respond. The person can then clarify, or the conversation can be over. Which in many cases is the real victory.

to help them turn down invitations to join pyramid schemes. Sometimes saying 'I'm not interested' is really hard!

Cat: I'm the designated witch in my family. I tell waiters they got an order wrong, call customer service hotlines, talk to managers, etc. It's less because I'm autistic and more because the rest of them are chickens, but autistic bluntness is quite helpful at times. My husband's not the witch of the family, but his job is to tell me the truth even if I don't want to hear it.

Strategy five is to lean into your unique communication style. Say exactly what you mean, and if people get offended, simply say you told the truth and ask if they'd prefer you lie. This is not a good strategy in most situations because it will likely come across as too aggressive, but sometimes there comes a point where it feels like nothing you do is good enough and you're wasting energy trying to bridge the gap. We can't tell you when to use this strategy, but we can tell you that you are not required to pretend to be neurotypical all the time. If you are constantly meeting people in the middle in a specific situation and they refuse to even try to meet you, we won't judge you if you stop trying in that situation.

Direct communication does not have to mean talking down to someone or talking to them like they're a child. A great example of direct communication among respectful adults is on display in the cult-classic fantasy movie *The Princess Bride*. In one famous scene a character is described as 'only mostly dead . . . [and not] all dead.'[27] This is an incredibly direct, blunt, and uncomplicated way to describe the situation. Fantasy movies tend to use complicated and flowery language. In another fantasy movie the character might have been described as 'comatose' or 'on the brink of death', or, even more poetically, 'death has come for him and almost taken him away'. So why doesn't this movie use that kind of language? By using a direct communication style, *The Princess Bride* subverts the expectations of the genre, making the film funny since unexpectedly truthful statements are one of the core elements of comedy and easy to understand. Everyone, regardless of age and neurotype, can follow what's happening. If you need a masterclass in direct communication, watch *The Princess Bride* and take notes.

AUDITORY PROCESSING DISORDER

Sometimes it takes a moment or two for the meanings of words to process in our brains. Sometimes words get lost and we have to put the meaning together from context. Sometimes we have no hope of understanding what someone is saying unless the person is nice enough to repeat themself. These are examples of auditory processing problems. If you have auditory processing problems, there is nothing wrong with your hearing, but complex sounds like speech, which have to be heard, translated, and then sent to another centre in the brain for a reaction, can get a little lost in translation. The brain lags, so to speak. Sometimes you have to try again. Sometimes you have to take a second to process.

If you have auditory processing problems, they might be significant enough for you to be diagnosed with an auditory processing disorder. Because we are not doctors, we won't be too specific about what falls into the category of a 'disorder' and what doesn't. Instead we want to discuss auditory processing issues as a whole.

HERE'S HOW IT WORKS

The sound waves of a person's speech travel through the air and into the ear canal. The little bones of your ear vibrate in response, and that pattern of vibration (imagine a little Morse code telegraph beep) is turned into electrical signals and delivered to your brain's auditory cortex after which the nearby Wernicke area of the brain works to pick up a meaning. As part of looking for meaning, your brain analyses the electrical signals as well as the person's tone, lip movements, and facial expressions. All of this information is then rushed to the prefrontal cortex to be understood as a unit in the context of your memories, experiences, and knowledge. From there your brain calculates a response, which is sent to the Broca area to be translated into speech.

It may seem like hearing happens automatically, but as you can see, there are a lot of steps to get the sound turned into something you understand! Sometimes, somewhere along the way, it gets jumbled.

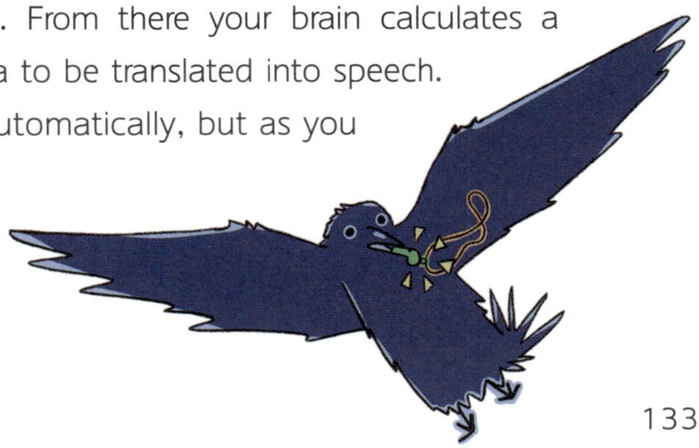

Maybe your brain cannot pick out important sounds (like someone talking to you) from other sounds (like a garbage truck in the background). Maybe you hear someone speak to you and you can't seem to understand what they're saying, even though you know you should be able to. Whatever it feels like, if you have auditory processing issues, you might be punished for them. People might accuse you of disrespecting them by 'not even listening', or you might interrupt more than you intend to because it's hard for you to keep track of the conversation. People might tell you that you need to 'try harder', but it's more complicated than that.

Cat: Usually the only way I can understand people is by repeating the sounds the person made back in my memory and translating from there. I also read lips, which I only found out during COVID when everyone wore masks and I couldn't understand anything they said. Even when there are subtitles on the shows I watch, I still occasionally need to pause and go back a few seconds. It's also extremely hard to get my attention because I don't respond to my name or to any one word in particular.

Auditory processing issues are common in people with ADHD and autism.[28] And it's important to know that it is not the listener's fault. You can be paying attention as hard as you can and still not be able to absorb the meaning of the words.

To people who have auditory processing issues: be nice to yourself. You essentially have partial hearing loss and need similar accommodations as a person with it. Here are some tips that might help:

- Ask for everything that you can in writing.
- When watching TV, put subtitles on.
- You can call theatres and ask when they are screening movies with closed captions on. If they don't offer that service, absolutely ask for the manager and request it. You are not the only one who needs it.

- Turn the volume up. Make sure it's not ear-damaging and everyone else is cool with it, but the noise does help you to focus more on that than anything else. You might also benefit from a voice-enhancing speaker.
- Focus on people's lips while they're talking. You might not think you know how to read them, but you might be better at it than you realise, and if not you will learn. This also solves the 'eye contact' problem that so many autistics have.
- Invest in comfortable headphones or earbuds, especially if they're noise-cancelling and can cut out background noise or isolate the human voice and emphasise it.
- Don't be afraid to ask people to repeat themselves. Just be polite about it. Most people will understand. Strangers might get frustrated. That's not on you. You're trying your best.
- Auditory processing issues are not super well known yet, so some people might not understand what you're talking about if you tell them you have one. If you need to explain why you are struggling to someone, it's okay to say you have a 'hearing issue'. It's not a lie and can save you time.

Elora: Sometimes as a kid I'd get in trouble for not following the rules because I hadn't even processed the rules in the first place. Like so many other times in my life, I told myself that I just needed to 'try harder'. But I couldn't! My brain, especially when I was a child, just wasn't capable of comprehending all of the rules and expectations that were set out in front of me, in part because of my auditory processing issues. If you've had experiences like this, please know that you're not alone.

To the people on the other end, please be understanding and kind. People might not feel comfortable telling you that they have autism or auditory processing issues. They're going to try their best. And they might not have auditory processing issues – they might just not speak your language that well, or they may want to make sure they didn't misunderstand. People all around us have trouble understanding speech all the time. It's more common than you might think, so be gracious.

Here are some tips for speaking with people with any kind of hearing issues, from deafness to auditory processing issues to second-language speakers:

- When someone asks you to repeat something, repeat the entire sentence. Don't repeat only the last few words.
- When repeating, speak a little slower and more clearly. But don't yell or drag out each syllable. That makes things worse by embarrassing the person who's trying to understand. Dragging out each syllable actually makes it harder to process the word, because the syllables get too far apart and can't be connected by the brain.
- If the other person says something like, 'No, I got that part,' be patient – they're trying to save you both some time. They're not interrupting to be rude.
- When someone asks you to repeat something more than once, use different words. This is helpful for non-native speakers, as they may not be familiar with the exact phrase you used originally.
- A quick 'That's okay!' before repeating what you said will reassure the person that you understand and are sympathetic.
- Repeat yourself, using different words, as many times as necessary. The other person absolutely hates asking for you to repeat yourself and is likely to give up and pretend they understand before you get sick of repeating yourself.
- Try to get someone's attention before speaking with them. If the other person is wearing headphones or is paying attention to something else, they might need a moment before they can fully engage with the conversation.
- When repeating yourself, avoid contractions. That little 'n't' can be hard to make out but creates an important distinction.
- Remember that they're not struggling to understand you because they don't care. They're trying their best.

There's no cure for an auditory processing disorder, but a specialist like an audiologists or a speech-language pathologist can work with you to come up with a treatment plan.[29] Auditory processing disorder is a disability that requires its own strategies and coping mechanisms. We all have to do the best we can.

NON-SPEAKING AUTISTICS

In order to engage in verbal communication with someone, you need to first be able to understand them. That takes hearing (or lip-reading) abilities, and even if you can hear, auditory processing issues can make things complicated. Then you need the mental capacity to understand them, and also the mental capacity to form a response. Those are two separate brain processes! A lot of different body parts need to work together at the same time to make speech possible. Part of that is breath control. You also need functioning vocal chords. On top of that, you need the mouth and tongue to make very precise movements to form the sounds. Even then, if you have all that, you might not be able to speak due to a mental block, from over-stimulation or trauma. And furthermore, some people just do not want to talk when you expect them to!

Reducing all these complex processes and skill sets into a marker of intelligence is shortsighted, at best. Though we cannot list all the factors that contribute to autistics' struggles with speech, some are obvious. Autistic people tend to be uncoordinated, and coordination is an important part of speech. Autistic people are monotropic, and performing multiple actions at once is also an important part of speech. Autistics are also prone to shutting down when overwhelmed and likely to experience trauma related to communication gone wrong. If you or someone you love struggles to speak, there are treatments available. A good place to start is to reach out to a speech therapist or occupational therapist and get their input. Not everyone will speak, and that is okay, but help is available for those who want professional support.

If you are non-speaking all or some of the time, you may want to invest in something that identifies you as such, like an enamel pin for your jacket or a seat belt cover for your car. Autistic people are sometimes assaulted by police and others because these people interpret stimming, lack of eye contact, communication difficulties, and melt-downs as proof that someone is not in their right mind and therefore (in their eyes) a danger to society. We hate that we have to tell you this, but if you struggle to speak, you are particularly in danger, and finding a way to inform people of your disability without speaking could save your life.

Autistic people can also develop speech differently from their neurotypical peers. Many autistic children are gestalt language processors,[30] which means they learn language in large chunks (gestalts) rather than individual pieces. The 'typical' way for a child to develop language is through what's called the analytic model. The child learns individual words and slowly learns to combine them into longer and longer sentences. A child may start out saying 'Mum', then graduate to two-word phrases like 'Mum, look', then build upon that to say 'Mum, look what I made'. Gestalt language processors, on the other hand, start with big chunks of language (sometimes taken from television and movies) like 'May the Force be with you'. The gestalt language processor then uses the phrase 'May the Force be with you' to communicate more broadly, perhaps in this case to express goodwill, instead of using more typical phrases like 'I love you', 'good-bye', and 'good night'. After some time, they break the phrase down a bit, substituting certain words out. They may say 'May the dinner be with you' to express excitement over dinner or 'May the Force be with Grandpa' to express their excitement over Grandpa coming over. Eventually, they learn to use the words in the gestalt individually.

There is still a lot we do not know about gestalt verses analytical language processing and this has been a very simple explanation. The point is that a child who repeats seemingly meaningless words, phrases, or quotes from media may be communicating in their own way. Try to discern the meaning of the gestalts if you can, and reach out to a speech therapist for further help.

Sometimes, people who can speak at other times are rendered unable to do so. Even allistics can be rendered speechless in certain situations. We don't know exactly how similar or different autistics' and allistics' experiences of speechlessness are, but we have no reason to doubt that anyone can, if overwhelmed, shocked, or frazzled enough, temporarily lose the ability to speak. Some people have lower thresholds than others.

Cat: I learned Italian and Spanish in formal classes but German from immersion only. I have very much learned German in a gestalt fashion, mimicking phrases that I hear, but I can't necessarily spell and don't always know the full meaning of individual words when I try to use them in different, similar contexts. When I've tried to string together the words I know, it's resulted in some hilarious errors. My son is learning German right along with me and he's doing exactly the same thing (only, frankly, better). It's just how our brains work best!

Sometimes an autistic's voice just turns off. This may be a stress response you experience during a difficult situation. It's called a 'verbal shutdown' and it can be terrifying. It can feel like your brain is making the loud static sound of an old TV or the noise between radio stations where some sound leaks through. Maybe you can still technically speak, but you mutter or stutter or trail off into silence. You look for words and they aren't there. It's like someone's yelling in your ear and destroying your concentration. It can feel like the walls are closing in.

An autistic person in verbal shutdown (with no injuries or auditory processing issues) might not seem frazzled or overwhelmed, but if they try to speak they may quickly become that way. Going into verbal shutdown is often a fight-or-flight response, and the anxiety of speaking in public – or to a stranger, or at all – might be enough to trigger someone's fight-or-flight response.

It's also possible that the autistic person simply has no control over how much they speak. Furthermore, the ability to speak is not like a light switch. Someone may have severe social anxiety and worry that anything they say will get them in trouble. Someone's voice may technically still be 'on,' but they can't bring themselves to say anything. Someone might choose not to speak in these situations, but that is certainly not the same as ignoring other people to be rude.

There are many different ways that autism and its comorbidities can limit speech. But no matter what the reason, people with limited speech still deserve to be included, respected, and acknowledged. What's important to know is that the non-speaking person can likely do some or all of the following:

- Hear you
- Understand you
- Understand what is going on
- Know what you want them to say back
- Know how to speak

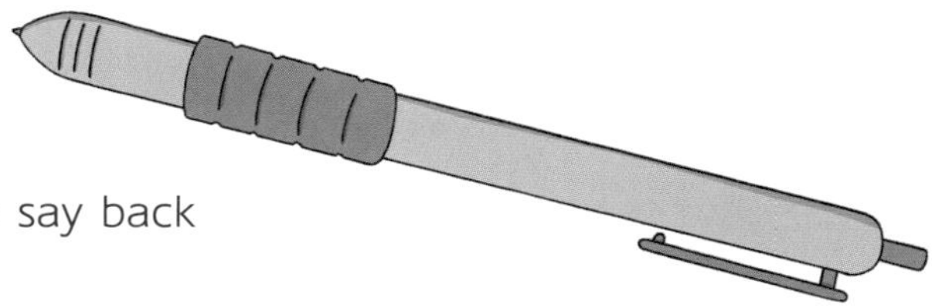

And most importantly, they are not less intelligent than someone who can speak. Stephen Hawking is a great example of an incredibly intelligent person who had difficulty speaking for much of his life. If one of the most celebrated minds in history needed assistance to communicate, why do we assume that difficulty communicating is a sign of low intelligence?

Being non-speaking is its own unique disability with many potential causes. But no matter the cause, the course of action for those around non-verbal people is the same.

1. Be respectful. Do not assume anything about a person's intellect or awareness of their situation.
2. Try to facilitate communication however you can. This may mean learning sign language or offering a speech-generating device, like a tablet, or another form of augmentative and alternative communication (AAC). There are many forms of this, including multiple phone apps.
3. Don't force communication. Even if a person is non-verbal due to something other than autism, like an injury or deafness, it might take a lot of effort for them to communicate, even with sign language or AAC. If it seems like they want a break, give them one. This is about them and their needs, not about you feeling awkward or wanting to be polite. If someone's communication issues are hard for you to handle, imagine how much harder it is for them.
4. Don't steal their voice. It might be kind of you to, say, order for the

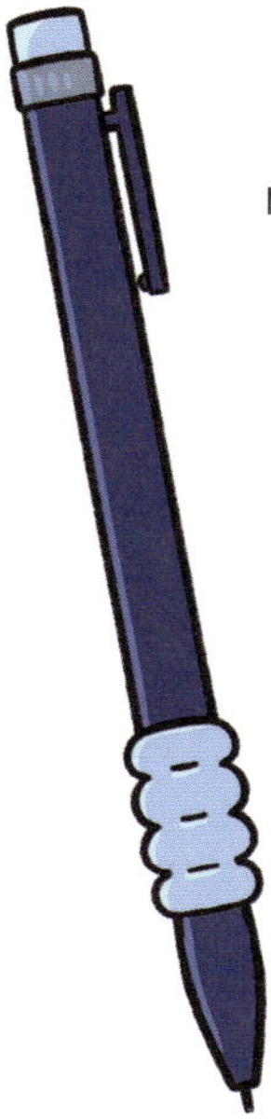

non-speaking person at a restaurant, but you should offer first, not just speak for them. Don't let anyone else do that either.

5. Don't activate their fight-or-flight response without cause. If simply having a normal conversation with someone is enough stress to trigger fight-or-flight, then being aggressively confronted or yelled at will definitely be too much for them.
6. Find some non-speaking autistics online and follow their pages or blogs. Learn about their lives and what they go through. Listen to what they have to say about being non-speaking.

COMMUNICATION TOOLS

Thankfully there are plenty of ways to communicate beyond speaking out loud. One popular method of communication is sign language. There is no one universal sign language. The United States and Britain, for example, have separate sign languages, despite English being the predominant spoken language in both countries. Learning whichever sign language is most commonly used in your area may help you communicate with others, both for your benefit and theirs.

Another popular method of non-verbal communication is writing. Some people use keyboards, like computers and typewriters. But you can do it the old-fashioned way and write down what you want to say with paper and pencil.

Yet another method of non-verbal communication is the use of communication boards and apps. There are devices that are designed specifically to help people with non-verbal communication, but there are also apps you can download onto an everyday device, like a tablet or smartphone, to help you communicate as well. People can communicate by pointing at letters or images on a physical piece of paper, book, or board. Some people even use a computer to track what their eyes are looking at as if that person has pointed at it. This allows them to use their eyes as a computer mouse and 'click' by holding their gaze on a part of the screen, blinking, or tapping a button. This technology can then be used to access other computer programs, like communication apps. Stephen Hawking managed to communicate quite a bit this way, so it could likely help you too.

Cat: Ever since moving to Germany, my primary mode of communication has been to type something into Google Translate and show someone the resulting German (at least until my actual German gets more intelligible). My deaf friend in the US does the same with her notes app. People usually do not mind.

All forms of communication are valid, but some are better suited for specific situations than others. Remember, just because you can talk some or most of the time doesn't mean you have to talk as your only form of communication. If you think something else would help you, then you have every right to try it out. A communication aid can be as mainstream as a writing-assistance program to help you figure out how to phrase your emails, or as unique as secret signals to use with your loved ones that mean 'I'm in overload' or 'My voice turned off'. It can be as high-tech as typed words that you have your computer read it out loud in a voice you chose, or as low-tech as a pointed finger at something you want. We all communicate differently, and there's nothing wrong with having multiple ways to communicate.

It is not your fault if you struggle to communicate or if people struggle to communicate with you. As difficult as it is, you sometimes have to accept that not everything is in your control, including how people interpret your attempts to communicate.

WHAT WE WISH ALLISTICS KNEW

Elora: I've spent my whole life full of things I wanted to say to the people who didn't understand me, who were dissatisfied with my work when I was doing my best, and who thought I was 'bad' because I was autistic, even if they didn't know I was autistic in the first place. Now that we are finally writing this book, it's a huge relief, but also exhausting. How are we supposed to coach normies in understanding autism? Even though I'm overflowing with things to say, at the same time I don't know what to say at all.

Cat: I don't know either, because I've tried and failed to explain it all to them in the past and it only gets worse. I get told I'm 'using autism as an excuse'. By now I feel like I'm running out of ways to make them understand, and I am frustrated with neurotypicals because of it. Why do they make things so hard for us? Why do we have to be the ones doing all the work and making all the effort? Why am I being held responsible for how *they* interpreted *my* words? It gives me so much anxiety to try to be understood by them and I know I'll mess up eventually. And I know they won't be nice about it.

Elora: I feel torn between being super hopeful and super pessimistic right now. So many normies are learning about autism and want to be inclusive and kind. The world is getting better. But I've also encountered people who say they want to be inclusive and then aren't. A great example of this is the trouble I encountered at my Christian college. My specific flavour of autism helped me think technically about ballet, and my college gave me a dance scholarship for it. Certain aspects of my autism also made me very impressive academically, and I got a scholarship for that too. But then other students would stop me on the way to class and ask to pray for me so

I could be 'healed'. My hip-hop dance teacher once spent the entire class lecturing us on how if we loved Jesus enough, we would all be rich and never get sick. (He injured himself a couple weeks later and had to use a cane on and off for the rest of the semester.) This is just the tip of the iceberg. I could go on and on with horror stories about my college experience, but the gist is simple – my autism was punished by the same organisation that had rewarded it. And now that so many people are eager to learn more about autism, I feel like I'm back in college again, undiagnosed and scared, wondering if any of the support is real.

Cat: Mine was the same. I got kicked out of my master's program after they questioned my 'fitness to practice' and found out I was autistic. It was a program to be a *therapist*. If they're not inclusive, who would be? So many people who claim to be supportive of autistic people have spoken to me like I'm a child or pitied me for having an autistic son like it's a tragedy.

I feel like we're fighting this huge uphill battle over everything they've been taught to believe. You can't logic someone out of a position they didn't logic themselves into. It really does feel like teaching won't do any good. That it goes in one ear and out the other and people treat us the same way as before. It feels like they don't want to learn and it's too much work to treat us with basic understanding and respect.

Elora: I hear you, but at the same time I don't think it's true. I'm choosing to believe that the world is full of good, kind people. I really, deep inside, think things are about to get better.

Cat: I do hope that if we can provide resources for people, then some of them will choose to make an effort and learn. That's all I want from neurotypicals, ultimately. Just to try.

Elora: I think it's important to remember what a difficult time this is for people as a whole. Financially, economically, politically, socially, ecologically, culturally, and personally, this is a difficult time to be alive. I want to see a positive change. I want individuals to step up and make a difference. But I also understand that for many people, they are at the end of their rope. Just because we have been hurt by normies doesn't mean all normies will hurt us, and even the normies who want to make things better might not have much to give right now. I want our readers to know that though we need to vent and be honest about our despair, we also appreciate every tiny change they make in their lives. Learning about autism makes a difference. Openness to clarifying questions makes a difference. Patience makes a difference. Pulling even one weed out of the garden matters. And though we are hurt, broken, and angry, we don't expect every reader to step up and save the world for us. We are asking for tiny steps forward. You never know whose life will be positively impacted by even the gentlest of changes.

AUTISM AND WORK

How has autism affected your ability to find and keep a job? How does your autism affect you in the workplace? How have workplaces accommodated you in the past or failed to accommodate you? What do you believe is the best strategy to approach autism in the workplace? Should you disclose it? Ask for accommodations? Keep it secret? Ask a friend for help? Have you been discriminated again? If you ever are, what will your recourse be?

BURNOUT (AND HOW TO AVOID IT)

Here's a maths problem for you: You have a lousy old phone that only charges at 1 per cent a minute. It takes 10 per cent of your battery to open an app, 30 per cent to perform a task, and 5 per cent to close the app. If you can only charge it for one hour at a time, how many times can you perform that task before the phone dies?

I'm sure most of you are just staring at this problem right now, trying to figure out if you actually need to do this maths problem. (And then there's the dorks who already have their scratch paper and calculator out. We love you, nerds.) But it doesn't really matter what the numbers are. The point isn't the maths. The point is that in this problem, the limit for how much you can do is really low. And like our phones, you have a limit too. It's hard to calculate what your limit is, but you know you're going to hit it quickly.

Burnout is the result of chronic, untreated stress that manifests as mental or physical fatigue. It can be hard to tell when you're in the middle of burnout or on the way to it, but in retrospect it becomes quite clear that you've been burned out. Most often we think about burnout in relation to work. Maybe you've been trudging along at a job you don't like all that much for a few years and haven't been rewarded for it. As a result you start dreading your days and feel out of control of how you spend your time. But burnout can also come from a stressful home life, like taking care of a sick relative for many months, parenting, or going through a divorce. Experiencing burnout is not the same as having a stressful morning at work, taking a lunch break, and then coming back feeling refreshed for the afternoon. Remember: the key word here is *chronic*.

Burnout is characterised by feelings of fatigue, cynicism, and sadness. You may feel tired all the time, dread waking up in the morning or fulfilling certain tasks, and feel empty or vaguely frustrated or disappointed in yourself. You might even confuse burnout with depression, due to how similar the experiences are. Unlike depression, however, burnout is not a medically diagnosable condition.

Anyone can suffer from burnout, but autistic people are particularly vulnerable to it. The world is built for neurotypicals, and while no one in this world has it easy, their batteries don't drain as quickly as ours do. Certain things can drain an autistic person's battery much more than an allistic person's, such as:

- Simply leaving the house. Why? Because social situations can be so much more taxing on us, even encountering other people can be exhausting, and we need to be home or in a safe space to recharge.
- Wearing shoes or restrictive clothing. Why? Because our senses are more alert, we feel the fabrics and fits of clothes more acutely. For instance, a shirt that feels rough to a normie may feel unbearably itchy to an autistic person. But many situations require us to wear clothes that are uncomfortable, either because there is a professional dress code or because a setting requires us to wear a specific garment, like a swimsuit in a pool. Spending all day trying to ignore the clothes on your body can be exhausting.
- Commuting. Why? Because crowds of strangers, smelly trains and buses, the need to stay alert in dark tunnels or rush hour traffic, and more all weigh on our senses and demand our attention. This can be a lot even for normies, but for autistics, who so often struggle to shift focus quickly, it can be downright draining.
- Being around strangers. Why? Because social situations are often full of unspoken tests, and you haven't had time to learn this person's quirks or pet peeves yet.

- Being around coworkers. Why? Because these are social situations that are related to your paycheck and livelihood, which adds another layer of anxiety and pressure to perform well.
- Being in an unfamiliar place. Why? Because new places come with unknown and unanticipated sensory inputs and social expectations. Have you ever been on a boat for a long period of time? At first, the rocking of the boat felt strange, and you struggled to walk and maybe got seasick. After a while, however, you got used to it all. That was a new and strange sensory experience (being on a rocking boat) that you adapted to after a while. In our personal experiences, encountering many new sensory experiences is similar to 'getting your sea legs' as the sailors say. You have to have time to adjust.
- Any change of schedule. Why? Due to our monotropic nature, autistics have difficulty transitioning from one task to the next. A set, familiar schedule helps us to mentally prepare for shifting to new tasks. If that schedule is changed or thrown off, we can feel rudderless, lost, and panicked.
- Masking autism. Why? Because masking is literally pretending to be someone else. Neurotypicals may have to mask occasionally (pretending they are interested, or professional, or heterosexual), but for many people with autism, masking is constant, all day every day with every word and action. When someone has an invisible disability, they spend a lot of time acting like they aren't disabled because people might not understand or be sympathetic. And since autism affects communication as well as sensory input, we don't just have to pretend to have neurotypical bodies – we have to pretend to have neurotypical minds. It's also important to note that masking at home and masking outside the home are two different stressors that need different amounts of energy. Autistic people need safe spaces to be themselves, and they can't recharge if they have to keep masking at home. If they're forced to mask in their own space, their batteries are always going to be draining.

We all find ways to recharge our batteries throughout the day in different ways. Physically we can rest, recharge with caffeine or a snack, or take a nap. Mentally we can meditate, watch something lighthearted and mindless, look at memes, read a book, etc. Emotionally we can have some alone time, focus on something other than our problems, or find something happy, like a video of a puppy, to lift our mood. Different things work for different people.

How much recharge time is enough? It depends on your battery – and your charger. But one thing is universal: if a person doesn't get enough time to recharge, their stress levels rise and eventually they burn out.

Autistic burnout is actually familiar to everyone. *Everyone* gets burned out, kids and adults, allistics and autistics. Sometimes you've just had enough. Maybe bystanders can't understand why, but that doesn't change anything, does it?

AVOIDING BURNOUT

Burnout happens over a prolonged, stressful period of time. If you don't keep your stress in check, you may need to take a lot of time off to fully recharge and start feeling like yourself again. To avoid that, remember that different stressors with their own timelines and scales can come at you from several directions at once. A simple but tedious routine task like doing the laundry might be annoying or depleting on its own. But when accompanied by endless days of masking, little time to yourself, and high pressure to conform to allistics' standards at work or school, that single load of laundry can start to feel like the end of the world. Making yourself dinner, working out, seeing friends, or talking to family – these can all start to feel like impossible burdens to keep up when you're burned out. It's staggering how much we juggle just to stay alive. But there are ways to avoid burnout and recover from it.

- Be kind to yourself. Burnout happens to everyone and is both real and serious. If you're experiencing burnout, treat it like an illness. If you can, spend some time in self-care, rest, and take a few days off.

- Prioritise your physical needs. Your to-do list is probably very long, but the most important things are eating regularly, drinking lots of water, getting sleep, and taking care of your hygiene. Putting some things on hold to get these physical needs taken care of is important.
- If a certain task is causing you a great deal of stress, put it on hold and move on to something else. Try to pick something that recharges you instead of draining you.
- Try to explain to someone else how your burnout feels and ask them to help you find solutions. If you're feeling burned out at work, you could talk to your manager or coworkers about what's going on and see if they can help you find a solution so you can keep working. A healthy workplace doesn't want you to burn out any more than you do. The same goes for burnout at school or home. The people who are close to you, like your teachers, parents, or partner, should want you to be healthy and present. If you are in a job, school, or relationship that does not value your health, consider whether it is possible for you to move on to something better.
- Try to keep a flexible schedule to accommodate burnout. Yes, this can be rough, especially because we autistics love our routines. But this can be as simple as keeping one evening a week free from commitments in case you need to do something that evening that you didn't have energy for earlier in the week. Maybe Monday is your grocery shopping day, and you keep Tuesday as your free evening. That way, if you're feeling burned out on Monday, you can postpone the shopping until Tuesday.
- Rest, in every way. Get lots of sleep, meditate, take time off work if you can. This is near-impossible for some people, but even a little rest is better than none.

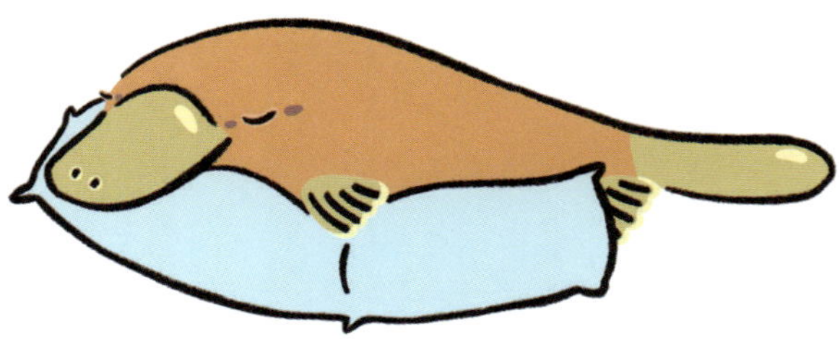

- Try to renew your focus on hobbies, special interests, and play. If you spend every day working in a lab looking at microbes, then taking up cello lessons, reading an entire fantasy series with a book club, or joining a soccer team will help you take pressure off your professional life and get your brain working in a different way. If your days are filled taking care of screaming children or arguing with people on the internet, finding an hour or two each day where you get to go be with animals or climb a rock wall adds dimension and moments of quiet and makes it easier to go back home.

- Be patient with yourself. Admitting to burnout is often seen as unacceptable by a society as focused on productivity and profit as ours. People may not be understanding, and they might not be able to do much to help you anyway. But whether or not other people will give you grace or deadline extensions or whatever else it takes, you need to give them to yourself if you can. Sometimes we literally cannot survive if we do not keep working, and we are not suggesting that taking breaks is easy, or always possible, but if shame is what is holding you back, try to let it go. It is frustrating to feel trapped in your brain, even though you need to be able to focus and work, we know. But being hard on yourself won't help.
- Evaluate where your self-worth comes from. If deep down inside you believe that you don't deserve love unless you complete a big to-do list every day to impress the people around you, you will always burn out.

We believe that we deserve to be kind to ourselves, even if the world around us disagrees. You can believe whatever you want to believe. But some beliefs inevitably lead to burnout, and we aren't going to pretend they don't. When we talk about preventing burnout and meltdowns, it's not for the comfort of others. Stress causes real damage, both physical and emotional. The stress hormone cortisol can cause long-term damage to the body. Burnout occurs when our bodies and minds decide they just can't ignore the stress anymore. It would be better if we didn't ignore stress in the first place but let the wounds heal as they come and then work to prevent them in the future.

Reducing stress is a lot of work for anyone, but it looks a little different for autistics. All the usual advice might still apply, but when you're hypersensitive, you need to take care of the little stressors too.

There's no dictionary for specific types of burnout, but there are some common types that we've observed friends, family, and other autistics experience. We've tried to describe them as best we can, but remember, there aren't official parameters for any of them, so different people may have their own definitions.

Autistic burnout: This is burnout specifically related to the extra effort it takes to survive as autistic. If an autistic person is forced to mask for too long or doesn't have a safe place to unmask and recharge, they will burn out quickly.

Gifted kid burnout: Burnout from growing up as an 'exceptional' child. 'Gifted kids' (kids who naturally do well in school were included in so-called gifted and talented programs in primary school) become used to everything being easy and don't know how to cope when something is difficult. Sometimes the people around them set them up to fail by assuming that the former gifted kid will keep up the impressive momentum they had in childhood. It comes with shame for only being normal at things and a disappointment in yourself for not being a superstar.

Holiday burnout: Holidays and vacations are fun but can also be stressful. Maybe you're away from home, around family a lot more, and have to wear special clothes and eat different foods. There may be a lot of activities, so you have less time take care of yourself. And there's bound to be at least one person who's a giant stress ball because they are keeping everything together. There's also the risk of a 'holiday

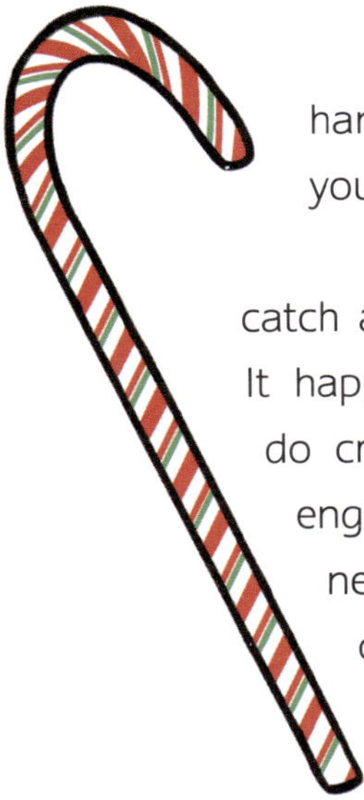

hangover'. That's when you burn out more easily after returning from your holiday because you haven't readjusted to regular life yet.

Artistic burnout: Hang around enough artists and you'll definitely catch at least one complaining of burnout or a creative block before long. It happens to all of us every once in a while. Whatever it is that you do creatively (and creativity comes in many forms, including things like engineering and product design), you run out of steam. Creators may need to take a long break and recharge, and experience art instead of creating it. However, some artists benefit from the opposite: stepping away, taking a break, and just breathing.

Job burnout: It doesn't matter how much you love your work – if it's a job, you can get burned out. Constant expectations, responsibilities, and demands are a lot on a person, and so is a forty-hour work week. Capitalism itself also adds plenty of pressure to have a job and keep it so you don't die, which adds a lot of stress onto all of us that we may not consciously realise. Job burnout is often the result of feeling a lack of purpose, drive, or support for your work. For autistics there's also a massive difference between a toxic work environment for everyone and a work environment that works fine for others but not for you. For a lot of autistics, *any* work environment can feel like too much, with it very stressful to be in a strange place with new expectations forced onto you for a huge portion of the day.

Have you ever experienced burnout?
What worked?
What didn't?

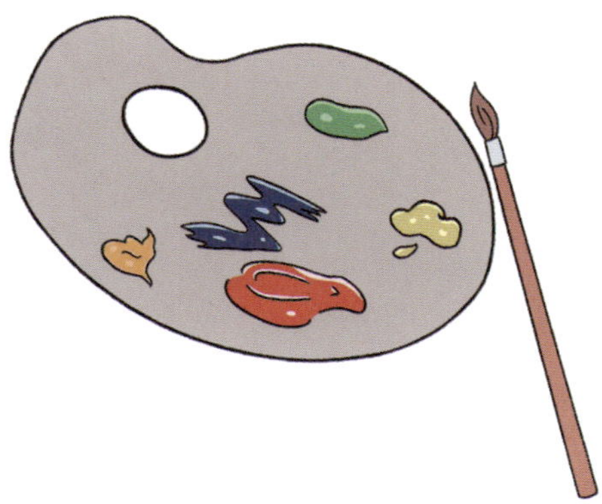

Journey to Burnout Mountain

Time for a game! It can be easy to fall into the mindset of 'I can do just one more thing', until you've pushed yourself the whole day and haven't gotten any rest. To visualise how life's many stressors can build up into burnout, move along the journey to Burnout Mountain as instructed. While many of these triggers for burnout aren't exclusive to autistics, they do tend to add up much more quickly for us.

- [ ] If you got less than eight hours of sleep last night, move two spaces.
- [ ] If you got less than four hours of sleep last night, move three spaces.
- [ ] If you *never* get eight hours of sleep, move three spaces.
- [ ] If you haven't eaten within the last five hours, move one space.
- [ ] If you haven't had a drink of water in the last three hours, move one space.
- [ ] If showering or bathing is stressful for you, move two spaces.
- [ ] If other hygiene-related tasks, like brushing your teeth or combing your hair, are stressful for you, move two spaces.
- [ ] If you struggle to find foods that don't cause sensory issues for you, move three spaces.
- [ ] If any part of your body hurts right now, move one space. If multiple parts of your body hurt, move one space for each body part. If you have chronic pain and you *always* hurt, move ten spaces.
- [ ] If you haven't taken a break to relax yet today, move one space. If reading this book is your break, that doesn't count. This is a fun book, but it can be overwhelming to read!
- [ ] If you have work to do, move one space for every hour of assignments you have left to do.
- [ ] If you have big projects you abandoned in the last month because you didn't have the energy to finish them, move two spaces for each project.
- [ ] If you feel you have to hide your autism often, move anywhere from two to ten spaces, depending on how much stress it gives you. If you have any other aspects of yourself you feel you have to hide (like being gay or part of an unpopular religion), move two spaces for each of those.
- [ ] If you recently failed at something that meant a lot to you, move two spaces.
- [ ] If your house is a mess, move two spaces.
- [ ] If you are so behind on laundry that you're out (or almost out) of clean underwear, move two spaces.
- [ ] If your living space has been infiltrated by a large sensory issue, like noisy construction next door or an annoying smell that you can't seem to get rid of, move three spaces.
- [ ] If you need to go grocery shopping, move one space.
- [ ] If you're the person in your family who always runs the errands and drives people where they need to go, move one space.
- [ ] If you can't engage in adult activities (like watching TV shows with mature themes or watching the news) because small children are around, move one space.

- [ ] If you have kids relying on you to take care of them, move two spaces for each kid.
- [ ] If you have elderly or disabled relatives who need you to care for them, move two spaces for each of them too.
- [ ] If you had a fight with a friend or loved one in the last week, move one space.
- [ ] If you personally know people who have died within the last year, move one space for each person. If any of the people who died were very close to you, move five spaces for each of them.
- [ ] If you're in debt, move one space. If you're in a *lot* of debt, move a second space too.
- [ ] If the current political climate in your country is making you stressed at least once a day, move one space.
- [ ] If you are worried about your health, move one space. If you are facing a health-related crisis like a cancer diagnosis, move five spaces.
- [ ] If you are worried about your loved ones' health, move one space for each person you are worried about.
- [ ] If you're going through a divorce or breakup (including platonic breakups like the end of a friendship or breaking off contact with a family member), move three spaces.
- [ ] If your living situation is currently changing or threatened, move two spaces.
- [ ] If the neighbourhood you live in or the place you work or go to school doesn't feel safe to you (it doesn't matter if other people say you shouldn't be worried; this question is about how you *feel*), move two spaces.
- [ ] Move one space for every day you spent hospitalised in the last six months.
- [ ] If you're regularly feeling physical symptoms from stress, like headaches, panic attacks, and nausea, move five spaces.
- [ ] If you feel lonely every day, move four spaces.
- [ ] If there's anything else you think should be on this list, add it here, and fill in as many blocks to move as you think are necessary. ______________________________

ELORA'S STRESS TAX THEORY

Have you ever had an experience like this? You're having a hard time at work or school, so you go home and try to distract yourself. You decide to bake a cake. As you bake, you think about the problems you're facing, but the fun of baking – and eating – the cake makes the problems bearable. It even distracts you a bit. You are using the task of baking a cake as a coping skill to deal with heavy emotions.

The next day you're still having a hard time, so you come home and bake another cake. Then you have another bad day and bake another cake. Then another, and another, and another. Day after day you bake cakes, and day after day those cakes help you calm down. You start to dive deep into baking, and it becomes a special interest.

Soon you're watching cake-decorating videos on your phone between assignments and you're daydreaming about becoming a professional baker. You buy a fancy set of frosting tips and an apron with your name embroidered on it and you're sure that this is the answer to your problems.

Then one day it just . . . stops.

You come home from school and yesterday's cake doesn't seem yummy anymore. You try to bake, but you're not interested – in fact, it stresses you out to think about it! Suddenly, you feel overwhelmed by the thought of baking a cake. The special interest has expired. It isn't useful anymore.

In my experience this is one of the worst parts of being autistic. The terrible experience of losing a special interest overnight and not knowing what to do with myself afterwards. When I think back to my own interests that faded, seemingly overnight, I notice a

pattern. Whenever I try to return to one of those interests, I notice old feelings and old memories from the last time I was truly obsessed with whatever the interest was. Awkward moments, stresses, confusions, and fears spring to mind.

Curiously, these special interests tended to be smaller than the special interests that truly define me. You might call them mini special interests, and they typically didn't last longer than a few months.

So I asked myself, 'What if the autistic brain's abandonment of mini special interests is a good thing? What if this is how we help ourselves let go of challenging emotions?'

That's what I call paying a stress tax. These mini special interests – baking cakes, playing *The Sims*, crocheting Christmas tree ornaments – are taxes your brain pays to let go of emotional stress. As autistics, we dive deep. The danger is that we might dive so deep into our problems that we struggle to come up again, to stop obsessing over them. So our brains force us to move on from whatever we are dealing with by obsessing over something else and then forcing us to move on from that too. When this works, by the time we lose interest in our tiny obsession, we've processed the emotionally taxing period and have perhaps forgotten it happened at all. In that way it's a form of self-protection. The special interest soaks up your stress like a sponge and then you simply throw it away. By getting rid of the interest, you're not losing a coping skill; you're letting go of the stress associated with the interest, freeing up mental and emotional space to take up a new interest that can address new problems. According to this way of thinking, your autistic brain needs to cycle through mini special interests in order to stay healthy.

So how do I use this theory of mine to make life easier? Instead of waiting around for my brain to pick an interest to sacrifice, I purposely give my brain something to pay the stress tax with! Because I know that my brain needs a mini special interest to throw away every so often, I make sure my brain has plenty of mini special interests to choose from! So rather than spending all of my time on things I enjoy wildly, I intentionally explore new hobbies and ideas that could become mini special interests. That way when it's time to pay the stress tax, my brain has a whole bucket of things to let go of.

And you know what? It works! One of the hardest parts of getting work done as an autistic professional is losing interest in the task I'm supposed to focus on, but since I started curating disposable mini special interests, I've dealt with that problem way less. Learning to pay the stress tax has protected the special interests I really need to keep, whether that's hyperfocusing on an important task, feeling joy with something I really need to learn, or just having fun with something I feel passionately about and don't want to lose. These are some ways I embrace new mini special interests:

- Starting to listen to a new podcast every so often.
- Going on YouTube deep dives about subjects I don't need to know about.
- Listening to educational audiobooks. (The book itself serves as the special interest – once it's over, it's automatically trashed. Easy peasy!)
- Listening to new music albums.
- Buying cheap craft kits I can do for a few days.
- Downloading new phone games to play for a few days.
- Throwing myself into an internet challenge that I know I'll obsess over and then abandon.

And these are some that Cat has found:

- Looking for pictures that spark her interest, or looking through ones that she's saved, to paint or draw.
- Working on papercraft projects.
- Buying craft kits, especially anything with laser-cut wood ('tis my weakness,' she admits).
- Sewing or crafting something from a favourite video game, like a stuffed animal or an outfit, which usually ends badly, but that's okay.
- Reading a new book.
- Picking some cool thing and doing a deep dive on where to find it and buy it.

- Cycling through the entire *Legend of Zelda* franchise, or *Minecraft*, or *The Sims*.

You never know if a mini special interest is going to end up being disposable or not. It doesn't matter. Dive into the special interest, and if you feel like it later, see if you can come back. And if not, it's okay. The special interest has done its job.

Stress tax theory is not an academic theory like monotropism. It's something I came up with by observing my own life and listening to others. But since it has yielded positive results in my life and the lives of those close to me, and is not hard to implement, I wanted to offer it up for you to try. If nothing else, it will help you discover lots of new interests, which I hope will make your life richer. Next time you lose interest in something that brings you joy, don't get mad at yourself for 'not sticking to anything' or 'giving up' – you just had to pay your taxes.

MELTDOWNS

A *meltdown* is often mistaken for a 'temper tantrum'. And in truth they're not that different. Tantrums have a negative connotation and are associated with toddlers, but the truth is, sometimes you've *just had enough.*

Adults have meltdowns too, but they can look very different from a child's meltdown. We tend to persevere through astounding amounts of stress before snapping, and the thing that makes someone snap might have nothing to do with all of the stress that had been building. Meltdowns are often the result of cumulative, compounded stressors layered on top of each other.

RALPH'S BAD DAY

Take Ralph. Ralph wakes up on the wrong side of the bed one morning. He isn't feeling well. Then his coffee maker breaks, which throws off his whole morning and he ends up leaving the house later than usual. The line for the coffee shop makes him even later, and the barista gets his order wrong. When he finally arrives at his office, his boss calls him out in front of everyone for coming in late with a Starbucks cup, even though the boss does the same thing all the time. A client sends him a rude email blaming him for something that wasn't his fault. His mother texts him yet another veiled demand for grandchildren, implying that he's a disappointment for not reproducing yet. A stressful meeting runs long, and his boss makes sure to clarify that even though the meeting

went late, he won't get paid for the extra hour at work. Traffic is horrible on the way home, and the driver behind him honks his horn repeatedly for about ten minutes, though it feels like an hour. By the time Ralph gets home, he's fried. Then his wife slips and breaks his favourite coffee mug, which he's had since he was ten. Ralph loses his temper and yells at her. He wants to stop, but feels like he can't help it, so instead he storms off to his bedroom and cries. Ralph has reached his limit and now he's having a meltdown.

Here's the thing: Ralph is normally a pretty chill dude. None of these things on their own would have been enough to make him lose his temper. He loves his wife and knows better than to yell at her. But all of these stressors added up and triggered a survival response in Ralph. His stress levels were heightened for too long, and as a result his body went into fight-or-flight mode.

Ralph is neurotypical, by the way. And, as long as he apologises to his wife for yelling at her and considers her feelings too, you might think he's being entirely reasonable about everything. After all, we all have our limits.

An autistic person can reach that same point of breakdown from stressors that other people don't even notice. Take Carla, who is autistic and works at the same office as Ralph.

CARLA'S BAD DAY

Carla wakes up feeling off, like Ralph. Her coffee machine is working, though, so she's got to be doing better than Ralph, right? Well, Carla's super-alert senses catch that the coffee tastes different today, and it throws off her routine. She doesn't know what's wrong, but it's bothering her and she feels the urge to fix it. So she doesn't go to the coffee shop. Instead she tries to find the problem. She checks the filter, puts fresh grounds in the machine, and brews a new cup. It still tastes wrong. She washes the filter and tries again. It still doesn't taste right. With each successive attempt at fixing the coffee, she becomes more and more worried that the machine itself is broken, and she doesn't want to have to deal with that possibility. This goes on for a long time, until finally Carla glances at the clock and realises she's late for work. She didn't just lose track of time. Her brain is hardwired to hyper-focus on things, at the expense of

everything else. When she gets to the office, she doesn't get chewed out by her boss like Ralph did, but she's as stressed as if she had, because she's worried about the coffee maker. She can't let it go. As an autistic person she relies on routine to feel stable, and the coffee maker is an important part of her routine. It might seem like a minor issue to someone else, but to Carla the fact that the coffee maker might be broken introduces the possibility that she will have to create a new routine and that every day from now on will begin uneasily. This uncertainty is intensely upsetting.

Carla doesn't get a rude email like Ralph, but because she's bad at reading subtext she thinks her clients *might* be mad at her. But she knows she can't ask them; that would be weird. Her mum texts her throughout the day, and Carla keeps checking the texts because she worries there is a family emergency. The texts are nice, but each one breaks Carla's focus.

Every noise in the office seems loud, the lights are too bright, and the textures are distracting, and her professional work clothes are too tight in places she didn't know existed. It's challenging for her to focus on her work, but when she does manage to get into a flow, her mum texts her and pulls her out of it again.

At a meeting a coworker politely asks her to stop fidgeting because it's 'distracting', so Carla spends the rest of the meeting focused on sitting still, which exhausts her because she needs to stim to concentrate. As a result she ends up misunderstanding some important information and embarrassing herself. Traffic isn't bad when she heads home, but it takes a lot more energy for Carla to drive than it does for Ralph. Her brain struggles to process all the information she has to digest in order to stay safe and follow traffic laws. When Carla gets home, her husband drops her favourite mug too, and it shatters. That mug was more than a cherished belonging; it was a comfort item, a tool she had used for years to ground herself, comfort herself, and cheer herself up when she was sad. She yells at her husband too and runs to her room and cries, just like Ralph.

The thing is, on paper, Carla *should* have had an okay day! She had coffee and time to get to the office. No one got mad at her and she even got cheerful, encouraging texts from a loved one all day. Her meeting wasn't as stressful as Ralph's, it didn't run long, and traffic on her commute home was light. But at the end of the day, Carla is every bit as stressed as Ralph

DIAGRAM OF A MELTDOWN

Meltdowns can look like:

- Shouting or snapping
- Crying
- Brain fog or an inability to focus
- Blank stares or dissociation
- The appearance or sensation of being 'broken' or 'shattered'
- Mental or physical exhaustion [31]

Everyone, regardless of neurotype, can have meltdowns, and they can look different from person to person. But autistic people tend to have them more often because of all the additional stressors and sensitivities we have to deal with. Add in the stress of masking and fulfilling neurotypical expectations, and it's a miracle we can hold it together at all.[32]

Some people differentiate between meltdowns (external breakdowns/emotional explosions with outbursts like crying and screaming) and shutdowns (internal breakdowns/emotional implosions with inner chaos like brain fog and an inability to speak). Since the line between them is fuzzy and there is a lot of overlap between them, we've grouped them together under the more commonly known term 'meltdowns'. You can think of meltdowns and shutdowns as variations of the fight/flight/freeze response. Meltdowns are fight, shutdowns are freeze, and elements of flight are in both. But regardless, they're both different expressions of the same panic.

BUT HOW DOES THIS AFFECT ME, THE MAIN CHARACTER OF THE UNIVERSE?

When dealing with an autistic person's meltdown, neurotypicals tend to get frustrated. They wonder, *Why can't this person hold it together? What do they mean when they say the lights hurt their brain and there's too much noise? Why are they crying in the middle of the drugstore? It's annoying, embarrassing, and inconvenient.* Even as a mere bystander it can feel as painful and frustrating as being trapped next to a crying baby on an aeroplane.

That's understandable. That's valid. But also whatever embarrassment and irritation a normie is feeling when the autistic person near them has a meltdown, it is probably nothing compared to how the autistic person feels. It's a terrifying, humiliating experience for that person, and they don't want it to be happening any more than the normie does. More often than not, being autistic means being pushed repeatedly to a breaking point you can't avoid. While a normie may be tempted to punish an autistic person for having a meltdown, that won't make the situation any better. If someone is so hungry that they collapse, they don't need punishment; they need food. If someone is so tired that they faint, they don't need shame; they need rest. If someone is so emotionally drained that they have a melt-down, they don't need judgement; they need a break.

Cat: I tend to dissociate when I'm having a meltdown. It feels like people are piling things onto me when they're just talking, and it can be hard to process what they're saying. I go into survival mode, looking to get through whatever I'm stuck in and do whatever I have to do to get home. Once I'm home I tend to find something to do that's mentally lightweight, like playing a video game or scrolling on my phone. I feel overwhelmed at the thought of doing anything, and it is an enormous struggle to tear myself away from whatever method of escapism I've employed. The strangest part is, I usually don't even know I'm having a meltdown until I'm analysing my own behaviour later. But my husband and I have developed a support system where one of us can take care of the basic duties around the house while the other recharges. Elora and I have developed a similar strategy for this book! One of us hyperfocuses, and the other one takes a break.

An autistic person who is having a meltdown might not know why they're having it. They might not even know that they're more stressed than normal. All they know is that they're yelling or crying. Some of us aren't great with emotions and can't identify when we're nearing our limit, so stressors pile up unnoticed until we shatter.

Imagine, if you will, that you have an extra sense – perhaps the ability to see extra wavelengths of light and sound. That means that any type of radiation would glow to your eyes, and something like a microwave or an X-ray would be blinding. You could see waves travelling through the air too, like thousands of beams of light crisscrossing the sky. Your house would be full of moving lights of every different colour. Maybe it sounds beautiful – but have you ever tried to get a good night's sleep on New Year's Eve? When you're already tired and have had enough, all those lights and sounds would have you clawing at your eyeballs to make it stop.

Autistic people feel like this pretty much all the time. It gets easier when you learn to control your environment through tools like noise-cancelling headphones and low lights. But 'easier' is different from 'easy'. Everyone has been in sensory overload before, but few people make the connection that autistic people feel that way often, sometimes even nonstop.

WHAT DO YOU NEED?

When having a meltdown, we do not need to be shamed, scolded, or otherwise made to feel worse. What we need is help.

An outburst of temper or a bout of brain fog can be a reaction to stress, like bursting into tears is.

And as an outpouring of emotion it often cannot, and sometimes should not, be controlled. Instead it should elicit sympathy and compassion from onlookers. That's one reason we cry – as a social signal to others that we are suffering. Crying also serves the biological function of helping us release stress and feel better. Plus, when you're used to pushing yourself to your breaking point, a meltdown signals that you've gone past your limit and forces you to rest. Melting down isn't only a consequence of intense stress; it can help make things better.

How can you help yourself (or a friend) who is having a meltdown? Everyone's different, and so are their meltdowns, so what helps one person might not help another. But here are a few things to try:

- Speak to the person melting down in a low, soothing voice. Do not raise your voice or use an angry tone. If you are the person melting down, ask people to speak calmly with you, if possible.
- Get yourself or the other the person a snack or drink. Everything seems more dire with low blood sugar.
- Remove as much stimulation as you can. Try to get to an area that is darker, quieter, and less overwhelming.
- Try to take something off of the metaphorical plate – either yours or the other person's. Take their crying baby for a walk, carry their bags, or run an errand for them.
- Let yourself or the person melting down do their thing for a minute or two. You might need to vent or take a mental break. Take a few minutes to recover.
- Listen. You don't necessarily have to retain any of the information. Just offer a sympathetic ear to the person melting down. Having someone listen to your concerns and say, 'Wow, that's a lot' or 'That sucks' can be a huge help.
- Focus on the real issue. Try not to get caught up in whatever little thing the meltdown is focusing on, even if that little thing is about you personally and feels like an attack.
- Being supportive and compassionate is more necessary than finding a solution. You may be tempted to solve the problem, but showing kindness to yourself or the person melting down and being considerate is often a lot more helpful.
- The person might say that they're okay after a little while, but it might still be best to wrap up what you're doing and go home. The person needs to recover and decompress properly in a safe place.

- Recovery from a meltdown might take minutes, hours, or days. Be patient with yourself or the person and give them plenty of space. You need some serious self-care and maybe some lifestyle changes, and to do that you need time and peace.
- The best fix is to prevent meltdowns altogether! It's impossible to stop them forever because they're a part of being human, but it *is* possible to have them less frequently.

PREVENTION IS KEY!

Preventing meltdowns requires self-care, self-love, and the emotional intelligence to recognise your own little habits and quirks. It will involve collecting data from your own experiences and tracking that data across time and different situations. However, if you can do even a little of this, you can prevent future meltdowns or lessen their severity and reduce your stress levels altogether. This is beneficial to your physical health as well as your overall sanity!

To begin try to track your stress levels and meltdowns. Keep mental notes of what causes stress for you, how much you can handle, what it feels like as you near your limit and then surpass it, and the specific triggers of your meltdowns. Try to see if there are connections between your stress levels and things like the day of the week, where you are in your cycle, if applicable, if it's trash day, if meltdowns have happened more since you started your new job, etc. Our brains make these connections unconsciously all the time, so looking for them consciously is not as overwhelming as it sounds. A journal may help, such as a daily log of how you're doing generally, or an app supporting mental wellness that lets you log your symptoms and moods. You could even put an emoji into a note on your phone that encapsulates your mood every day. All data is valuable and useful, so collect as much as you can. Your family and friends may have noticed patterns that are useful to you, so you might want to ask them for their input.

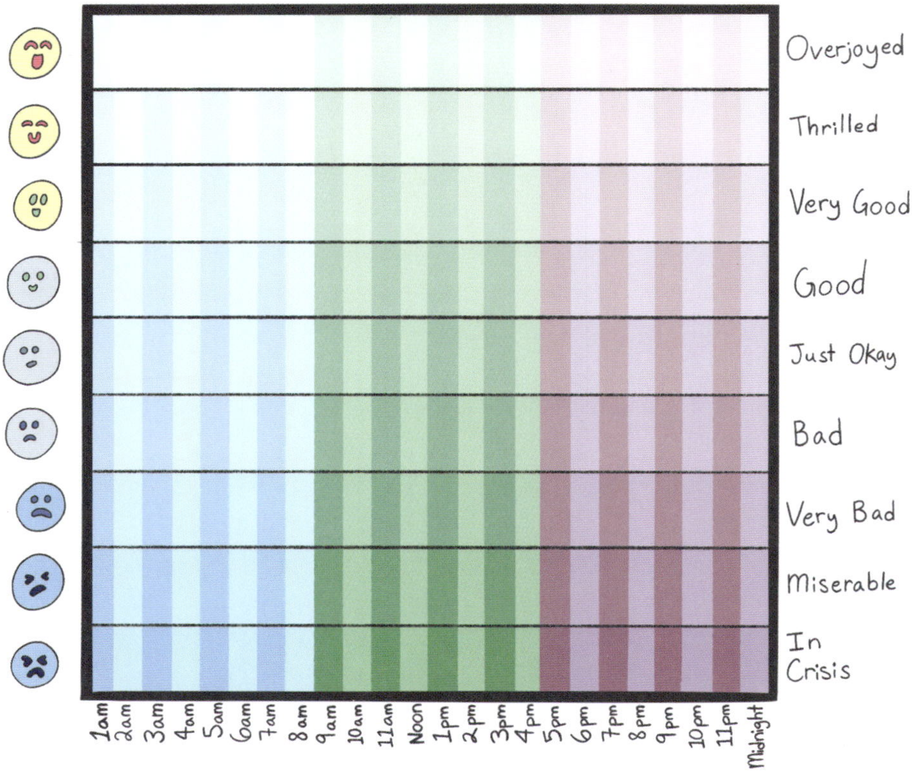

Once you recognise your own patterns a little better, you can start developing strategies to prevent overloads, meltdowns, and general stressors. Do you often forget your wallet and doing so ruins your whole day? Take steps to help yourself remember it, like putting it next to your keys or writing 'WALLET!' on a sticky note and putting it on the door you leave from. Did you start a new medication? Keep that in mind when your significant other is being super annoying all of a sudden. Have you had frequent meltdowns since moving apartments? It might be time to make some changes to your environment or your commute and help yourself adjust. Information is power, and with data we can make informed decisions.

Here are some general tips and strategies.

- **Have a routine.** Autistics thrive on routines, which are useful for making sure that important things aren't forgotten. A routine can help you eat regular meals, take your meds on time, and remember important items like a wallet or keys before leaving the house. Remember, a routine doesn't look the same for everyone. A routine can be an hour-by-hour setup of your day, or it can be as simple or as specific as the order you do things in. For example, Elora's hourly schedule changes constantly, but she tries to get an afternoon nap in most days and that helps her a lot. Certain things she does are 'pre-nap' activities, while others are 'post-nap' activities. It's a simple structure, but it helps her significantly. For Cat, she absolutely *must* start her day with breakfast and medicine. That is so deeply ingrained in her by now that she does it automatically. She then checks her schedule for appointments, and if there are none then she arranges her day as she wants. As long as her meds are taken on time, everything else tends to work itself out.

Here are some repeatable tips:

- **Know your limits.** Don't plan two errands on one day or two events on one weekend unless you're sure you can handle it. Schedule a whole day for big stuff like travelling or seeing a new doctor.
- **Set a schedule.** You need to get enough food and rest. Set a phone reminder so you remember. Does anything else need to occur at a certain time or at certain intervals? Do you need to take meds at a certain time, or do you keep forgetting to brush your teeth, or do you only remember to make phone calls when places are all closed for the day? Set reminders for that stuff too.

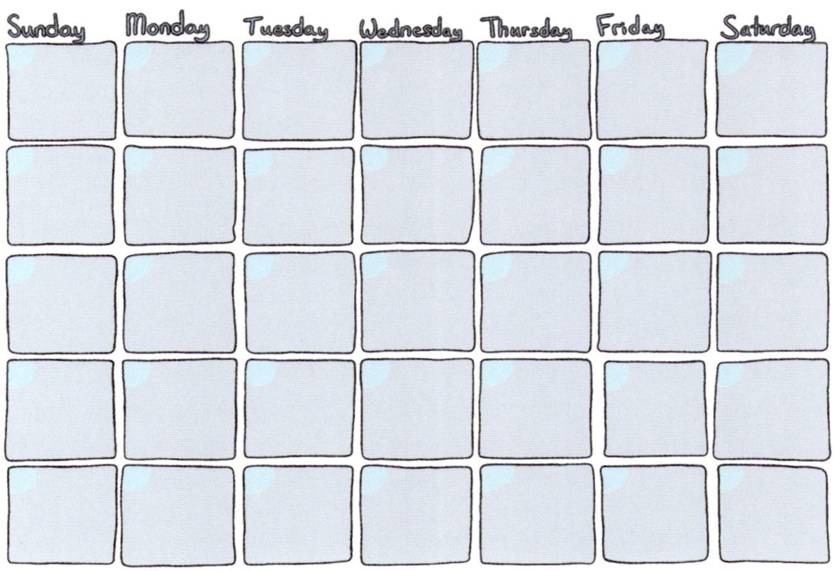

Cat: Routines can be agonisingly painful for ADHD people. So if you have autism and ADHD (a condition often informally referred to as AuDHD), creating and holding yourself to a routine is the *worst*. I know it sucks, but you just gotta do it. It'll be so much better for you, and it gets easier, I promise!

- **Eliminate extraneous stressors.** Is your volunteer job at the shelter thankless, tedious, and horrible? Quit. Does the thought of doing another Dungeons & Dragons session tonight fill you with dread instead of joy? Quit. Do you and your kid both hate soccer practice with every fibre of your beings? Q-U-I-T. Free yourself from as much nonsense as you can so you have room for what brings you peace and joy. You might disappoint a couple of people, but they'll get over it, and the slight sting of rejection is much better than the pain of doing something you hate. Freeing up room to breathe is underrated but so valuable. The exception to this is when something makes you feel good but you still dread going to do it. A common example is exercise. If you always feel energised after a yoga class but hate getting ready to go, maybe you just hate getting ready to leave the house and should still go to yoga.
- **Eliminate extra stimuli.** Turn off things that make noise, get a more soundproof bedroom window, or use white noise machines. Turn off overhead lights and lamps and install curtains, even blackout curtains if you need them. Wear comfier, softer clothes, take off your shoes inside the house, put a pillow on your desk chair. Whatever you have to do to reduce noise, light, and discomfort, do it.
- **Choose what's important.** The stress of certain chores isn't worth it. If cleaning spots out of the white sofa is too much stress for you, then get a gray one, or a cover, or just let your sofa be spotty.
- **Learn to say no.** There's nothing wrong with helping people out. If you have the bandwidth to do these things and want to, then do them! But don't say 'yes' to everything. Get comfortable with turning people down and disappointing them. You might even find a strange, thrilling freedom in saying 'no' and setting boundaries.

- **Prioritise.** Being an adult is like juggling, and people keep throwing extra balls in for you to keep in the air. But some balls are glass and others are plastic. Glass balls are things like picking your kids up from school, going to doctor appointments, and making sure your bills get paid. You *have* to catch them. Plastic balls are things like cooking a healthy dinner, taking your kid to karate practice, or watching your friend's cat. You can order pizza, Braydyn can skip karate, and your friend can find someone else to watch Fluffles. These things aren't life or death.
- **Show as much love and concern for yourself as you would for anybody you love.** You're a part of your family too. When you have a significant other, you clean up their messes and take care of them when they're sick because you love them. When you have a baby, you get up every two hours to make sure they're breathing, buy an expensive stroller, and do hours of internet research to make sure they're only crying because they're gassy. And you never resent them for it. You try to be kind to other people, so why not be kind to yourself?

- **Stand up for yourself and your needs and communicate them clearly when you can.** If you can get your needs met, your life will become easier and less stressful. Not everyone around you will respect your needs, but they can't respect them if they don't even know about them!
- **Do not let other people dictate the life you lead.** Don't let anyone pressure you into dressing, acting, or doing things a certain way just because it's their preference for your life. You do not have the energy to know everything, research everything, and care about everything. Prioritise what you value. Give yourself permission to take breaks, step back, and rest. You aren't invincible and your energy is finite.
- **Make time for the things that bring you peace and joy.** Find time for yourself every day to unwind and do what you love. It's critical for your mental well-being.

EXPLAIN YOURSELF? IN THIS ECONOMY?

If you're nearing a meltdown or *having* a meltdown, how can you explain this to those around you? Especially when you're having trouble communicating at all. Let's list some strategies to signal to others that you're overwhelmed.

- You can be honest and say, 'I'm overwhelmed right now' or 'I need a break'.
- Give an example of one of the things that are contributing to the meltdown and say you're overwhelmed because of it. If in the past two months your dog died, political news has kept you stressed, and you've had bad allergies, when you're having a meltdown you can share one of those things and say you need a break because of it. It's not a lie to refrain from listing the twenty different things that are bothering you.
- Simplify and say there is something on your mind that's bothering you.

How would you describe how your last meltdown felt? What do you want the people around you to know if it happens again?

DEFLECTION

When a person has a meltdown, it may appear to be over something tiny, like being asked to take out the trash after a long day. But it isn't about that at all. The person's brain is simply choosing a target to focus all its stressful energy on. When trapped in fight-or-flight mode, a person needs something to fight. So a person or object may find themself the unfortunate recipient of someone's pent-up emotions.

Deflection is the act of shifting focus from the primary issue onto an unrelated, often smaller issue. This protects the person from facing what's really bothering them, instead offering them a smaller, easier target to shoot at. And believe it or not, deflection can be helpful. If your house is messy, ignoring the giant puddle of dog vomit in the hall to focus on washing the windows might help you work up the momentum to tackle that bigger issue. Ignoring big problems in the long-term only makes them worse, but setting aside big problems in the short-term can help you gain the strength and confidence to face them.

Deflecting is more useful if done with intention. Tell yourself, 'I am not dealing with that right now', and focus on something else. Give yourself a break. Calmly shut down any conversations about something you aren't ready to deal with until you have gathered your thoughts on the subject and know what to say and do. Try to deflect in healthy ways instead of taking your frustration or anxiety out on someone else. And if someone shouts at you or overreacts, they might be deflecting too. Try not to take it personally.

Feel like there's no time in your day? Here's a great tip a friend gave me as someone who works from home on a computer: make some tasks computer activities and some tasks phone activities, and set specific times for each task. This is going to look different for everyone, but essentially I designated social media and email as phone activities and I check my phone while I have my morning tea and when I leave the house in the afternoon. I do not have those things open on my computer at all – only the documents I need for work. I also have a separate browser profile for writing than I do for research and related tasks. I have terrible object permanence, so when I minimise a program, it's like it doesn't exist and I use that to my advantage. I bring my work to the forefront and make everything else disappear. It's amazing how much it helped me to make these small changes.

DISSOCIATION

So there's this thing called dissociation. Unlike 'zoning out', dissociating is typically involuntary and triggered by stress. It cannot be 'turned off' by sheer force of will. Everyone dissociates in different ways. Sometimes it looks like daydreaming, except you can't snap yourself out of it. Sometimes it feels like being trapped in your body and watching someone else move it. It has been described as being stuck in a hamster ball or a bell jar and seeing the world through a clear plastic wall or a layer of glass – everything is one step removed, all the sounds are muffled, and it feels like you're not really part of the world.

Everyone dissociates from time to time. Sometimes you'll be driving and realise you don't remember how you got where you're going. But dissociation can also be a trauma response. The brain tries to protect you by drawing back and putting a shield between you and reality. In essence, your brain is taking you out of reality when reality feels too stressful, and you can't always choose to come back. Dissociation (not to be confused with dissociative identity disorder, which is a different thing) is common in people with post-traumatic stress disorder.

It's also common in autism. This might have something to do with the intense and long-term trauma many autistics experience as a consequence of being disabled in a world that's not designed for them. It may be that autistic people's brains dissociate in order to protect us from overstimulation, which can lead to a meltdown or panic attack. By mentally removing oneself from the noises, movements, and chaos that is causing distress, the autistic person could be unconsciously softening the stimulation and therefore lessening the distress and strain on their mind. Remember when we explained that autistic brains are like an octopus that has to use all eight of its arms to do the same thing?

One of the things that normies assume autistics can do is to dedicate one of their brain's octopus arms to tuning out the sensory inputs around them. Normies don't even realise they are doing it! They have one of their octopus arms dedicated to tuning out the world. But autistics can't dedicate an octopus arm to running that program in the background. Maybe this is part of the reason that so many autistics disassociate. It may also have to do with why we tend to verbally shutdown under duress. If you are incapable of using part of your brain to tune out the world, maybe your brain takes you out of reality altogether.

There is no automatic 'fix' for frequent dissociation. Some strategies that have helped the two of us are avoiding overstimulation and taking psychiatric medications in consultation with our therapists. We can also sometimes snap ourselves out of it by using grounding meditation, taking a nap, or focusing on something relaxing for a little while to rest our brain.

If someone is dissociating around you, they may not be able to tell you or may not even know themselves. But if you know or suspect that that's what's happening, give them some space. Take some stuff off their plate and give them a chance to rest. Let them have some quiet time and accept that they're in their own little world right now. And if they like hugs and you're very close with them, a hug wouldn't go amiss. Sometimes it can squish their brain back into place and ground them in reality.

PAY ATTENTION!

Did you know that the brain uses 20 per cent of the body's resting energy?[33] You need a certain number of calories a day just to maintain life, and using your brain simply to think burns about three hundred twenty calories a day.

> **Cat:** I've gone through many a twelve-hour study session where I could feel my blood sugar deplete and my brain go foggy. The brain definitely needs fuel!

If someone was sewing all day, you wouldn't blame them for taking a break, pausing to flex their hand, or wearing a brace. If someone was on their feet all day, you wouldn't blame them for sitting and resting for a few minutes or even a few hours at a time once they were done with whatever was keeping them on their feet. But when it comes to the brain, suddenly we're all sweatshop owners, working our bodies to the breaking point and refusing to allow a moment's rest. A lot of people think that even kids need to push themselves to work their brains all day every day.

If you don't give your brain a rest every now and then, it will run out of energy. It will start to drag and struggle like it's trying to perform a complex dance routine after running a marathon (or, for some of us, jogging farther than thirty feet). It won't work properly. And you're not helping anyone by trying to force it. You won't absorb what you're studying in that state, and your work will be shoddy with mistakes.

Thinking takes energy, and people have different energy needs. Some people need a little downtime, or a nap, or a snack to recharge; some people need to focus on something else for a bit; some people have an hour or two of difficult brain work in them a day, and then they're done. *Paying attention is hard work.*

An autistic person usually has more stimuli to juggle and a harder time pretending that everything's fine when it's not. We are burning a lot more energy just to mask, or to keep up with the conversations and social nuances going on around us. Let an autistic hyperfocus on their special interest and the person might pay attention for twelve hours straight without so much as a bathroom break. But force an autistic to pay attention to anything else and results can't be guaranteed. So what's the takeaway from this section? That there is a basic physiological reason for you to take mental breaks. Your brain is not invincible, just like your legs, lips, stomach, and liver are not. Thinking is work! So rest when you can – you really do need it.

Draw a self-portrait of you as a superhero, because you're doing hard work!

EMPATHY

'Empathy' is a word that can mean a lot of different things in a lot of different contexts. Most people use it to mean 'the ability to care about other people.'[34] [35] Those same people, however, will bring their assumptions about what 'caring for other people' looks like to the way they use the word. Let's look at an example.

'My boyfriend did not even cry when his grandmother died. What a total lack of empathy!'

What this woman is trying to say is that she thinks her boyfriend does not care about other people, but she has made a lot of assumptions along the way.

- She did not see her boyfriend cry about his grandmother's death.
- Therefore, she assumed her boyfriend never cried about his grandmother's death.
- And she assumed that if you do not cry you are not sad.
- Then she assumed that you are supposed to be sad if your grandmother dies.
- Then she assumed that if you do not have the emotions you are 'supposed' to have, you are incapable of having the 'right' emotions in other situations, which is her specific definition of 'empathy'.
- Finally, she assumed that if you do not have the 'right' emotions, then you do not care about other people.

Exhausting!

But maybe the boyfriend did cry, in private. Maybe he cried and the woman never noticed. Maybe he is still in shock from the death and has not been able to cry yet. Maybe he has been trying very hard not to cry because he is self-conscious about his emotions. Maybe he just does not cry much, even when very sad. Maybe his grandmother was dying for a long time and he had already grieved her before she passed. Maybe he did not know his grandmother well. Maybe his grandmother was a terrible person who burned down orphanages and poached baby seals, and his feelings about her death are complicated because of that. Maybe the boyfriend is not a very emotional guy. Maybe having specific emotions, or no emotions at all, has nothing to do with whether you are a kind person. And maybe that's a good thing.

As an autistic person, you have probably experienced this kind of stigmatisation. People constantly label autistics as selfish and uncaring because we do not pass the secret emotional 'tests' people set up for us without us knowing. In fact, they do not seem to know they are doing it either! Before we go any further, we want to take a moment to acknowledge how much that might have hurt you. We need you to know these important truths:

You are not a monster.
Having different emotional experiences from the people around you can be a good thing.
You deserve to be treated with respect, without having to put on an emotional show.

Instead of talking about empathy as one big complex term that everyone uses differently, let's look at seven different factors that people will lump under their individual definitions of 'empathy' and see how mental and emotional diversity is actually a strength. This is not any sort of clinical or definitive list. This is just a list of elements we have seen people pick and choose from time and time again to build their own Frankenstein's monster of cognitive phenomenon that they use to judge whether someone has any kindness in their heart. We see beauty in all these unique ways of existing, even if others do not.

1. SITUATIONAL AWARENESS – THE DETAILS WE NOTICE

How observant are you of the world around you? Do you pick up on little details in your environment or stay shut off in your own world? That is your situational awareness.

Imagine that your friend Shawna recently borrowed something from you and promised to give it back. Unfortunately, she's been a bit distracted since then, because she is getting divorced. She did not tell you about it, but she stops wearing her wedding ring. A couple weeks later, when you remind her for the fourth time to return your item, Shawna yells, 'You don't have any empathy, do you? I never would have asked you for anything if I knew you were so selfish!'

Shawna made an assumption here that you would notice her wedding ring was missing, but you did not. She connected that with your bugging her to return your belonging and decided that you were intentionally pushing her during the worst time of her life. Based on that evidence, she (incorrectly) concluded that you are self-absorbed and unkind.

The funny thing is, being super observant can make you a better friend, but so can being unobservant. Sometimes it feels good to have a friend play detective and find all the clues so that we do not have to explain our complicated lives. Other times, it is nice to spend time with someone who is oblivious to all the drama, so we can just escape.

Having low situational awareness does not make you unkind, and it can even be a comfort in times of trouble.

2. COGNITIVE EMPATHY – THE FEELINGS WE FIND

'Cognitive empathy' is a scientific term used to describe our ability to read and understand the feelings of others. Autistic people tend to have low cognitive empathy when they try to understand allistics. Likewise, allistics have low cognitive empathy when they try to understand autistics.

Cognitive empathy is another way Shawna might have expected you to discover what she was going through without her mentioning it. Maybe her facial expressions and body language have implied that she is sad. Maybe she has hinted that she is struggling and expected you to read between the lines to pick up on it. Maybe she has used a strained tone of voice whenever talk of relationships comes up, and she thought you would connect all these hints together and conclude that she was going through a dark time in her relationship.

It is obvious that strong cognitive empathy is an asset, but low cognitive empathy can be beneficial too. If you do not understand what people are feeling, you have to ask them about their feelings to understand. This is not in any way a failure. On the contrary, having to express and verbalise those feelings helps the other person process how they feel, as well as helping both parties become more emotionally intelligent as a result. These conversations are valuable and needed to build healthy relationships. High cognitive empathy gives you a shortcut to connecting with other people. Low cognitive empathy forces you to be intentional.

3. EMOTIONAL EMPATHY – THE FEELINGS WE SHARE

Emotional empathy (also known as affective empathy) is another scientific term that refers to our ability to feed off of other people's emotions. Have you ever been to an event, like a concert or a party, where everyone else was so hyped that you got pumped up just because you were near them? Have you ever been near someone who was so jittery that you started to feel on edge just by observing them? Have you ever held the hand of someone who was crying and you started to tear up too, because you could feel their sadness? That is emotional empathy, the ability to feel what someone else is feeling. Autistic people can have a wide variation of levels of emotional empathy or even levels that change depending on the situation.

Far too many autistics have lived the same horror story. Someone you love is upset and you try to comfort them, but they get angry that you are 'so heartless'. What made you heartless? They wanted you to feel sad with them, but you did not. You just listened, and that was not good enough. Or maybe you have faced the opposite problem. You are watching a movie, and it all gets too real. The character does something embarrassing and you feel overwhelmed with shame on the character's behalf. It's like you are living the story. Then a character dies and you start sobbing because it is just so real for you. Sure enough, everyone around you starts rolling their eyes at you for being 'too much'.

But having low or no emotional empathy is useful in an emergency when being overly emotional can overwhelm you and cloud your judgement. Having high emotional empathy can help you connect with others. Having empathy in the middle, or empathy that changes, makes you versatile.

4. SYMPATHY – THE FEELINGS WE OFFER

Sympathy is similar to emotional empathy, and they overlap a lot. Emotional empathy is the act of feeling someone else's feelings, but sympathy is the act of feeling *for* someone else, regardless of whether they feel it too. For example, if a young mother is widowed, and you cry with her as she cries, you are experiencing emotional empathy. You are feeling her pain. But if you see her toddler son playing happily with blocks on the floor and feel very sad for him, you are experiencing sympathy. The child is not sad. He does not understand what death is. But you know that something terrible has happened to this child, and you feel terrible for him because of it.

But what if you do not feel it? What if something terrible happens in front of you and you feel empty, or even happy? Are you a monster?

Nope. It is impossible to hold enough grief for all the evil or loss in the world. Being sad about all the things you are 'supposed' to feel sad about is not a realistic goal. And feelings are extremely complicated! There are no 'good' or 'bad' feelings, only feelings that are generally assumed to match certain situations. Sympathy is just an emotional arrow that points you towards problems that need to be solved. You do not need the arrow to help someone. If you have a lot of these emotional arrows, that can motivate you to help. If you do not have many, or any, of these arrows, then they will not drain your emotional energy, and that leaves you with more resources to help.

5. PERSONAL EXPRESSION – THE WAYS WE EXPRESS OUR FEELINGS

Two people can be feeling the same emotion and express it in completely different ways. We all have individual facial anatomy that makes our expressions unique. We come from different cultures that influence us to express ourselves in specific ways. We subconsciously mimic the mannerisms of other people. We have unique personalities and energy levels.

Sometimes people demand that you 'show a little empathy', but what they really mean is 'show a little emotion', emphasis on the 'show'. Part of masking our autism is learning to perform the 'right' emotions for others so they do not punish us. Many of us learn to flip through exaggerated smiles and artificial frowns because the people around us refuse to trust us unless our feelings are easy for them to read at all times. Others of us learn to tone our self-expression down because we are just 'too much'.

But having a flat affect has advantages! People who express themselves in subtle ways are uniquely qualified to handle pragmatic situations where big displays of emotion would overwhelm people or escalate a situation. They can hide their emotions if an emotion isn't suited to the situation, such as controlling their anger or frustration when they know it is unwarranted. On the other hand, people who express themselves in dramatic ways are uniquely qualified to be entertainers, work with small children, or provide emotional support to those in their lives who require a visible cue.

6. COMPASSION – THE DESIRE WE HAVE TO HELP

Compassion is our motivation to help other people. Sympathy may be the arrow pointing you in the direction of the problem, but compassion is the desire within you to do something about it. It might be an emotional response for you, or an impulse, or a desire. All that matters is that you have it. When other people hurt, is there a part of you, even a little bit, that wants to help them? Or maybe you feel that you cannot or should not help them, but you still want someone else to? If you answered yes to either of those questions, congratulations! You care. You have compassion. That's a good thing. You do not have to perform it, or feel it in a certain way, or be overcome with emotions about it. It exists. That is enough.

7. ACTIONS – THE STRATEGY WE CHOOSE TO HELP

Regardless of what we notice, feel, want, or show, what really defines us is our actions. Someone can feel sorry all day long for people in pain, but whether they do something is what reflects who they are. You do not need to cry a single tear for anyone else in your entire life. You do not need to share anyone's pain even once. You do not need to express your feelings in ways other people can read. But we have a responsibility to, at a bare minimum, not make the lives of those around us worse – and, if we can, to make them better.

So much of this book centres on the ways we get hurt as autistics. Our lives are betrayal upon betrayal. Our families, communities, and governments abandon us constantly. Systems of power make it unsafe for us to embrace who we are. The way we are treated is not fair. That is just a fact.

So what are we going to do about it?

You may have heard of the improvisational theatre concept called 'yes, and'. When actors are making up a scene as they go, they react to each other with 'yes, and' as their guiding principle. Instead of changing or negating what the other person has just done, they accept it, no matter how ridiculous – that's the 'yes'. The 'and' is to add onto whatever the other person just said, as in 'Yes I killed the duke, and I killed the butler as well!' As autistics in a world that was not built for us, we do not get to stop the pain we face. We cannot say 'no' and stop the scene and negate what just happened. The hurt keeps coming, and we have to accept it. We have to say 'yes'. But we can choose to say 'and'.

Yes, and.
Yes, you assume the worst of me,
and I will look for the best in others.
Yes, you call me evil for being different,
and I will call others special for being different.
Yes, you treat me cruelly because you think
I have earned it, and I will treat
others kindly without their earning it.
Yes, you hurt me, and I will not become like you.

Knowing how complicated people's conceptualisations of empathy are can help us evade some judgement, though not all. Many people have not considered how diverse human brains and personalities are, and your loved ones may be excited to learn how your brain works. Sometimes all you have to do to improve a relationship is explain how your brain is different from the brains of the people around you. Other times people refuse to adopt the new perspective and call you a monster for explaining that you think and feel differently.

There is no easy, light, and fluffy way out of this mess. The best you can do is explain your brain to the people you trust the most, and show yourself the respect that others refuse to give you. Knowing that you are not emotionally broken will not stop people from being cruel to you. What it can do, though, is stop you from being cruel to yourself.

Affirmations are sayings that you tell yourself repeatedly to help you internalise a message. Try these out:

- Emotions are not good or bad. They just are.
- My emotions do not define me. My actions do.
- My emotions are part of me. They are not all of me.
- Assigning a moral value to what I cannot control is setting myself up for failure.
- My emotions do not have to be 'correct' to be valid.
- I have human dignity and worth regardless of my ability to communicate.
- The people who care about me value my honesty over my ability to perform to their liking.
- Life is too short to waste time trying to please people.
- I am not a trained actor in my own life. I am not required to lie to please others.
- My gut reaction is out of my control. How I react to it is the true display of who I am.
- My emotions are trying to tell me something. It is up to me, and only me, to determine if that something is important.
- Empathy and sympathy are not required to be a good person.

PARENTING AS AN AUTISTIC BY CAT

My main worry as a new autistic parent was sensory overload. I can barely stand the sound of a distant lawnmower, so I couldn't image how I was going to function with a constantly whining toddler. How would I keep my temper? How could I watch a kid twenty-four seven when I spend most of my time zoning out and daydreaming?

But the age I was dreading most (my son's eighteen- through thirty-six-month toddler period) came and went, and I did so much better than I'd thought I would. I have a few coping mechanisms (like listening to something on my headphones while I play with him because, let's be honest, some of these baby games are *boring*), and I have my iPad on standby if I need a minute to work.

Cat: My son was 18 months when I started writing this. He'll be four when the book comes out. Old me was dreading the wrong age group.

When I was younger I was a nanny, a day care worker, and a Tae Kwon Do instructor. It was great that I had those experiences before I became a parent because they made it so that having a child of my own was much easier than I'd expected. Parenting isn't necessarily difficult; it's just endless. It doesn't matter what the task is: if you're performing it for sixteen hours a day on minimal sleep, you're going to get overwhelmed. We've all been there. Although my husband is helpful when he's home, I have been my son's primary caretaker since his birth, and for the most part being a work-from-home parent has been amazing. It did, however, get much rougher when we moved to

Germany. My son had just turned two, and I was alone with him all day every day without a support system. My son wanted me to play with him *constantly*, and all the fun of getting to watch him grow was utterly negated by how stressed out I was. It was too much. Some people function better in this situation than others. It's like a track meet – some people are better at marathons (consistently going strong), and some people are better at the hundred-metre dash (short intense bursts). I'm a hundred-metre dash person. Once my son could go to kindergarten, both of us were much happier: he wasn't bored, and I was able to do things for myself.

Don't feel guilty if long days of solo parenting burn you out or you have to rely on child care and leave the kids at home with a babysitter for part of the day to cope. We're all different and that's okay. What isn't okay is judging each other.

A better approach to discipline is to try to understand *why* a negative behaviour is occurring before you start handing out consequences. Practice compassion. It may be that something is going on with the child that they don't know how to handle.

Autistic children in particular get overwhelmed, overstimulated, or confused about what to do.

Recent studies have come out that give us a few great, if sometimes difficult-to-swallow, parenting tips.

Never spank or hit your child. It wires their brains in the same way as physical abuse, and causes children to perceive the world as more threatening.[36]

Try your best not to shout at, demean, or insult your child.[37] The occasional raised voice or thoughtless word will not destroy their psyche, but verbal abuse is real abuse. It is easy to dismiss it as 'not real abuse' when compared to physical abuse, but the effects on the brain are still devastating.[38] If you feel out of control, excuse yourself if possible, apologise for your temper, and take responsibility.[39]

Too much kindness and support will not 'spoil' a child. Children need boundaries, but those boundaries do not have to come with condemnation. Being warm and loving with your children puts them on a path to lead a much better life.[40]

Even autistic adults get overwhelmed and lash out. While it's instinctual to snap back or start punishing, you owe your child love and kindness when they're distressed.

Making it clear that a behaviour is not okay is often enough to stop it, but if it's not, take time to address the feelings behind the behaviour. Sometimes a child's tantrum isn't about them not getting their way; it's about them standing up for their needs. One day my son threw a tantrum when we were putting his shoes on for school. It was an unusual response for him, so when our attempts at calming him down failed, I watched him closely and realised that his freaking out was actually starting at the sock stage of getting the shoes on. Those socks were new and pretty cheap and he'd only worn them once. I switched out the socks and suddenly there was no issue. The new socks were uncomfortable for him and he couldn't stand to have them on again. I could have wrestled with him and dealt with him screaming for half an hour on the way to school, but instead I figured out the problem and addressed it. Just because he didn't deal with it the way I would have liked didn't mean his problem didn't matter. Autistic kids have issues with things like this all the time and can't articulate what's wrong. Even as an adult, I have these experiences. Sometimes being strict is necessary, but sometimes the best thing you can do is be understanding.

For behaviour that is actually harmful to your child, other children, or property (and not just irritating or inconvenient), putting your child in a time-out or taking away privileges are good tools to have in your kit. The best consequences are natural consequences, related to the behaviour; for example, throwing the toy means the toy is taken away. Regardless, you can condemn a behaviour without rejecting your child, and you can provide consequences for an action without causing harm.

Redirection is the best tool in your arsenal for littles. Give them something else to focus on so they don't do the thing that's causing problems. If you know stopping one activity will upset them and cause them to scream or throw things or work themselves up, short-circuit the tantrum entirely by suggesting a different activity that they'll enjoy. Instead of commanding, make tasks into a fun game. If they're upset that it's bedtime, distract them from the meltdown by suggesting they pick out their books, pyjamas, or stuffies. Nobody wins in a power struggle with a toddler, so just sidestep it completely.

My son gets soothed and told it's okay during tantrums. If he does something specifically harmful, like hitting or throwing, we make it clear that behaviour is 'not nice', but otherwise we understand that he's trying to handle his feelings. We don't believe it's good for him to cry for very long, regardless of what he's crying about, because while he needs to learn how to process his emotions, there's no need to abandon him with elevated stress levels. So even if it's a tantrum over something silly, we hold him in a bear hug and try to distract him out of it. He's since developed a coping mechanism when he's upset: he lies on the floor, puts his hands on his mouth, and calms himself down. Telling him it's okay to be upset has worked, and now he understands that he can feel his feelings, take a break, and then get back into the game when he's ready – or even go to sleep. He is definitely allowed to fall asleep. In fact he has my blessing.

I'm by no means an expert parent, but a little bit of sensitivity and understanding can go a long way, especially for autistic littles. I hope that by citing the times it made my life easier, I can help inspire others to parent with compassion.

Cat: My son continues to age, and is, as of editing, a threenager. These same tips apply, but holy cow does he require more patience. Not only does he have strong opinions that don't often coincide with reality (sorry, buddy, but we cannot create a vacuum inside your toy train to make it implode, no matter what you saw in *Mythbusters*), but he has strong emotions as well. He is incredibly sensitive to rejection or correction by adults, even if it's kind. It is so frustrating how many tantrums he throws over the littlest things and how much time we waste dealing with the fallout when it would be so much easier and faster for all of us if he just *did the thing.* But alas, his brain can't make those connections yet, so patience is needed. A lot of patience. The biggest struggle for me has been to implement a more structured routine when putting him to bed got too difficult. I have ADHD as well, and routines feel like torture to implement. He thrives on routine, and so do I, even if we hate it.

Here's some more little-kid parenting tips from one autistic to another:

- Don't deny yourself what you need to cope. If sugar and caffeine help you, and your body can handle them in a healthy way, then go ahead and load up. If having a movie on in the background or in your earbud helps you focus, do it. If free play is easier for you than structured play, then babyproof an area, dump out some toys, and let your kid go to town. If your kid's noisy toys are too loud, take out the batteries.
- Have a pocket full of something your kid loves, like fruit snacks, and offer them one if they start to get grumpy or need a distraction.
- Don't be afraid to put a screaming baby in a safe spot and leave the room for a few minutes. They'll be okay, and you can't take care of them if you're about to have a meltdown. Put on your own oxygen mask first!
- Take your meds, keep current with your doctor's appointments, and be responsible about your basic health needs. Eat well, get rid of your addictions, and go to therapy, *regardless of whether you think you need it,* because therapy is self-care. A happy, healthy, mentally stable parent is the best gift you can give your child.
- Playtime is how kids learn best. Some parents get really into playtime and this is great fun for everyone. But if you have the opposite problem, I get it. Kids' games and toys can be frustratingly boring. If you're struggling, adjust. Try moving your kid's play area to a more engaging setting (like a bathtub or a sandbox), get them more complicated toys (like building blocks or marble runs, the sort of thing that older kids and younger kids both find fun), or get them a toy you're interested in.
- Attention is a need just like food and water. A child wanting attention is perfectly normal and healthy. It can be extremely overwhelming for you to fulfil those attention needs, however, which is absolutely normal. This is where other family members and playdates and the like come in. Just because your child needs attention and stimulation doesn't mean it all has to come from you!

- Being 'touched out' is a thing. Small children and babies want to touch you and climb on you *all the time* and it can overstimulate you really quickly. It can't always be helped, because physical touch is a comfort that children desperately need, but it is totally natural to be sick of it and overwhelmed by it by the end of the day, and that does not make you a bad parent.
- Make time for things that bring you joy. It will help your sanity. If you include your littles in your hobbies too, that's perfect! Two birds with one stone.
- Nap when your kid naps if you are home with them and no other child needs supervising. Seriously. Make sure to get a nap a day as often as you can until your kid is down to one nap a day, and even then I suggest you use that time to rest. You need it to recharge your brain. Sometimes you'll have to skip it, but if the opportunity comes to take a nap, leave the dishes to fend for themselves and go have some you time.
- Ask for help. People are surprisingly willing to help you out when you have a baby. Whether it's your in-laws babysitting or someone in the grocery store parking lot lifting a heavy bag for you because you only have one arm free, let people help you and don't be afraid to ask for help. You have a kid; they get it.
- Lean into whatever type of autistic you are. If you're a quiet autistic, keep the house quiet. If you're a music autistic, play music. If you're a going-places autistic, go places with your kiddo. If you're a stay-at-home autistic, stay at home. It's good for kids to get new experiences, but it's not really beneficial if you're on edge and overwhelmed the whole time.
- Similarly, learn to cut back on playdates and commitments if it works better for your family. Our tips for preventing burnout work for parenting too. Leave an evening a week free, simplify your life as much as you can, and focus on what's important. Remember: glass balls stay in the air; plastic balls are allowed to fall.
- If you're not the default parent (whoever stays home with the baby all day), it can be tempting to let the default parent keep parenting when you get home because you're tired, or have things to do, or are getting

overwhelmed. Fight that urge as much as you can because taking care of a small child all day is exhausting and the default parent needs a break. It can be easy to give in to sensory overload or sensory issues (you might not want to change a dirty diaper because the smell makes you sick), but the default parent has been in giving mode all day without the opportunity to give in to sensory overload and take time for themself. This is a good time for communicating and practising compassion even when it's hard. Parenting is about doing things you don't want to do when you're super tired. If there is no default parent because you both work, then the child care should be equal.

- Autism is highly genetic. If one family member is autistic, chances are that one or both of the person's parents are and also one or more of their children. Take that information how you wish and adjust your parenting accordingly.

And as always:
be the parent you wanted for yourself.

AUTISM AND FAMILY

Do you think your parents did a good job raising you? What family related wounds are you still nursing from your childhood? How has autism affected your familial relationships, especially factoring in the genetic nature of autism? How has your family responded to your diagnosis? Do you have trouble communicating with your family? What does the ideal version of your family look like to you?

ON LOVE BY CAT

Love is work. That's something we don't always understand, and we may prefer to ignore as often as we can, but connections with other humans do need to be maintained. And part of the work of loving someone is learning how to be around them. You learn that they like their coffee a certain way, that their English might be flawless but they don't always understand idioms, or that they like jokes as long as they're not too dark. Learning someone's nuances, preferences, and boundaries, and honouring them is one way we show people we love them.

Sometimes the work of loving one person is harder than it might be to love another. Babies, for example, are easy to love. Parents love their children so hard when they're babies. But as people grow and become, well, people, that love must shift and change along with the child. It is sometimes hard for me to reconcile that with my own child – to see the road from how I have loved him to how I will love him in the future. Realising that my parents travelled the same road with me and that my child and I will face similar struggles to the ones my parents and I encountered. My son isn't easy to care for, but he *is* easy for me to love. Sure, he has opinions on things like Cheetos and the vacuum cleaner and mornings, but he and I aren't going to argue politics around the dinner table anytime soon.

Here's the thing though: you're not *supposed* to make yourself easy to love. People aren't supposed to diminish themselves or be 'low maintenance' or agree about everything to earn love. Love means being loved for who we really are. It means being ourselves – our authentic, messy selves. It means showing the people we love every side of us, even if it's not very pretty. It means drawing lines in the sand and expecting people not to cross them, and respecting their boundaries in turn.

It takes work to maintain a relationship, especially in a family.

Sometimes my parents feel like they can't do anything right. They say things that offend me too often. I correct them on how I want to be treated or how I want to raise my child. They try their best and are perfectly willing but still seem to trip up. I draw lines in the sand that seem unfair and too harsh and don't take their feelings into account, proving that I don't really understand them. But here's the secret: I feel exactly the same way about them. I also feel like I can't do anything right. I also feel like I'm walking on eggshells and am scared to trust them with my anxieties or limitations. It's not that I don't understand where they're coming from, because I've absolutely thought about it – overthought it, even. I just can't express any of this in a way that makes them see. But after being diagnosed with autism, I finally found the words to just tell them that I *can't* find the words. I helped them realise that I was trying to reach out so that they realised they had to listen a little harder. And though we still have our disagreements, we keep trying, and keep hashing it out, and keep drawing boundaries and respecting them and damaging our relationship and repairing it again, because love can be messy, and it can be hard work, but it's work worth doing.

Relationships are work at both ends and it's supposed to be a fifty-fifty effort. But asking someone to put in more effort is difficult. They might not like it. It might feel like a punishment or criticism. And when you're autistic, it may be even more work. You will have to teach people how to treat you, and they may resist. I don't allow people to shout at me or around me or my child anymore; I insist on instructions being written; I work on things at my own pace; I speak my mind bluntly, and I make it clear that I don't mean any offence. And the people who really love me? They come through. They put in the work. They adjust. They understand that it's a give and take, and they're willing to give.

The people who don't really love me don't put in the work. They don't make the effort to understand me. They react badly when I try to be myself, which means I mask around them, which is exhausting. That's why most of those people aren't in my life at all. It's okay if they don't like me, but I can't stand acting like a different person anymore. I know they don't like me enough to allow me to be myself and that hurts. It's honestly a relief when people admit that they don't like me, because the pretending makes me feel like I'm going insane. By not putting in the work to understand me, they prove that they don't like or love me. So why pretend?

But that's the beauty of it – you can't fake love. Because love is caring about someone, putting them first, doing things for them, thinking about them, and putting in time and effort. Love is about changing, growing, and learning. It's my parents finding out I'm autistic and driving for hours to attend a conference on the subject to understand me better, and it's me making sure they can FaceTime their grandson anytime they want. It's my husband saying 'I love you' before hanging up the phone after years of him not being comfortable saying it at all, and ordering more of my vitamins when I mention I'm running low, and quietly doing hours of research to fix a problem he knows has been bugging me. It's me taking care of my son without complaint (okay, without complaining *much*) so my husband can work late on his pet project, and responding with excitement instead of exasperation the ten millionth time my son tells me about his trains, and working with half my screen taken up by Bluey and a toddler in my lap and crumbs all over me. It's me being hard to love, and my friends and family doing it anyway.

People will prove that they love you if you're looking for it. And they'll also prove that they don't. It's up to you to decide what kind of relationships you have. But you deserve to know one thing: you are worth the work it takes to love you. Every bit of it.

PART THREE

Autism Every Day

LIFE WITH AUTISM

Elora: People think that the only options for autistics are 'hide your autism forever and live a lie' or 'hide nothing and be super vulnerable'. On the contrary, there are so many ways that many of us can meet our autistic needs without painting targets on our backs!

Cat: Very true. I have taken to saying I'm 'bad at conversation' or something else mildly self-deprecating, almost a joke at my own expense. It explains to the other person that I'm not being socially inept on purpose and puts them more at ease without talking about autism at all. As far as I know, they don't pick up that I'm autistic just from that. That being said, I do tend to live my life more on the authenticity side because I have so much trouble masking. I try really hard but the results are never really what I want, and I really like to know the people in my life like me for me. But I do wish I was better at faking just to have the option.

Elora: Different people will see different sides of us as autistics, and that's okay. But taking control and choosing which side of us we show them is a way to be both authentic and calculated at the same time. We are not in a war against our autism. We are in a war against the challenging world we live in, and autism is the field we fight on. For better or worse, this is the terrain where we must do battle, so what are we going to do with it?

Cat: Yeah, it's no use wishing we were different! Goodness knows I've tried to be. It will slowly drive you insane trying to hide and change who you are. It's just exhausting. Putting a label to it helped so much, though. Upgrading from 'broken neurotypical' to 'pretty average autistic' was a mental shift that probably saved my life.

Elora: It saved my life too. I didn't want to live anymore because life felt like a never-ending checklist of duties I could not fulfil. Realising that the standards were impossible from the start freed me. I could finally start living my life, instead of the life other people forced upon me.

Cat: That's how I feel too. Everything was always harder, and it still is, but now I know why and I can take steps to make things easier on myself. I know my limitations a little better. It seems from the outside like I'm setting up extra rules and boundaries on myself, or making life too difficult on purpose, but it honestly feels like freedom. I don't get as many panic attacks or feel overstimulated all the time. I can just be.

Elora: Life is best when you live it. It sounds corny, but it's true. Life isn't an assignment, it's an adventure.

AUTISM AND FOOD

TERMS TO KNOW

Half Food: a term we invented to describe a quick, simple safe food that requires little to no preparation to give basic calories to an autistic person until they can eat a full meal.

Same Food: a term used by the autism community to describe a food that an autistic person eats every day (possibly multiple times a day) for many days in a row.

Safe Food: a safe food is a food that an autistic person knows they will be able to eat and enjoy even if other foods are difficult to eat.

Autistics' super-sensitive senses can make eating complicated, putting a lot of autistics at risk of eating disorders. Some people say we are 'picky eaters', but the truth is that eating with high-intensity senses comes with a lot of variables. Behold, the 'parfait problem':

- That glass looks pretty full – will it drip on me? Will my hands get all sticky?
- Is it still cold or has it gotten warm? What if it's too cold and hurts my teeth?
- Is this parfait going to make gross noises in my mouth?
- What sound will the spoon make in the glass?
- Does that granola have raisins in it? Is it flavoured or plain?
- Is the granola so hard it hurts to chew or has it gotten all soggy?

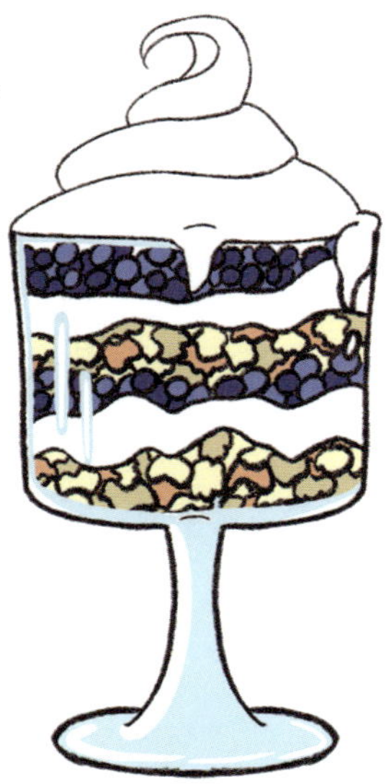

- Is that whipped cream or yoghurt?
- Are the blueberries sweet or tart?
- Are the strawberries firm or are they deflated and mealy?

Whether or not a normie enjoys a parfait might just depend on 'Is it yummy?' But for autistics, our parfait experience is more complicated.

A GENTLE REMINDER

Food is fuel and your body needs it to function. Your body's purpose isn't to look a certain way. It's your vessel to experience the world and that's it. It's more important to eat something than to eat the 'right' thing.

Because eating can be so complicated, autistics tend to develop 'safe foods'. Your safe foods are the foods that you eat because you know they will be just right. You don't have to worry about the taste, texture, or sound of the foods – they're easy to eat. Your safe foods can change over time. Sometimes a safe food won't taste the same and you'll stop eating it suddenly. That's normal for autistics.

Did you know? A lot of autistics have favourite forks. This makes sense, as the utensils you eat with are a very important sensory aspect of a meal. Do you have a favourite fork (or style of fork) that you prefer to use?

FOOD STRUGGLES FOR AUTISTICS

There are lots of reasons autistics might struggle with food. Here are just a few.

- Restaurants and family meals can be loud, chaotic events and may lead to sensory overload.
- Social expectations around mealtime can be complicated, so it can be difficult to eat when you're focused on masking.
- You might hear other people chewing or slurping and be bothered by the sound.
- You might be afraid to offend someone by adjusting the food (for example, by adding salt or pepper). It may seem obvious to a normie that a certain cook is fine with adjustments, but if the cook does not say that explicitly, the autistic might not know. One cook may be fine with guests adjusting the food or asking for things that aren't on the table, like tomato sauce, but another cook may be offended. If an autistic person has to read subtle social cues to know whether they're allowed to adjust the meal to their taste, they might never know.
- Grocery shopping can be overwhelming and lead you to avoid buying food.
- You may love the taste of something but be bothered by some other aspect of the food, like:
    - The texture
    - The appearance
    - The sound the food makes on the plate when moved
    - The sound the food makes in the mouth when chewed
    - The smell

- Smell is more closely linked to memories than any other sense, and food is an incredibly smelly affair. Food might remind you of past painful experiences more easily than you realise. Considering how intense social expectations are at the table, and how many tense family gatherings

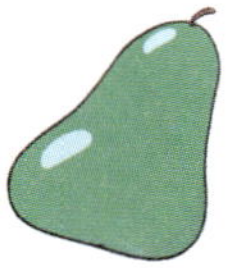

happen around tables, it is entirely possible that you have a traumatic memory around food that other people wouldn't notice. Sometimes the moments that wound us most deeply are the moments no one else notices. If you smell a particular food, it could bring you back to a difficult experience and increase your tension.

- Food is often linked to personal value. Some people struggle to eat without being ashamed of every 'bad' food they eat and feel awful because of it. This could be even worse for autistics, who struggle so much with social expectations as is and may be carrying a huge burden of shame already.
- Keeping your teeth clean is a whole other sensory struggle that can affect when or what we autistics eat. For example, you might not be able to eat after brushing your teeth because nothing tastes right. Or if you have to brush your teeth each time you eat, you might lose the desire to eat at all because you don't want to have to brush again. Or your favourite food might be really sugary or hard on the teeth. The struggle between autistics and dental health is real.

AUTISM AND EATING DISORDERS

Eating disorders are conditions that prevent people from interacting with food in a healthy way. They are serious and can even be fatal in extreme cases.

A few eating disorders you might hear about include:

Anorexia nervosa: A restriction of calories or avoiding food altogether.

Avoidant/restrictive food intake disorder (ARFID): A heightened sensitivity to the food one eats and/or having little interest in eating at all. This is not the result of low self-esteem or a desire to lose weight.

Binge eating disorder: The consumption of an excessive amount of food in one sitting. Unlike bulimia nervosa, this disorder does not involve purging.

Bulimia nervosa: Cycles of binge eating followed by purging, perhaps by vomiting or extreme exercising.

Orthorexia nervosa: An excessive preoccupation with healthy eating. Officially this is only a *proposed* eating disorder (so it is not yet recognised in the DSM-5), but it is starting to be recognised more by clinicians.
Pica: The consumption of something that is not food, like ice, paper, dirt, or skin.
Purging disorder: The act of purging by using laxatives or inducing vomiting. Unlike bulimia nervosa, this disorder does not involve binge eating.

Eating disorders are more common than you might expect. According to the Strategic Training Initiative for the Prevention of Eating Disorders, based out of Harvard University, 9 per cent of Americans will develop an eating disorder at some time in their life.[41] And if you have one it's not your fault. Food is complicated. The social expectations around food are complicated. Our society's toxic beauty standards have a lot to do with food too, so it's not surprising or shameful if you find yourself in a bad place with regard to food.

We learn more about eating disorders every year. In the previous edition of the DSM, anorexia and bulimia were the only conditions listed, while the rest were classified as EDNOS (Eating Disorder Not Otherwise Specified). In the current edition of the DSM, most of the eating disorders we listed earlier have their own listing. Our clinical understanding of eating disorders is growing rapidly, but that doesn't mean our relationship to food has become any simpler. Everyone is different, and even two people with the same eating disorder might not experience it the same way.

Many common autistic traits can make having a healthy relationship with food difficult. Our sensitivities can make us 'picky eaters', while our lack of interoception, or the ability to understand what's happening in our bodies, might mean some of us can skip meals without feeling hungry or overeat without feeling too full – or at least without *identifying* our discomfort as being hungry or being overfull. We may use food for comfort, grounding, or stimming, which isn't inherently bad, but can be taken to unhealthy extremes. And we like predictability with our food – meaning if we take a bite of something and it doesn't taste how we want or expect it to, we might not want to finish it. This isn't pure wilfulness; this is finding food physically repulsive if we don't 'vibe' with it at the time.

We also tend to have same foods, or foods with which we may replace other foods, even to the point of eating that food exclusively for nearly every meal for long stretches of time. Not every autistic does this, but if you do and if this food is lacking nutrients or calories, caffeinated, or otherwise a poor choice for frequent consumption, this could be considered disordered eating as well.

And we autistics are not immune to the better-known factors that contribute to eating disorders in general, like body image issues and the need to feel in control.

All of this combined makes us very susceptible to eating disorders. Any unhealthy, out-of-control relationship with food could be considered an eating disorder if it impacts your life in a negative way. Eating should be a sustaining experience that brings you joy, or at the very least gives your body the nutrition it needs. Food should not be linked to fear, panic, or shame. That is why we're spending so much time talking about food. It's important to have a healthy relationship with food that fits your autistic needs so you get the nutrition that your body needs. Therapists, doctors, and nutritionists can help you recover from eating disorders, and some even specialise in eating disorder recovery. If your relationship with food is damaged to the point of causing you mental or emotional harm, reach out to one of these experts for help. (For more information on finding a qualified nutritionist, see our section on intuitive eating.)

FOOD HACKS FOR AUTISTICS

As we've said, eating can be difficult for autistics. Whether you struggle with sensory issues, lack of awareness of what's going on in your body, forgetfulness, or the often chaotic social environments around eating, know that you are not alone. We've put together a list of tips and tricks that we hope will help.

Let's talk about basic nutrition first, which is something everybody with a body should understand. You should know this not to make yourself feel guilty but to help you understand how your body turns food into energy and why it works the way it does. This will also help you figure out what makes you feel good and what doesn't.

All food items are tools in your arsenal, and you'll want to be prepared to whip out the exact one you need in any situation.

This is a *super fast* guide that is *not* comprehensive, but it's a great starting point.

The three pillars of a rounded diet are proteins, fats, and carbohydrates. You need these in roughly a 20/30/50 ratio, though the exact proportions change from person to person.

PROTEIN comes from animal products like meat, fish, eggs, and cheese along with plant products like tofu, nuts, and beans. There's also protein in bread and grains (gluten).

FATS are found in things like oils and oily foods, dairy, and also certain fruits, like avocados and bananas. It can also be the actual fat of an animal, which is often present in the meat you eat. Our body needs fat to help absorb vitamins and nutrients from other foods.

CARBOHYDRATES, or carbs, are sugars, starches, and fibre. The sugar you buy at the store is a simple carbohydrate; other carbs, like breads, are complex carbohydrates, which break down into sugars down the road. Carbohydrates are in basically everything to some degree and give your body energy.

Most foods aren't entirely one category. Beans, for example, are sources of protein and carbohydrates. Bread has protein but is mostly a carbohydrate. Yoghurt and milk have fat, protein, and sugar. Meat has protein and fat.

Sugars aren't all *sugar*, as in the white powdery stuff you put in cookies. There are three simple sugars that all other sugars and carbohydrates are made of glucose, galactose, and fructose (the sugar found in fruits). These combine to make sucrose (table sugar), lactose (milk sugar), and maltose (found in beer, bread, and molasses). They all taste different and are digested differently. Sugar is added to all sorts of foods you wouldn't expect, like salad dressing and condiments.

Fruits and vegetables are basically vitamins, fibre, and a little fructose suspended in crunchy water. Fruits and veggies are recommended so highly because (1) they have small amounts of the vitamins and minerals that you need and used to be the only place to get them before fortified cereals and bread; (2) they contain a lot of water, and many of us don't drink enough water; and (3) they're mostly fibre. *Fibre* is indigestible plant matter. It basically comes in and then goes right back out but makes you feel full and clears out the intestines, like swallowing a steel wool sponge. If you struggle to eat enough fruits and vegetables throughout the day, you can supplement your diet with a decent multivitamin and more water, but fruits and veggies are the best way to get nutrients and are super tasty, so give them a shot!

If you're picky about produce's flavours or textures, things like apples, oranges, onions, and potatoes have a wealth of different varieties, so experiment to find one you like. Try out the organic or local varieties too. They may be pricier, but it can make a big difference in quality, especially in something like berries. Finally, if you think you don't like a certain kind of fruit or veggie, try it when it's in season. You may be surprised at how tasty it is when it's most ripe.

Cravings are a universal human experience of wanting a particular food. Cravings usually don't mean that we are lacking something; that's rarely the case.[42] What's more common is that a craving is a desire for a 'comfort food', something that makes us feel safe and satisfied. Our bodies and brains are saying, 'This! I want to feel this again!'

It's great to know how the body works outside of the framework of diet culture, with no shame or judgement. It's important to remember that our bodies have their own goal: to gather and store energy so we never run out. And if we listen to our bodies, we can cooperate with them and work in harmony with them instead of constantly fighting them.

No matter how much you know about food, understanding the various categories and their pros and cons can still be overwhelming. Here are some of our top tips to help autistics manage food.

- Metal and ceramic dishes and silverware can make tense screeching noises when they scrape against each other. Using dishes and silverware made from softer materials, like bamboo, plastic, silicone, and wood, can help you avoid these noises.
- Scraping noises can also be limited by having a little sauce, butter, or oil

in the dish. The surfaces are less likely to scrape loudly if they're slick.

- Strongly flavoured condiments and seasonings can sometimes cover up strange flavours. If a meal tastes off to you, try adding a strong flavour you already love – you might not notice the bad flavours anymore.
- Condiments can also be used to change the texture of a food.
  - * Adding cheese to a hot dish will make the whole thing stick together more, so you might not notice crumbly, grainy bits so much.
  - * Coating a bite in sauce can make the texture of a food less obvious.
  - * Mixing sauce, dairy, or oil into food can make it looser and creamier.
- Toppings can be added to foods too, and there's a lot you can do with them!
  - * Adding croutons to a salad can make every bite feel crunchy and distract you from the slippery bits.
  - * Topping a medicine you have to drink with a little dollop of whipped cream will coat your mouth with a good flavour to help distract from the bad.
  - * Fried onions or crumbled crackers on top of a casserole can make it feel less like mush.

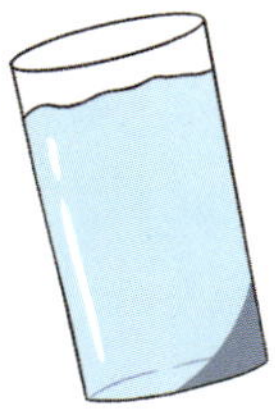

- A timer can help you stay fed if you're someone who forgets to eat. Try setting a timer for every three to six hours and getting a snack each time it goes off.
- Body-double with a friend or family member if you forget to eat! Also known as parallel playing, body doubling is the act of sharing a space with someone else, even if you're not interacting with them, because you want to be alone together. For example, maybe your grandpa would love to have breakfast with you in the mornings. Ask him to call you at the same time every day. Having the reminder of a phone call can help you get up to eat, and having someone to body-double with can help relieve the stress of remembering to eat.
- Keeping a wide variety of non-perishable foods in the house gives you lots of options for those days when you don't find your normal meals appealing. And because they're non-perishable, you don't have to throw them out if you forget about them for a while.

These are some great non-perishable foods:

- Staying stocked up on your safe foods can help you eat when you're struggling. As long as you're getting enough nutrition, there's nothing wrong with having a whole shelf of the same thing if that's what you like. Variety is a very modern, very Western idea, but for most of history there was nothing wrong with eating the same thing every day, and there's nothing wrong with it now.
- Keep 'half foods' in your house no matter what (we'll talk about those more in a minute).
- Give yourself permission to eat foods that don't make sense together. You don't have to make a dish. You can eat a handful of sandwich meat

and half a cucumber, and that's a fine meal! Meals don't have to be complicated. And if you like to eat jelly on your hot dogs, who are we to judge? Sometimes the hardest part of trying something new is the guilt you feel if you don't like it. If you're autistic, you likely will dislike a lot of foods, and that's okay. Give yourself permission to dislike foods when you try them. Remember: trying a food and hating it is a *success*, not a failure, because now you know whether you like it or not. You might find yourself becoming more adventurous with food with a new, shame-free outlook, and that's a good thing! The more foods you try, the more likely you are to find something new that you love.

- Often the worst part of trying a new food is how new it is. You might spend so much of your brain power trying to understand the texture, taste, smell, sound, and look of the food that you don't have any energy left for its enjoyment! It's okay to be a bit stressed by trying new foods. A good way to alleviate this when you're trying new foods is to ease yourself into a new dish by keeping some parts of it familiar. Some examples:

    * Substitute a single ingredient in a dish you like, but keep the rest of the ingredients the same. For example, you could try a new kind of noodle in your favourite soup or dip your trusty chicken nuggets in a new sauce.

    * Try a new food prepared in a way you already know you like before you try it in a strange new context. Let's say you want to try pickled okra, but you're afraid that the intense vinegar flavour and the newness of the okra will freak you out. If you know you love fried foods, why not try fried okra first? Then once you're comfortable with that, move on to pickled okra.

    * Analyse a strange food a little first and try to visualise what it will be like to eat it. You can cut it open with your fork to see what it looks like on the inside, smell it to guess the taste, and compare it to other dishes you've eaten to get a ballpark estimate of the overall experience.

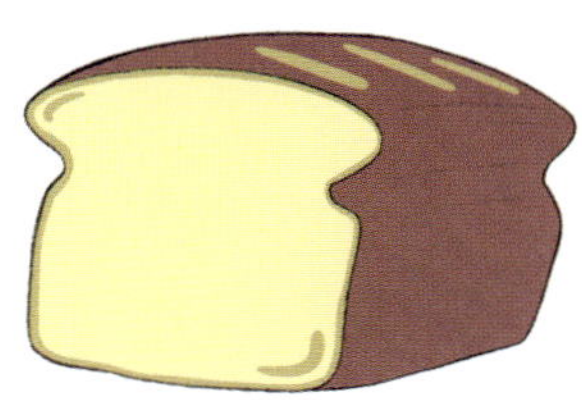

- If there's a category of food you really love, you can try learning as much as you can about that style of dish, rather than trying to get good at cooking a lot of different things. For example, if you really love sandwiches, learn to make a bunch of different kinds of sandwiches. The things you learn from making one sandwich can be applied to all the other sandwiches you make, so you'll get much better at making sandwiches you love. Plus, you'll be able to use similar ingredients for all the dishes, which makes grocery shopping easier. You could eat sandwiches every day and still be really healthy because there are so many different kinds. Some examples of food categories like this include the following:
    * Dumplings
    * Pasta
    * Soups and stews
    * Smoothies, malts, and blended drinks
    * Salads
    * Breads
    * Crepes
    * Pizza
    * Tacos

- You can eat breakfast food for dinner, or sandwiches for breakfast, or whatever you want whenever you want. Food is food. The only good reason to limit when you eat foods is if you feel sick or get bad dreams when you eat certain foods at certain times (for example, Elora sometimes gets nightmares if she eats spicy food right before bed. Cat had the same reaction to wild blueberries, inexplicably).

Sometimes low blood sugar or hunger pangs can send us into sensory overload, making it hard for us to eat and meet this need in the first place. It can be incredibly stressful to get caught in this cycle. You can break out of this cycle with half foods.

HALF FOODS

Half foods is a term we came up with for foods that help ease you into eating when you're feeling too overwhelmed to eat. When you're in sensory overload, putting something into your mouth might be the last thing you want to do, *which makes sense.* After all, if you're already hearing too much, smelling too much, or feeling too much, then forcing yourself to hear, smell, and feel food on top of everything that goes along with tasting it is a big ask. This is unfortunate because hunger can make sensory overload worse. Sometimes food is what you need to lessen the overload.

So what do you do? You find a food that is so easy to eat that doing so takes only half the normal effort.

The point of a half food isn't to be a whole meal. The point is to reduce your hunger enough that you're less overwhelmed and have the mental energy to prepare whatever more complete, more nutritional, or satisfying food you actually want or need. Don't judge yourself based on your half foods!

Half foods are either prepared ahead of time or don't take much preparation – typically taking less than a minute to get ready – and they're easier to consume than other foods. They might have a simple, consistent texture. They might have only one flavour, not a bunch of different flavours throughout. Their texture/s and flavour/s are ones you've had before and know you love. Some great half foods are cookies, crackers, chips, popsicles, bananas, or even a squirt of whipped cream right into your mouth!

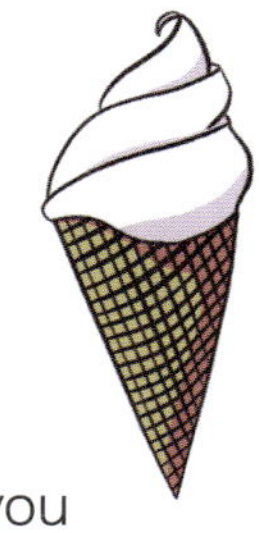

People often say that dessert should come at the end of a meal, but we think that's silly. We don't think you should force yourself to eat foods you don't like as a requirement to get the food you want. Also, we believe anything can be a dessert if you love to eat it! Dividing foods into 'good' and 'bad' and then assuming the bad ones always taste better is so ridiculous! And sometimes you need that really yummy food to coax yourself to eat when you're in overload.

Do what you need to do to get food in your stomach. Remember, there's not a single food that is worse for your body than starving it would be.

More tips:

- Set alarms if you forget to eat. It's totally fine to wait to and try to work up an appetite, but if you wait too long, you'll feel sick or depleted. Keep snacks nearby, and when the alarm goes off have one.
- Fats and sugars are calorically dense. Use that to your advantage when you're having trouble. Foods like granola bars, cookies, and bananas will get a lot of energy into your body quickly.
- Don't worry about eating at any particular place. It's no fun to sleep in a bed full of crumbs, but that doesn't mean you need a full-on dining

table. Dining tables are frequently more trouble than they're worth unless you have a spacious house.

- Take advantage of the wide variety of foods in the Western world. We know you may want to eat the same food for every meal of every day, and with a lot of foods that's totally fine, but if you have variety in your diet, you're more likely to get all the nutrition you need. You might even try new things and find a new favourite food!

INTUITIVE EATING

We have both suffered from eating disorders in the past, heavily influenced by our autism. As we said, it's a common problem. So how do you get past that? How do you develop a healthier relationship with food? Ultimately, you'll have to find your own path. But the principles of intuitive eating might be helpful in starting to recover from cycling through different diets and weight fluctuations and feeling bad about yourself.

Intuitive eating is an approach to food created by dieticians Evelyn Tribole and Elyse Resch. They introduced the world to their methods in their 1995 book *Intuitive Eating: A Revolutionary Anti-Diet Approach*. They have updated the book throughout the years, and the latest edition was published in 2020.[43]

Oh great, you might be thinking, *another diet. What are the rules?* Good news: there are no rules. Instead, get used to listening to your body and make decisions based on what it is telling you. That's it. That's the whole thing. Trust your body to make food choices that feel good for you. But at the same time, pay attention and explore how different options make you feel. There are lots of reasons we eat, like hunger, a sense of obligation to 'clean your plate', and simply the enjoyment of a good taste. There are also lots or reasons we do not eat, like feeling full, feeling like we have not 'earned' the food, and fearing we might be eating a 'bad' food. Intuitive eating means looking inside yourself and sorting through these complicated feelings so you can discover what your body is actually telling you. It is letting go of the food expectations other people have placed upon you, finding out what you are feeling, and responding to that.

Cat: I wanted to fix my relationship with food before I had my children so I wouldn't give them the same issues I had. When I ran into intuitive eating, it sounded like a break from diet culture that I desperately needed to recover from my eating disorder. I didn't expect it to become a lifelong philosophy – but since it's about reconnecting with your own body, it's not really a 'diet' to follow at all. Just by making small changes at first like eating yoghurt instead of ice cream as a half food helped me reprogram my taste buds over time, and now I crave much healthier foods. It took time and work but it was well worth it.

You can research intuitive eating on your own – and if you struggle to have a good relationship with food, we highly recommend it. It requires no money, no equipment, no expensive ingredients. Just the ability to pay attention.

If intuitive eating is not the right choice for you, that's okay! One major trait of autism is difficulty listening to what your body is telling you. Intuitive eating works for us but it may not even be an option for you. If you want to find a healthy way to approach your eating habits that still honours your unique body and mind, you might benefit from reaching out to a qualified dietician or nutritionist. Legally, anyone can call themself a 'nutritionist' in the United States, regardless of qualifications, so make sure you find someone with a degree in the field. Unfortunately, a lot of multilevel marketing schemes selling dangerous diets and unproven supplements call their distributors 'wellness coaches', 'nutrition experts', 'diet consultants', or other deceptive names that echo legitimacy. These people mean well, but they can damage your mental and physical health. Do not listen to them! Reach out to an actual qualified dietitian for help, and they can help you create a food plan that works for you.

MY FOOD STRATEGIES

If I don't feel like eating, I can drink:

If I have trouble drinking water, what can I add to it that will make it more palatable?

If I feel queasy, these snacks will settle my stomach:

What are my go-to half foods?

If I don't like a food, what are condiments or toppings that can make it better?

I can remind myself to drink water by

If a food is too:	I can fix it by:
mushy	
crunchy or tough	
inconsistent	
overwhelming	
weirdly flavoured	

I can convince myself to eat more vegetables by:

My favourite same foods:

TIPS AND TRICKS

There are plenty of things that autistics struggle with that we're just too shy to ask about. So here are some nifty tips and tricks that we've come up with to help you through your day-to-day routine.

HYGIENE

Just as autistics struggle with food, so too can we have a hard time with personal hygiene. Thankfully, it's incredible how much you can simplify your hygiene routine. All you really have to do is wash your body, wash your hair, and brush your teeth. Everything else is a luxury to enjoy. Here are some tips to make your routine more enjoyable:

- Try showering in the dark! By removing light, you'll cut out an additional sensory input.
- Try using a reusable makeup remover cloth to wash your face or body. A lot of companies make supersoft and gentle washcloths, pads, and puffs that are meant to remove your makeup with water alone and are softer than normal washcloths.
- There are also many types of loofahs and sponges. Try different products, textures, and sizes until you find something to wash your body with that you're comfortable with.
    * Washcloths can be washed and reused over and over for years. That said, they don't have a lot of structure, so if you hate the feeling of wet fabric, a washcloth may not be for you.
- Baby washcloths are softer and smaller than adult washcloths and make

another great option. In general baby stuff can be great for hygiene-related sensory issues – baby nail clippers, baby shampoo, baby laundry soap.

* Scrub brushes with long handles are useful for cleaning parts of your body that are hard to reach, like your back, and they exfoliate well. However, they can be rough.
* Natural sponges are harvested from simple, plant-like animals that live in the ocean. The sponge can be harvested without causing harm to the animal. They can hold a lot of water at once and are softer than a scrub brush. They're also biodegradable.
* Plastic loofahs turn bodywash into foam when you rub them and then exfoliate without being as rough as a scrub brush. They do need to be replaced regularly though to prevent bacterial growth. Some people avoid them because they cause plastic waste.
* Natural loofahs are often assumed to be from the ocean, like natural sponges, but actually they're from the plant family that gives us cucumbers, and their fruit is dried out to make a natural loofah. You can grow loofah (also spelled luffa) vines in your garden and harvest your own sponges if you want.
* Silicone bath brushes are a sustainable alternative to plastic loofahs. They are easy to clean and not rough at all! That said, they don't create the same amount of foam as a plastic loofah.

- Whatever you use to wash your body, be careful to replace or clean it regularly to avoid bacteria buildup. Also don't let it stay wet when you aren't bathing – whatever it is, it needs to dry out between uses to prevent bacterial growth.
- Instead of having one hygiene routine, try having several. You can have your normal hygiene routine and also other routines that you can use when your energy needs call for it. For example, on a great morning you might brush your teeth, wash your face, put on sunscreen, apply lotion to your hands, and brush your hair. On a rough day, you might just brush your teeth and pull your hair back. You might think that giving yourself permission to do less work would make you forget your hygiene, but in our experience

it's actually the opposite. Because we know that we can do an easier routine if we need to, we're less likely to become overwhelmed or melt down. This has helped with more than just hygiene!

By giving ourselves permission to do an easier version of whatever is overwhelming us, we have become more productive, wasted much less energy fighting ourselves, and felt far less shame.

- Try different hygiene products. If you hate the smell of a product, try one with a different smell. (There are also unscented versions of lots of products.) If you hate the texture of a product, try one with a different texture. For example, shampoo can come out of the bottle as a liquid or as a foam. You can even pour a product that doesn't foam into a bottle with a foaming pump if you prefer a foamy texture. There are also creamy textures for a lot of hygiene products, like conditioner. As sustainability becomes more of a focus for companies, a lot of products are being released in bar form. You can buy a shampoo bar now, just like soap.
- There's no rule that says you can't multitask in the shower. Brush your teeth in there if it makes your life easier.
- Take baths instead of showers if you find that more enjoyable. Getting clean is the important thing, not the method.
- Try using special products to make your hygiene routine more luxurious, like bath bombs, which perfume and colour the water in a bath; shower steamers, which emit fragrances into the shower; and bath confetti, which often comes in pretty paper-like shapes that dissolve in water. There are also plush shower mats, shower chairs, bath pillows, bath shoes, and a wealth of other items – there's no limit to the products that can make your bath or shower more opulent.
- Change your showerhead. You may prefer a shower that feels like a gentle rain, or one that feels like standing under a Hawaiian waterfall, or one that massages that hard-to-reach muscle under your shoulder blade. Different showerheads can be easily installed to achieve all those effects.

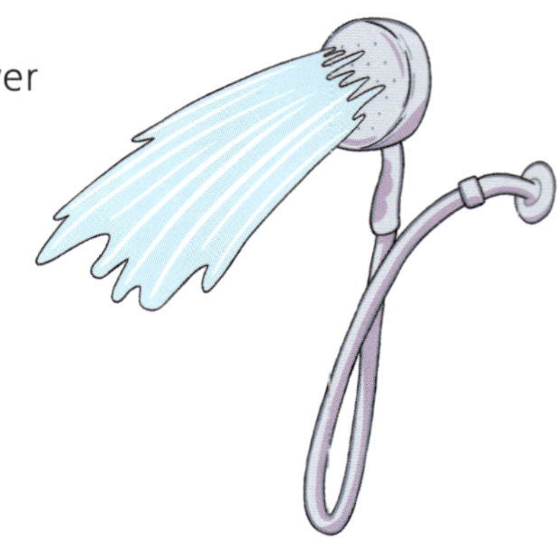

- Incorporate your special interest into whatever is stressing you out, including hygiene. If you like sharks, get a shark bathrobe. If you like art, get bath crayons to draw on the shower walls. You don't have to feel ashamed for liking 'kid stuff'. If something makes you happy, let it make you happy.
- If mint toothpaste is an uncomfortable, intense flavour, try unflavoured toothpaste or kids' toothpaste, which often comes in gentler flavours like bubblegum and berry.

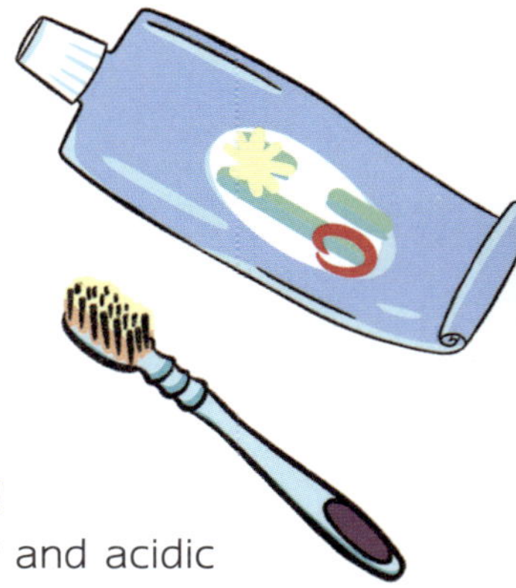

- If your teeth are sensitive and hurt sometimes, especially when they get cold, try using a toothpaste for sensitivity.
- You do need to take good care of your teeth. The rules about cleaning your mouth are not silly social rules – they're practical guidelines to keep you healthy. Problems with your teeth can be painful, overwhelming, and expensive. If you're bad about brushing your teeth, a good diet can help. Getting more calcium and Vitamin C in your diet and avoiding sugary and acidic drinks like soda can help prevent damage to your teeth. Drinking milk can also be helpful because it neutralises acids and protects your teeth a little better. None of this, however, is a substitute for regular brushing and flossing.
- If you hate clipping your nails, you can file them. If you prefer to clip but struggle with doing so, try one of the many products for baby nails that work for adults too. Long nails can be an uncomfortable sensory experience for some people, but if you like them, they can be very fun to stim with. Just remember to keep them clean!
- If your ears are all clogged up with earwax, don't reach for the cotton swabs! Putting cotton buds into your ears can be dangerous and make the earwax more compact and tougher to get out. Thankfully, there are a lot of safe ways to remove earwax. There are special earwax removing drops you can buy at the drugstore. If you can't hear and the earwax drops aren't working, you should go see a doctor. A medical professional can flush out your ears with water or use a special vacuum to get the wax out. Fair warning though: this can be uncomfortable, so clean your ears regularly at home if you can.

- If hygiene practices feel overwhelming, it's okay to use your phone or laptop for entertainment. For example, if brushing your teeth is stressful, you could watch YouTube videos while you brush. If showering is overwhelming, you can play music in the bathroom while you shower. Just try to sanitise your gadgets regularly.
- Your hair doesn't have to look any certain way, but there are two big 'musts' for hair safety.
    1. Keep your hair clean enough to avoid bacteria. It's okay if your hair is oily or tangled, but big, unbrushed clumps can get musty and even mouldy if left for too long. It's best to detangle and wash your hair regularly, whether that's every day, once a week, or once every few weeks. The exception for this is if your hair is in a protective style, like box braids or twists, which require regular cleaning but on a different scale and frequency.
    2. Do whatever you need to do to avoid head lice. Head lice are tiny bugs that live in your hair, and dealing with them is a sensory nightmare. Try to avoid shoving your head up against the heads of strangers, and don't share pillowcases, hats, combs, or anything else that touches the head with anyone who has head lice. If you do get lice, try to remain calm! There are all kinds of ways to get rid of them, from special shampoos to fine-tooth combs to home remedies. Getting lice does not mean you are dirty or did anything wrong, but they are a real pain that can spread to people around you. So be proactive to avoid lice and treat your scalp quickly if you get them. If you get overwhelmed by caring for your hair, consider wearing protective styles like box braids or twists. They can be left for weeks with minimal care, saving you time, energy, and stress. If your hair is straighter or smoother, you can try one or two big braids, though you may need to take them out and refresh them more often. People across cultures and time periods have used protective styles and head coverings to protect their hair.

- If you want the look of having a specific hairstyle but don't want to maintain that style, consider investing in a wig. One of the cheapest options is a headband wig, which is a wig attached to a headband that's easy to take on and off. Wigs still require some maintenance, like washing and detangling, but you might discover that you prefer styling hair that doesn't hurt your head if you pull it.
- Shave your head if you want to, or cut your hair short, or wear wigs, or wear your hair the exact same way every day. You are not required to spend a lot of time and effort on your hair.
- You don't need to do your hygiene routine at any particular time. If you remember to brush your teeth at two in the afternoon, go ahead and brush them then. Of course, some things have ideal times to do them (like brushing your teeth before bed so the gunk doesn't sit on your teeth all night), but it's better to do them at an unusual time than to not do them at all.

BEAUTY

- Experiment with your appearance. People joke a lot about how 'embarrassing' their old haircuts or styles were, so it's easy to get the feeling that it's shameful to look a way that you wouldn't want to look forever. But guess what – it's not! In fact, joking about old style choices is a way some people connect with each other. Experiment with your appearance as much as you want. It's your body.
- Whether or not you shave your face, legs, or anywhere else on your body is completely up to you. Some people love the slick feeling of bare skin. Some people hate it. The hair on our bodies moves when it touches something. By shaving it, we get rid of that wiggly hair feeling whenever we are grazed by something. For example, you might find yourself less bothered by the feeling of the wind or standing close to strangers if you shave your arms. But shaving can also irritate sensitive skin, so it might be a better choice for you to leave hair where it grows in.
- Ask yourself who is telling you that you need to use or buy a certain

product. Is this someone you trust to know what you would like? Is this someone who makes money from your purchase? If you're ever unsure if you actually need a product, start by considering the motive of whoever is recommending it.

> **Cat:** Many beauty standards, such as the 'ideal' body shapes, skin tones, facial features, and hair textures, are deeply rooted in racism, classism, misogyny, and transphobia. If you're nervous about breaking social norms, it might make you braver to know that many social norms deserve to be broken.

- If your skin feels painfully dry, super oily, has a lot of acne, has a rash, or has some other issue that causes you distress, your soap may have something to do with it and there might be a special soap that can address the issue. When in doubt, always seek help from a dermatologist. There are soaps that are made specifically for your skin type, extra-gentle soaps for babies that could work for you too, soaps to get rid of pimples, soaps to smell sweet or not smell at all, soaps for sensitive areas, and more. So use whatever works for you, but remember that you have a plenitude of options.
- The same goes for hair products. There is a seemingly unlimited number of options for different hair types, textures, and even colours. You can use a bunch of different products, or a three-in-one shampoo, conditioner, and bodywash. Some ways to find what works for you are to ask your barber or hairstylist what they would use on your hair, ask a trusted friend to help you create a hair routine, and take online quizzes about your hair. You can learn a lot through multiple-choice games. But remember, you don't need every product that's advertised to be hygienic or healthy, and you don't need the most expensive ones either.
- Makeup is ten thousand per cent optional. Anyone can wear any amount that they want at any time for any reason. Whether you wear no makeup, only cover-up, only lipstick, a full face, drag makeup, clown makeup, or something else is completely your call. You do you. The same goes for nail polish

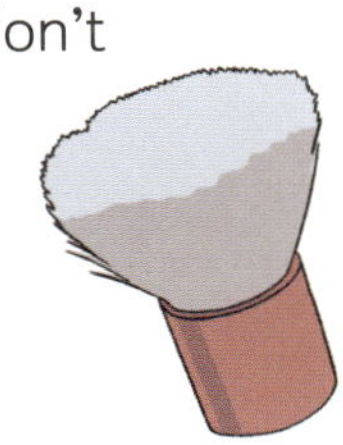

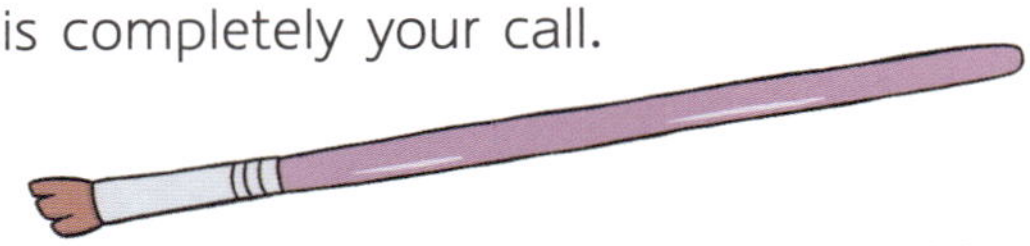

and hair dye. Of course if you're trying to achieve a specific goal with make-up, like blending in with the normies, looking professional, or winning a beauty pageant, then certain looks will be more useful than others. But that doesn't mean you have to wear makeup all the time or even at all.

- Exfoliating and moisturising your skin both make it feel softer. If that's a sensation that makes you feel good in your skin, try using an exfoliating scrub in the shower and then moisturising after the shower. Don't overdo it though – too much exfoliation can irritate your skin and make it appear red and puffy.
- If something about your skin bothers you, there are products out there to help change it. Moisturisers can make your skin softer, retinol can partially heal scars and smooth out wrinkles, sunscreen can prevent sunburns, acne treatments can reduce the size of painful zits, and more. But remember, many of the 'issues' the beauty industry might take with your skin (and your body in general) are only important if they bother you.

- Jewellery, like many other beauty and fashion items, is not necessary. It is up to you whether you want to wear it. If you find that the metal in some jewellery irritates your skin, avoid nickel, stainless steel, and pewter and instead aim for gold, platinum, titanium, and sterling silver, the purer the better.
- Jewellery and fashion accessories make great subtle fidget toys. If you need to fidget in public, try doing it with a ring, scarf, keychain, pair of gloves, or even a hand fan. Some companies even make jewellery in a variety of styles and types specifically for fidgeting.
- Wedding rings can be made from every type of material, including stone and silicone, and you can get a tattoo if you *really* want to commit but don't want to wear a ring. Or you can skip this tradition entirely. Not wearing a wedding ring doesn't make you any less married.

Elora: I use a retinol cream on my acne scars because my face feels the most comfortable when it's soft and smooth. Slowly healing those scars has made my face more comfortable for me to live in. However, retinol is often marketed as a beauty product, so I check in with myself from time to time to make sure that I'm using retinol for my own sake and not because I feel ashamed.

Cat: I don't like the sensation of washing my face, so I wash it in the shower but otherwise leave it alone. For the most part, that works okay. Some people have low-maintenance skin, and unnecessary products make their skin worse. My bare-bones, broke-college-kid hygiene routine works for me, and it means I can use all the same products as my husband and toddler with no issues.

CLOTHING

- If clothing tags or seams bother you, you can turn the item inside out. This is especially useful with socks.
- If you want to remove your tags completely from the base, not just cut them off where you can reach, you can use a seam ripper to break the stitches holding the tag into the clothing and then resew the seam with a needle and thread.
- Loose, soft, comfy clothing is far less likely to cause sensory issues for some people. If you like oversized clothing, go ahead and wear it. Don't worry about the size on the tag.
- Alternatively, form-fitting and stretchy clothes can be sensory heaven for some people, because they can feel like a second skin. Don't worry about those being your size either. If you like it tight, ignore the tag.
- If you love to go barefoot, some shoes more closely mimic the feeling of being barefoot than others. Try breathable sneakers with mesh panels and thin soles if you want the closest thing to being barefoot while still wearing shoes and preventing things from touching your feet. You can also wear sandals or flip-flops in many situations!

- Certain activities require more specific footwear. It can help to break in these types of shoes by wearing them for an hour or so at a time on several occasions before you wear them for the intended event or activity. This will make them softer and more bearable when you need to wear them for a long period of time – for example, when hiking or dancing.
- If you really like a specific item of clothing, buy multiples of it. Don't think of it as repeating the same outfit; think of it as your signature look – cartoon characters, video game avatars, and fashion designers often wear the same outfit all the time. Steve Jobs famously wore the same outfit all the time to reduce the decision fatigue involved in picking an outfit every day, and it can help you in the same way.
- Movies and TV shows often send the message that certain people are perfectly dressed and everyone agrees about that. In reality one person's perfectly dressed is another person's dumpster fire. So don't be discouraged by people who hate how you dress. Somebody else probably loves it.
- You've probably heard of style rules like 'find your colour season' and 'dress for your shape'. These rules are based on psychology, cultural preferences, and sometimes prejudice. Luckily being stylish is not necessarily about following a bunch of rules. Being stylish is about making an impact and saying something about

Cat: My husband hates shoes. For a solid ten years he only wore flip-flops unless other shoes were required, even in the winter. We lived in Texas, so he could do this safely and it didn't strike most people as odd for most of the year. He was the 'flip-flops guy.' Maybe some people thought it was weird, but other than some good-natured teasing, nobody made fun of him and it didn't limit him in any way. He's a great example of how, sometimes, breaking social norms doesn't actually hurt anyone. In many cases people don't even care.

yourself through your look. Fashion rules can help you decide how to make that impact, but you don't have to follow them unless you want to.

- If you're trying to be adventurous with your fashion but need something you can take off in public in case it starts to bother you, try a hat, headscarf, or something else that goes on your head. If it starts to annoy you, you can remove it.
- Feel the fabric of clothing when shopping and learn what kinds of fabric you like or dislike. This will help you decide right away if clothing is a good sensory experience or a bad one. Remember that some fabrics feel better during certain times of year. If it's going to be really hot outside, you might want to wear something lighter, like linen or cotton, and if it's going to be freezing that day, you might want something heavier, like flannel or wool.
- A lot of shops, especially boutiques, will be happy to help you find sensory-friendly clothing. It can be nerve-racking to tell someone you're autistic, but if you take that leap you might get some great help.
- Bras serve three main purposes: support the breasts, hide the breasts, and keep the breasts warm in cold weather. Ask yourself which of these you need, if you need one, and bra-shop accordingly. You might need a lot of support but not worry about getting cold and get a bra with thin material but strong support. You might not need support at all but feel really uncomfortable wearing clothing without that extra modesty layer and get a bra that's relaxed but double-layered. There are more kinds of bras than you probably realise, and if you're willing to search the internet for a while looking for one that suits you, you'll likely find a lot of unique options to choose from. You can get bras custom-made or even experiment with bra alternatives like corsets and stays. Or you might not want to wear a bra at all, and that's okay! Skip it.

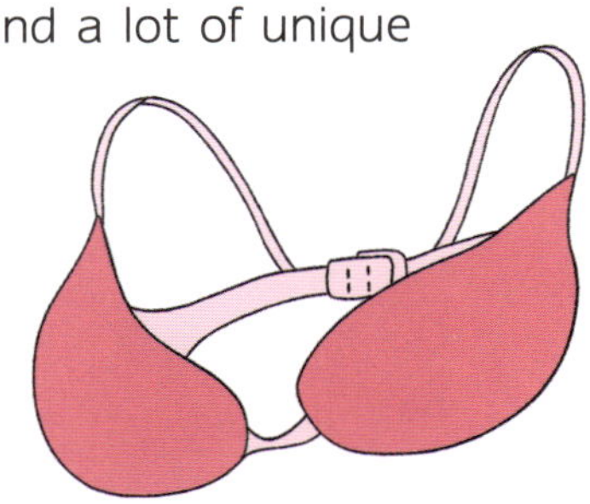

- It can be comfortable for autistics to wear tight clothes that feel like a second skin. Unfortunately, wearing underwear that is too tight can give you a painful infection. If you like underwear that feels like a second skin, look for underwear that is made with a thin, stretchy material rather than a very tight pair. This will help it lie flat on your skin without crowding your crotch. Try different cuts of underwear to see what level of coverage makes you most comfortable.

- There are also a million kinds of socks to wear! There are socks with seams, socks without seams, tight socks, loose socks, thick socks, thin socks, socks with grips on the bottom so you don't slide on your floor, fuzzy socks, and probably even socks with your special interest on them.
- You are allowed to dress ridiculously. You can wear Halloween costumes all year round if you want to, or dress like you're from the 1800s, or wear shiny outfits covered in glitter. In certain situations, however, wearing flamboyant clothes can put you in danger. If you're going into a situation where people with a lot of power will judge you based on your appearance (like interviewing for a job, appearing in a court of law, marching in a political protest, or just existing in a prejudiced environment) weigh the risks carefully. There is nothing wrong with dressing in your own unique way, but there's also nothing wrong with blending in.

FASHION 'RULES'

If you don't understand a fashion rule that other people seem committed to, try to understand where the rule is coming from and why it exists. For example, we don't wear white to a wedding because the bride will wear white and letting her be the only one wearing it is a nice way to make her feel special. It's also practical because it will be easy to find the bride during the event, so you can go over and say congratulations – just look for the only person wearing white! Plus in all the photos of the wedding, the bride will stand out. 'Don't wear white at a wedding' makes sense, has a practical purpose, and doesn't require a massive effort from the guests, so we would argue that it's a good rule and we follow it. On the other hand, let's look at another rule about the colour white: don't wear white after Labor Day. No one actually

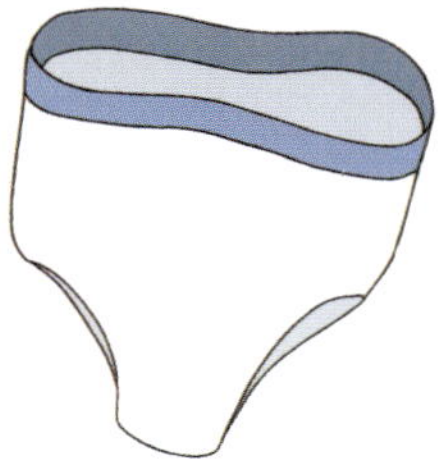

knows where this rule comes from, but one theory is that it exists because white is harder to keep clean, and back before we had laws to limit pollution, the snow could get very dirty in the winter, creating a months-long muddy sludge that would stain any white it touched. Nowadays it only seems to serve as an unspoken test to see who is fashionable and who isn't. This rule helps no one, is only practical if you walk through muddy sludge all winter, and requires you to keep an entire colour out of your wardrobe circulation for nine months of the year. That's a big ask! Plus, the elitist mindset of something being a secret fashion test rubs us the wrong way. We think this rule is a bad rule and won't be following it now or ever.

PICKING AN OUTFIT

'There is no bad weather,
only bad clothing.'
—German expression

If you're not sure what to wear for the day, here are some great questions to ask yourself to help you decide:

- What will the weather be like? Do I need to wear something waterproof? Something warm? Something that I can use to change how warm I am, like a jacket I can take off? Do I need to wear a special fabric to keep me cool or warm?
- Is there a dress code? Will I get in trouble if I don't follow the rules?
- If there are unspoken clothing rules for this event, what do I think of these rules? Do they serve a purpose? Does it take a huge effort for me to follow them? Will following them make other people feel

respected and will breaking them make other people feel offended?

- Do I care what the people at this event think of me? Do I need them to think I'm normal? Do I want them to see the real me right away?
- If I'm not sure what to wear, is this an event where I can copy someone else? Can I just pick out an outfit close to what my parent, friend, or coworker is planning to wear?
- Do I need to wear certain clothes to be safe? Do I need a wetsuit to go surfing or special boots for a hike?

- Will there be photos at this event? Do I want to look a specific way in those photos?
- Am I trying to make a statement at this event? Dressing in certain ways can send an unspoken message that you are rebellious, innocent, scandalous, mourning the dead, rich, artistic, and more! If you want to learn more about secret messages that clothing can send, search 'how to dress ______________' online, filling in the blank with whatever kind of message you want to send.

CLEANING AND HOUSEWORK

- Robots and machines can make cleaning our homes and their items much easier. There are washing machines and dryers that clean and dry our clothes. There are dishwashers to clean our dishes. There are robot vacuums and mops that clean our floors. There's even a machine that sprays down the entire shower after you use it. New machines are being invented every day to make cleaning easier. If you can afford it and don't mind the sounds these machines can make, you can collect a little army of household machines to help you. You can even name them if you want to! (Cat: I gave mine googly eyes and a name and title. Highly recommend.)
- Try taking a picture of a room right after you've cleaned it. That way you and everyone else in the house can use that photo for reference so everyone knows exactly where everything should go and what 'clean' actually looks like.
- Sometimes the problem with housework isn't the work itself – it's how boring it is. Try trading places with a friend. You might find that cleaning each other's mess is much easier than cleaning your own.
- Put on dance music while cleaning. Sing loudly and badly and shake your butt. It makes it way more fun and it's a lovely serotonin boost.
- If you're having trouble completing a task, try body doubling! Just hanging out in the same room as someone else can help some people get work done. At our house we have a laundry party, where we all hang out in the same room and keep someone company while they fold laundry.

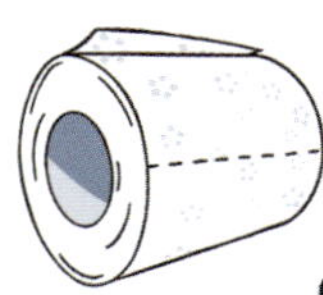

- Little bits of cleaning add up and are a practical approach to cleaning if longer efforts exhaust you. Fill the sink with hot soapy water and toss all the dishes in, and then go about your business. If you're lucky enough to have your own washing machine, use it as a hamper so you don't have to gather all the clothes when it's time to wash them. Put all of your paperwork into one pile until you have the energy to

sort it out. If you do a tiny bit every day, the mess is less likely to sneak up on you.

- Avoid getting overwhelmed by allowing yourself flexibility in where you start. There's no rule that says you have to do the biggest job first. What's most important is that you get started by doing *something*. If you don't know where to start cleaning, pick up all the dirty clothes and put them in the washing machine. Or pick up all the trash. Or move all the dishes to the sink – or to a bus tub like a restaurant uses. Any of these will make everything else look more manageable. You can also take a first step that will make the next steps easier – like rinsing off dishes but saving the soap-and-water stuff for later, or sorting the laundry into categories but not folding it, or picking up clutter from the floor but not vacuuming. Future you will thank you!

Cat: I hate doing dishes after dinner every night. But you know what? It does help. Dedicating a specific time in your schedule to a specific chore and making it part of your routine might work well for you too. It is the worst but it really does make your life better to build a little cleaning into your routine.

- Clutter isn't necessarily a bad thing. By clutter we mean lots of stuff being out and visible, instead of neatly organised and hidden away. A lot of us (especially people with ADHD) think better with clutter around. Having something visible also reminds us that it exists, which is useful for medicine, healthy snacks, etc. Don't ever let anyone make you feel bad about clutter. Mess isn't the worst thing in the world. If there aren't bugs or mice living in it and nothing is attracting mould and no one is in danger, you're fine.
- Use disposable plates, cups, and utensils if you want. It's a lot easier than doing the dishes. Paper goods are biodegradable or compostable and there are plenty of eco-friendly options.
- If you can, change your home air filters every few months, or at least a couple times a year. And yes, you probably *do* have home air filters. They're in the vents. If you have a heater or air conditioner, check your vents and see if the filters look

CLEANING GAMES

- Assign 'points' to each task and see how many points you can get.
- Write your to-do list onto a blank bingo card (one task per square) and try to get bingo!
- Pretend your favourite stuffed animal is trying to get around your house (or across a table) and try to make a 'road' for them by cleaning a path.
- Make up an imaginary situation (like being a detective in a magic castle who has to clean to find the clues) and play as you clean.
- Set a timer and see how much you can get done in a certain amount of time.
- Race a friend or family member to see who can clean their room fastest.
- Take a picture of your mess and then take another picture when you're done cleaning for the day, and see how much you can make the pictures look different.

gross. If you don't have central heating or AC, mould can become an issue, so watch for that and consider dehumidifiers or air purifiers, and be sure to open your windows to let in fresh air as needed.

DRIVING

- Take your time. There's no need to rush. Even on a 320 km-trip at high speed, going 8 km an hour over the speed limit the whole time would typically save you less than twenty minutes. It's not worth the risk. Other drivers might be irritated, but that's their problem, not yours.
- Limit your sensory input as much as you need. Wear sunglasses or a hat to block the sun and ask passengers to save conversation for later if that helps you.
- There's no shame in using GPS, even if you know the area well. If it helps you find your way or makes you feel less anxious about having to think about directions while focusing on the road at the same time, then use it!
- Listening to something in the car can help some people focus. You might find it distracting when

you're a new driver and later find it a necessity in helping you focus. Some ideas for listening material are music, podcasts, audiobooks, radio dramas, and radio news. You could even make a playlist full of sounds that help you stay calm and alert. But remember, focusing on the road should always be your top priority.

- Eating and drinking on car trips can be relaxing and help you focus by keeping you from feeling hungry or thirsty and by giving you a way to stim. However, food and drinks can be a safety hazard if they distract you or cause you to take your hands off the wheel too often. If you find yourself swerving or drifting when eating or drinking, limit yourself to eating and drinking when parked or waiting at stoplights. It's not worth risking your safety.
- You can do so many loud things that other people don't like when you're alone in a car. You can sing, quote movies, yell in imaginary fights, talk your feelings out, or just make fun stimmy sounds. Take advantage of that and have fun.
- Pay attention to your physical needs. Driving when you're tired can be dangerous. Stop when you need to. Turn down trips when you need to. It is okay to cancel plans if you're too tired to drive. If you absolutely have to drive but are tired, see if a friend or family member can come with you and drive part of the way or talk to you to keep you awake.
- Learning how to drive well is not something that can be rushed. If you spend three years in driving school, there is no shame in it. You will be happy to have learned.

- The experience of driving can be overwhelming, especially when you are new to it. But over time driving can become instinctual, easier, and even relaxing. Some autistics even consider driving a stim!
- If you own your own car, it is your own space and you should make it fit your needs or style. You can put covers on the seats or

Elora: One fun way to learn to drive is to have a specific fun destination in mind and drive there and back, day after day, with your driving teacher. My dad and I used to drive to my favourite drive-in restaurant over and over. The repetition helped me get into a rhythm. The snacks and drinks made the whole situation feel fun, even though it was sometimes stressful to learn.

the steering wheel to change their textures. You can fill the glovebox with snacks. You can use air fresheners to make it smell like a rainforest or a meadow. You can draw on the inside with markers. You can cover the walls with stickers. You can add bumper stickers about your special interest. You can even buy a custom licence plate from the transport department. It's your car – make it your happy place.

- You're not immature, or embarrassing, or problematic if you can't drive. It's a difficult skill to master and in many places driving isn't necessary. If you can move to a walkable city, use public transportation, or carpool, all the better for you. Mother Earth will thank you for it.
- Never drive while under the influence of alcohol or drugs. It is never worth the risk.

DATING AND RELATIONSHIPS

- Be yourself. If someone doesn't like the real you, a relationship with them won't be fulfilling, even if you're lonely.
- It is okay to ask someone on a date without a magical build-up of flirting and special moments. You're autistic so you might miss subtle cues anyway. Sometimes it's best to just ask.

- You do not have to want a relationship. You are not broken if the idea of being partnered or falling in love isn't that interesting to you. You are not missing out on happiness either. There are thousands of ways to be deliriously happy, and romantic love is just one of the most popular ways to find that happiness. It doesn't mean it's the only one.
- A relationship will never solve all of your problems. Being in a relationship is like going on a special adventure with someone, but that adventure might still be hard. You're only setting yourself up for trouble if you expect a romantic relationship to make up for pain in all the other relationships in your life. Sometimes life hurts. Having a special someone won't make the hurt go away. What it *can* do is give you someone to face the hurt with.

FLIRTING

Normies tend to be more subtle with their compliments, while autistics are more direct. Normies sometimes avoid eye contact when they are nervous or make unusually strong eye contact when they are excited, while autistics often avoid eye contact by default or make uncomfortably direct eye contact as an attempt to mask. Normies will sometimes get awkward when they are nervous, while many autistics are perceived as awkward all of the time. Because of this, some people think autistics are flirting when they're actually just being themselves. And autistics might not even notice when normies are flirting with them for the same reason. When a normie nervously plays with their hair, tells someone they're beautiful, and looks deep in their eyes, they're probably flirting. For an autistic, that might just be a normal conversation. There's no magic way to avoid these misunderstandings, but knowing that they exist might help you avoid them, or at least explain yourself if you find yourself in one.

DEALING WITH REJECTION

- **No means no.** If someone says they don't want to date you, kiss you, or even talk to you, that's all there is to it. It might be disappointing, or feel unfair, but access to someone's body and heart is never up for debate. The same goes for you. If you reject someone's advances, they need to respect your boundaries.
- **You don't need someone else to prove your worth.** If someone rejects you, you are as wonderful as you were before they rejected you. If someone dumps you, you are still as valuable as you were when you were dating. If someone doesn't love you, you are as lovable as if they did. Lots of terrible people are in relationships and lots of amazing people are single. Whether you have a significant other or not does not reveal anything about your character or value.
- **Some people are pickles. Some people are cake.** Maybe you love pickles. Maybe you love cake. But do you love pickle cake? Maybe some culinary genius could make a tasty pickle cake, but most people agree that pickles and cake do not go together, even if they like each of them on their own. In life some relationships don't work out. That does not mean you are defective. You might meet people who feel uncomfortable around you from the beginning. Maybe you remind them of someone who hurt them, you communicate in different ways and keep misunderstanding each other, or all your favourite stims annoy them. You might both be amazing, but you don't get along. Or maybe you and the other person simply don't blend. Not every duo makes a good couple. That's okay. As an autistic, you'll end up in a lot of pickles-and-cake situations. It's exhausting, but it doesn't mean you are bad, broken, or low-value. You're just the cake to their pickle.

RELATIONSHIPS AND SAFETY

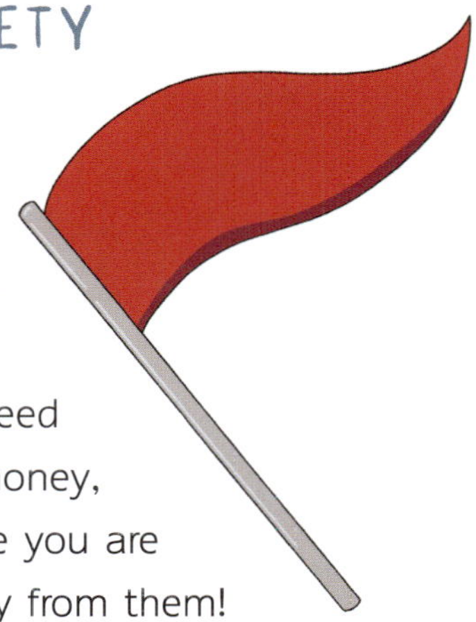

- Remember that as an autistic person, you are vulnerable. That does not mean you are childish, immature, or not ready for love – it means that people might try to take advantage of you. If someone you're in a relationship with tries to convince you that they need control over your life (like demanding access to your money, deciding who you are allowed to talk to, limiting where you are allowed to go, or going through your phone), get away from them! It's okay if you need help managing your money, making daily decisions, and communicating with people, and it can be really sweet when a romantic partner shows that support; however, if someone starts demanding control of those things rather than offering help when you need it, they are not to be trusted.
- Another way autistic people can be vulnerable in relationships is feeling desperate for acceptance. Often we have spent our whole lives trying to change ourselves to be 'good enough'. Finally, being loved for who we are is the best feeling in the world. Remember that there are lots of people who will treat you decently. You may not have found them yet, which can feel heart-wrenching, but don't let anyone try to convince you that they are the only one who will treat you well. That simply is not true. Someone who really loves you will see you as a gift to the world.
- As autistics we often spend our whole lives confused about what is expected of us. We may live in a constant limbo of ignoring what makes us feel safe and comfortable in order to make other people like us. We might even experience teachers, family members, or medical professionals touching us to control us, get our attention, punish us, or stop us from doing something. We are used to being touched in ways we don't like, forced to do things that make us feel uncomfortable, and told that unspoken social rules should control our behaviour. One way predators or other toxic people operate is by convincing their victims that something

is normal when it's not. They might say that touching you in a certain way is normal or that you owe them something because they were nice to you. You do not owe anyone access to your body. You do not owe anyone a romantic relationship. You do not owe anyone your heart. Under no circumstances do you have to give someone access to you – physically or emotionally. If someone doesn't respect your boundaries, you also have a right to defend yourself, through physical self-defence if necessary.

- It is never your fault if someone assaults you. If this does ever happen to you, you have a right to talk about it with people you trust and the police. You may be vulnerable, but that does *not* mean that being assaulted is your fault. If you have been assaulted, we strongly recommend reaching out to a therapist for support.

- If you cannot safely say no to someone's request to access your body, it's not a real choice. Somebody who truly cares about you will respect your right to refuse and will not give you any negative consequences for refusing, including being angry with you or scolding you. This is not only for your body; it applies to any boundary you set.

AUTISM AND RELATIONSHIPS

As an autistic person, is it harder to make friends or find significant others? Have you struggled with rejection or miscommunication? Have the people in your life been willing to accommodate your autism? What do you think you need in your most important relationships?

SCRIPTS

Have you ever wished that real life had video game dialogue and when someone spoke to you, four dialogue options to choose from would pop up in front of you? Well, good news! Neurotypical conversation actually does work that way!

In conversation, neurotypicals follow scripts. They have predetermined, widely agreed-upon lines that they recite to each other, each person playing whichever part is required of them in the moment. A script looks like this:

Neurotypical A: Hey, B!
Neurotypical B: Hey, A! How's it going?
A: Hanging in there. How about you?
B: Doin' all right!

This script is so ingrained it's practically built into a neurotypical person's bones. They know the diction, tone, cadence, and rhythm. From the outside it all seems pleasant and polite. But do A and B like each other? We have no idea. Are both of them actually doing well? B has adopted a relaxed and informal tone that suggests that yes, they are, but A's response, 'Hanging in there', can mean anything from 'It's the end of the day and it hasn't been bad but I'm looking forward to five o'clock' to 'This job genuinely makes me want to die'. If they actually said either of those though, it would disrupt the script and take the conversation in a direction they might not both be ready for.

When an autistic interprets these scripts literally and responds honestly, it can throw neurotypicals off. The neurotypical is now frantically riffling through their mental notecards for something to say that will put the conversation back into comfortable territory. The problem is that scripts are not really meant for heavier topics.

Neurotypicals often get frustrated with autistics for deviating from the script because they don't like feeling flustered and having to improvise. It makes them feel nervous, off-kilter, put on the spot. Is it logical to be upset with a person over this? No, but it's not logical for autistic people to be so on edge in social situations either. Just as we like our routines, neurotypicals like their scripts.

And the fact that these scripts exist? This is a good thing for us. It means we can learn to talk like them, because following the script is predictable and will get approval across the board. If we learn these scripts and when to use them, we can effectively 'speak neurotypical'. We can study all the possible responses to simple questions and all the acceptable questions to ask in turn, and learn both parts and play both parts. We can do it. We just need to learn in *our* way, not in theirs.

STARTING A SOCIAL CONVERSATION

A: Hey! All conversations start when one person captures the other's attention. The goal of a greeting is to acknowledge the other person's presence in a friendly way.
B: Hi! How are you? Sometimes people say 'How are you?' as a polite greeting without actually wanting a response. They aren't trying to be rude. That's just the script. A good way to tell if someone really wants you to respond is to see if they stop what they are doing, look at you for an answer, or wait for your response. If someone is passing by you and doesn't break their stride, just respond, 'Fine; how are you?' If they actually seem to want a response, tell them how you are, but briefly and gently. Having a conversation with a normie is a lot like taking a shower – you have to wait for it to warm up before jumping in.
A: I'm good!/I'm doing all right./Just doing my thing./Rough, but I'll survive. Since the conversation hasn't warmed up yet, you don't want to share any emotionally heavy details, but it's okay to be honest if you're not doing well. If you mention that you're doing poorly this early in the conversation, be generic and pair it with something dismissive like '. . . but I'll get through' or '. . . but that's life', so that the normie doesn't read subtext there that you want them to 'fix' your bad situation right off the bat.
B: That's great!/That's too bad./What have you been up to? When normies talk to each other, they frequently acknowledge what the other person has said. Sometimes this can feel like empty chatter to autistics, but normies feel most comfortable in a conversation when people take turns being 'it,' like a game of tag. Little phrases like 'That's great' or 'That's too bad' don't just let normies know that you're paying attention and that you care; they keep the rhythm of the conversation going. Autistic conversations tend to be more like a relay race: one person goes for a bit, then the other. Normies prefer more of a back-and-forth. The next bit, 'What have you been up to?', demonstrates that this person wants to hear more about the other person, even if they don't have anything to say. They're essentially saying, 'I care. Now it's your turn again.'

A: Oh, you know, just busy with the kids (or some other snippet of information)! How have *you* been? The conversation still hasn't warmed up much, so the response is still brief and not too serious. Now they're giving the other person a turn to share a little bit about themself.

B: I bet. My little niece wears me out and I don't even have to put her to bed (or some other brief response to their snippet of information)! I'm doing fine! Responding to the snippet of information shows interest and encourages further responses. Notice how B used the opportunity to add a little bit about themself into the conversation, this time without an invitation. The conversation is slowly warming up. Each person is adding to the conversation in small responses, one at a time, and the more each shares, the more the other person is open to sharing. It might help to think of normie conversation like a nice meal out at a restaurant. You start with drinks, then appetisers, then the main course, and you finish with dessert. Drinks are like the greetings: they're simple, usually sweet, and help people relax. The appetisers are like small talk: they're fun, easy, and shared with the group. The main course is like serious conversation: everyone has their own thing, and it might be heavy, or light, or complicated, or strange, and that's okay. And dessert is like a goodbye. End with something sweet, even if it's just 'I hope things get better for you.'

ORDERING FOOD

A: Hello. I'd like to place an order, please. The goal here is to capture the attention of the worker and state your intended purpose. There's no need for small talk because this is not a social conversation. Even if the other person makes small talk anyway, you don't need to say much. Just acknowledge what they said, maybe ask them how they're doing, and then move to the reason you're there.

B: Sure. What can I get you? You have successfully captured their attention and they are confirming that it is, in fact, your turn to order.

A: Can you tell me what's in the soup of the day? You can skip right to ordering if you want, but you are allowed to ask any questions you have first.

B: That's our potato broccoli soup. It has potatoes, broccoli, cheese, cream, and pepper. Restaurant employees don't usually tell you every ingredient in a dish. They aren't trying to deceive you; they just think you want a general idea of what it tastes like. If you need a more specific description, you can ask them if they have a full ingredients list you can see.

A: Okay. I'll have the cheeseburger. You don't have to explain why you chose one dish over another. This is your chance to give the necessary information on the dish you want. If you need help remembering what to say when you order, just think 'NASA'. Normally NASA stands for National Aeronautics and Space Administration, but here it stands for 'Name, Add or Subtract, Special Requests, and Allergies and Dietary Restrictions'. Start an order by giving the *name* of the dish you want. Then clarify what you want *added* to the dish ('I would like extra cheese, please') and/or what you want *subtracted* from the dish ('Can you make it without onions?'). Then give any *special requests* ('May I have the pickles on the side?'). Finish off by informing your server of any *allergies and dietary restrictions* you have. This is for your safety. If you just don't want the bread, a few crumbs won't hurt you. If you are allergic to the bread, a few crumbs could make you seriously ill and the restaurant wants to know that.

B: That comes with fries or salad. Which would you like? This is the server's chance to ask clarifying questions. Blunt, direct answers are best here. Don't overthink it.

A: Fries.

B: Okay. Is that all for you today? This is a standard polite way of asking if you have more information to give that is relevant. If you haven't gone through your NASA yet, now is your chance. If they skip this and go straight to the price, you are welcome to stop them and provide that information anyway. You won't get in trouble.

A: Oh, I'd like a drink. If you are at a fast-food restaurant, repeat NASA as necessary until you have ordered all the items you want. If you are at a sit-down restaurant, place your order for drinks, any appetisers, and your main course at one time and you will have the chance to order more items, like dessert, later.

B: Got it. Altogether that will be [price]. Receiving the price means you are concluding your transaction and you both have all the relevant information. At a fast-food restaurant, this comes right away. If you are at a sit-down restaurant, the bill will come at the end, once you've finished your meal.

A: Okay. *pays*

B: *hands you the receipt* Thank you. Have a nice day! Servers are usually required to give you the receipt, although sometimes there isn't one or you can have it emailed or texted to you. They might also ask if you want to leave a tip. You may like to leave a tip if you had an exceptional experience, but it's generally not expected in Australia. If you would like to tip, leave an extra 15 per cent to 20 per cent of what your meal costs.

A: You too! You can also say thank you or give any polite farewell. It is not required of you, but it's nice.

MAKING AN APPOINTMENT

B: This is Dr. X's office/X hair salon/X location. They say this to make sure you've called the right place.

A: Hi. I'd like to make an appointment, please. Get right to the point. No need for small talk. You can also clarify who specifically you want to make the appointment with, if there are multiple professionals working in this location and you know you want to see a specific person or type of practitioner.

B: For what purpose?/What do you want done?/What kind of appointment do you want? Different kinds of appointments take different amounts of time and require different people to complete them. The person you're speaking with will need to know your purpose so they can schedule you at the right time.

A: I need to have my annual physical./I want to have my roots coloured./My car is making a weird sound. Give a very brief description of what you need. The person who answers the phone only needs basic information to give to the person you're going to see.

B: Okay. Our next available appointment is [date and time]. They may ask instead when you want to make the appointment.

A: Do you have anything in the afternoon? If you can only do certain days or times, now is the time to tell the person. You are allowed to ask for a different time than what they offer. Try to suggest a category (like Tuesdays, or mornings) rather than a specific slot you want (like Tuesday morning at 8:30).

B: Yes. I have [date and time].

A: That will work.

B: And your name?

A: [Give your name. For a doctor's appointment, make sure it is your full name.]

B: Okay. I have you down for [date and time]. They are confirming that you heard each other correctly. Make sure they say the date and time you agreed upon.

A: Thank you!

B: Have a nice day. Bye-bye. *hangs up* It is typical of people who make appointments to be brief and seem curt. It is not a reflection of you; they are very busy.

ASKING FOR HELP IN A STORE

A: Excuse me, do you work here? If you're not sure and don't want to offend someone, you can ask this.

B: Yes, I do! How can I help you? Retail workers are encouraged to have good customer service skills and are likely to be helpful.

A: I'm looking for [whatever you need]. No need for small talk.

B: Certainly. That would be in aisle seven. Let me show you. Sometimes the worker will just give you the aisle number. Sometimes they will tell you the aisle and which side the item is on or what it's next to. In this scenario they are walking you to the product.

A: Oh, thank you!

B: Here it is! Can I help you with anything else? They are offering you a chance to ask for a specific brand or for any other items you are missing, or to ask general questions like 'How late are you open?' or 'Where is the bathroom?'

A: No, that's great. Thank you!

B: Of course. Have a nice day!

ASKING FOR DIRECTIONS

A: Excuse me. Do you know where City Park is? Not only is no small talk needed, but it's best to get right to the point. Sometimes people approaching strangers in public are scam artists or asking for money, especially in big cities, so some people might not want to talk to you if you don't clarify what you need right away. They may even be rude or refuse to answer you. If so just say you're sorry for bothering them, walk away, and ask someone else. It's not worth starting an argument over.

B: Of course. It's one block down.

A: Thank you. The signs pointed that way, but I can't find the entrance. This is your chance to get more detailed instructions if you need them.

B: It's tricky to find! The easiest way to get to the entrance is to head down that way and take the steps. Then it'll be straight up ahead, past the construction. If you're the one giving the directions, give clear, specific directions with landmarks.

A: Thank you. That helps!

B: My pleasure.

COMPLIMENTS

Unsolicited compliments (e.g., to a stranger you are not already having a conversation with) might make someone uncomfortable, especially if you're a man giving them to a woman. It is still fine to give them; just try to be casual, so that the other person doesn't feel pressured to give you anything in return. Be on the lookout for things to compliment in people. It's good for your mental health to see the best in people! The more professional a setting is, the better it is to give compliments related to the work. Saying someone has great shoes is a good compliment in a casual setting, but when they just presented research that they spent the last six months working on, it's best to compliment the research instead, so they don't think that you are ignoring all the hard work they've put in.

A: I love your outfit! It looks so nice! This is a good compliment because it recognises the effort someone has made in creating an outfit and shows you have a good impression of them.

B: Thanks! The dress was on sale, and I had a lot of fun putting it all together. It is common to offer a fun fact about an item when it is complimented. You can also take this opportunity to brag a little bit ('I made it myself!') or offer a generic piece of advice in case the other person wants to emulate you, like how they can get the thing too ('I got it at Macy's!').

A: I like your septum ring! Complimenting individual aspects of people's appearances is usually fine, as long as you stay away from their body. While you could be okay with certain comments on someone's body, for example saying someone has 'beautiful eyes' can be lighthearted and kind, other comments on a person's body can come across as creepy, such as saying someone has a 'beautiful bust'. Intentional choices in appearance, like tattoos, piercings, outfits, and hair, are usually the safest choices.

B: Thanks. B is giving the bare minimum response here, which is fine.

A: I've been thinking about getting one. Did it hurt to get yours? A is giving the conversation a chance to continue.

B: Oh, not at all. It hurt less than getting my ears pierced. You just have to take really good care of it. I went to this great piercing studio . . . At least for now, B is happy to keep the conversation going on this subject.

SMALL TALK

Small talk might seem inane, but it serves an important purpose. It puts people at ease, gives them a sense of what kind of person you are, and keeps a conversation running smoothly in situations where a conversation is expected, required, or simply preferable to silence. If successful, it can certainly lead to deeper, more personal talk. If you want to keep a lighthearted conversation going with someone, there are plenty of things to talk about. Some examples of small talk scripts are:

A: What did you think of [culturally relevant piece of media such as the Grammys, the Super Bowl, a popular TV show, or a newly released movie]?
B: I didn't see it. Was it good?
A: It was excellent! Having been given an invitation to elaborate, you may proceed to give a *short* summary or endorsement. Try not to infodump.
B: I'll have to check that out!

A: The weather has been so awful lately. The weather is always a safe and relevant topic.
B: It really has! It's not usually so nasty in March, is it? Discussing past weather trends is standard.
A: It wasn't like this last year, but this winter has been colder than usual, so I'm not surprised.
B: I hope it clears up this weekend. Discussing the forecast is also standard.
A: I checked the weather forecast and it should!
B: Thank goodness for that!
A: Do you have any pets?
B: Yes. We have a dog.
A: Nice. What kind? This is usually all the prompting people need to gush about their pet. People love talking about their pets.

Asking someone what they do for fun, what they do on weekends, or if they follow a certain sport or team is also great for small talk. People also enjoy complaining about traffic or construction, especially if there's one particularly terrible highway or endless construction project that everyone hates. If they mention a recent purchase, like a car or some furniture, or a recent move, you can discuss that. There are plenty of mundane daily-life things to talk about!

Exiting a conversation is mostly about finding an excuse. Luckily, there are plenty of acceptable ones. You can simply say, 'I have to get going' or 'I gotta go', and the other person will have no choice but to accept it. You can mention an errand you need to run, say you have to get home to a family member or pet, say you have to catch a bus, or just comment about how late it's getting. All of these are normal and accepted ways to exit a conversation.

Remember, it's not entirely a two-way street. Many autistics struggle significantly with some of the communication paths that we are expected to follow. Sometimes we cannot fill in the blanks. It's not a matter of not trying hard enough; some types of communication will always be foreign to us! Sometimes the normie is going to have to make the bigger sacrifice in communication because that's the only way. However, that doesn't mean autistics can't adapt our communication either. Even if you only know how to be blunt, you can still bluntly say things like 'Just to be clear, I'm not mad at you' and 'I'm being direct, but it doesn't mean I'm upset'. It throws people off because it's not in the script they've always followed, but it helps.

Furthermore, just because you know a script doesn't mean it will be easy for you to follow it. You have a monotropic brain, and if your brain registers 'thinking about the script' as a different task from 'having a conversation' then it will be difficult for you to do both at once. It also may be high effort for you to follow the script, at least at first. Give yourself grace.

CONCLUSION

When we learned we were autistic, we found a sprawling, confused web of anecdotal evidence, conflicting viewpoints, and bits and pieces of disconnected fact. But what we needed was exactly what is in your hands now: a field guide for everything autism, especially how to live with it. What autism is, or is not, can be hard to define, and though we have tried to answer these questions, we cannot give a definite answer, because none exists. But life with autism? That, we can help with.

As the subtitle says, this book is by no means definitive. The more we learn about the human brain, neurotypes, and genetics, the more we will likely discover about autism, and this book will be rendered outdated and obsolete. Both of us welcome the day this happens, because it means that progress has been made, and science's understanding of autism is greater than it was.

But what will not change as we learn more is the way people diagnosed with autism, now, in the present day, might be struggling. Right now, autistics are facing threats and discrimination across the world. Right now, we don't need a genetic marker for autism, or a neural map of the autistic brain. Instead, we need community, education, support, and acceptance. We need to join together, share resources, and support one another.

We can't fix it all with just this book. But by putting this guide in your hands, we hope we can help, just a little.

What's most important to us, in the end, is not any one fact or tip. It is how this book makes you feel. We want to give you the reassurance that you are not broken, you are not bad, and you are not alone.

WHAT'S NEXT?

Elora: We haven't figured it out yet. This is a book to help people like us, not a roadmap to a perfect life. During the years we spent writing this book, at one point I got so stressed I threw up blood. Seriously. I sometimes shut down to the point where I just can't work for weeks. I lose motivation to talk to anyone and let friendships fizzle out. I spiral into dark places, so fast. But I have faith. Faith that this is the beginning, not the end. We've written our book. Now it's someone else's turn. I hope we can help other people navigate the struggles we've managed to survive. I hope they can help us navigate ours as well. Autistics don't need a messiah to lead everyone into the sun. We need each other. And for the first time in history, we can find each other.

Cat: My original vision for this book was something that I thought already existed: education about autism. 'So you've been diagnosed as autistic. Now what?' But I looked and couldn't find anything. When I posted about my autistic experience with my little fish cartoons, people looked to me as if *I* was a source of knowledge. And I saw a need for this sort of thing, something I badly, badly needed. Maybe I struggled to learn it all, but with a bit of luck, others won't have to.

Elora: One of my biggest fears writing this book is that we wouldn't make something good enough because it couldn't be perfect. But we knew from the start that this book would not be perfect! The question is, is it enough?

Cat: 'The perfect is the enemy of the good,' as they say. We have become very good at picking apart every little detail of something and criticising it, often in bad faith, with no intention of helping

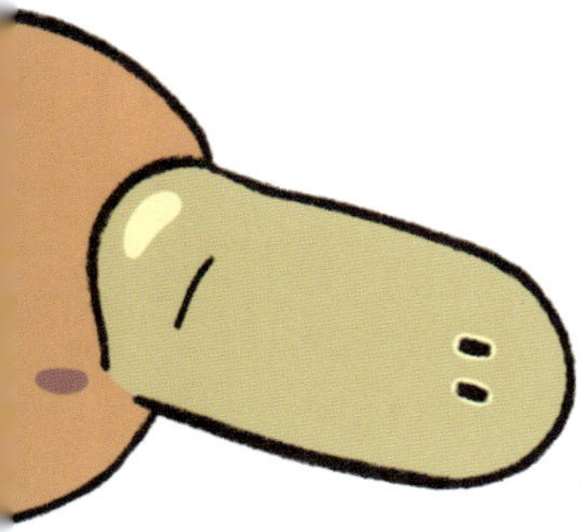

anyone do better. But people still create. They still put themselves out there. You have to. It's what makes us human: to put our flawed and messy selves in front of other people and say, 'Here I am! Mistakes and all. Being a work in progress is okay.' We've said several times that we hope we are one day proven wrong on all counts in this book. For my kids' sake, I hope this book is ancient and irrelevant by the time they're old enough to need it. I hope we live in a more understanding world where it's not necessary. But until then, we all need something, because having nothing is just so tough. I always think about my kids with these things. What do they need? What would they want? What can I do to help them? What did I want in their position? And this is it.

Elora: When I was in college I intervened in some other people's mental health crises. I might have saved some lives. The reason I was able to do it was because I was open and honest about my issues, leading other people to be open about theirs. The school I went to had a very toxic culture around mental health. Putting myself out there felt like volunteering as a target. But I did it because I wanted to help others, and I did. I helped a lot of people. I'm realising that being vulnerable is not a relinquishment of your power. It is stepping into the power you already have, the kind of power that comes from pain, and can only be awakened with courage.

Cat: Personally I think real vulnerability is much braver than tearing people down for showing it.

We have more in common than we do differences. If we can agree on the big things – that people deserve respect and support, for example – then it's worth having a reasonable discussion about the best way to go about that. You can study all the psychology and sociology in the world, but what you did – offering real connection – is what really helps people. That's what we all want: safety, connection, and support. There's real power in helping someone feel less alone, and seeing and loving them for who they really are. It's not easy. But it's worth doing.

Elora: And that's what we have done. No matter how this book is received, I'm really proud of us.

NOTES

1 K. Shaw, A., S. Williams, M. E. Patrick, et al., 'Prevalence and Early Identification of Autism Spectrum Disorder Among Children Aged 4 and 8 Years — Autism and Developmental Disabilities Monitoring Network, 16 Sites, United States, 2022,' *Morbidity and Mortality Weekly Report: Surveillance Summaries*, 74, no. 2 (April 2025): 1–22, http://dx.doi.org/10.15585/mmwr.ss7402a1.

2 Robert T. Muller, 'Why Women with Autism Are So Often Misdiagnosed,' *Psychology Today*, May 2, 2019, https://www.psychologytoday.com/intl/blog/talking-about-trauma/201905/why-women-with-autism-are-so-often-misdiagnosed.

3 Casey Rentz, 'Black and Latino Children Are Often Overlooked When It Comes to Autism,' NPR (website), March 19, 2018, https://www.npr.org/sections/health-shots/2018/03/19/587249339/black-and-latino-children-are-often-overlooked-when-it-comes-to-autism.

4 Camilla Gesi, Giovanni Migliarese, Sara Torriero, Martina Capellazzi, Anna Caterina Omboni, Giancarlo Cerveri, and Claudio Mencacci, 'Gender Differences in Misdiagnosis and Delayed Diagnosis among Adults with Autism Spectrum Disorder with No Language or Intellectual Disability,' *Brain Sciences* 11, no.7 (July 2021), https://pmc.ncbi.nlm.nih.gov/articles/PMC8306851/.

5 Brandon S. Aylward, Diana E. Gal-Szabo, and Sharief Taraman, 'Racial, Ethnic, and Sociodemographic Disparities in Diagnosis of Children with Autism Spectrum Disorder,' *Journal of Developmental and Behavioral Pediatrics: JDBP*, September 10, 2021, https://pmc.ncbi.nlm.nih.gov/articles/PMC8500365/.

6 Osagie K. Obasogie, 'Legacies of Eugenics: An Introduction.' *Los Angeles Review of Books*, April 17, 2024, https://lareviewofbooks.org/article/legacies-of-eugenics-an-introduction/.

7 Dinah Murray, Mike Lesser, and Wenn Lawson, 'Attention, Monotropism, and the Diagnostic Criteria for Autism,' *autism* 90, no. 2 (2005), https://journals.sagepub.com/doi/pdf/10.1177/1362361305051398.

8 Bozena Zawisz, 'What Is Monotropism?' *Psychology Today* (blog), March 31, 2023, https://www.psychologytoday.com/us/blog/nurturing-self-esteem-in-autistic-children/202303/what-is-monotropism.

9 Hannah Rapaport, Hayley Clapham, Jon Adams, and Wenn Lawson, '"In a State of Flow": A Qualitative Examination of Autistic Adults' Phenomenological Experiences of Task Immersion,' *Autism in Adulthood* 6, no. 3 (December 2023), https://www.researchgate.net/profile/Wenn-Lawson-2/publication/376693155_In_a_State_of_Flow_A_Qualitative_Examination_of_Autistic_Adults.

10 Ashley Bell, 'Is Autism Genetic?' UCLA Medical School (website), April 10, 2004, https://medschool.ucla.edu/news-article/is-autism-genetic.

11 Lawrence Brody, 'Gene Expression.' NIH National Human Genome Research Institute (website), September 9, 2025, https://www.genome.gov/genetics-glossary/Gene-Expression.

12 Dae-Wook Kang, James B. Adams, Devon M. Coleman, et al., 'Long-term benefit of Microbiota Transfer Therapy on autism symptoms and gut microbiota,' *Scientific Reports* 9 (2019), https://doi.org/10.1038/s41598-019-42183-0.

13 J. Leask, A. Leask, and Natalie Silove, 'Evidence for Autism in Folklore?' *Archives of Disease in Childhood* 90, no. 3 (February 2005): 271, https://doi.org/10.1136/adc.2003.044958.

14 'Euthanasia Program and Aktion T4,' United States Holocaust Memorial Museum (website), October 7, 2020, https://encyclopedia.ushmm.org/content/en/article/euthanasia-program.

15 *Last Week Tonight with John Oliver*, season 8, episode 10, 'Vaccines,' written by Jonathan Appel, et al, directed by Paul Pennolio and Christopher Werner, aired May 2, 2021, on HBO.

16 Harriet Hall, 'Vaccines & Autism: A Deadly Manufactroversy.' *Skeptic Magazine*, January 1, 2009, https://www.skepdoc.info/vaccines-autism-a-deadly-manufactroversy/.

17 *Last Week Tonight with John Oliver*, season 11, episode 19, 'RFK Jr.,' directed by Paul Pennolio, aired August 4, 2024, on HBO.

18 'Extraordinary Minds: The Link between Savantism and Autism,' *The Transmitter*, January 13, 2016, https://www.thetransmitter.org/spectrum/extraordinary-minds-the-link-between-savantism-and-autism/.

19 Katie Rose Guest Pryal, 'The Barriers to an Adult Diagnosis of Autism,' *Psychology Today*, November 25, 2023, reviewed by Ray Parker, https://www.psychologytoday.com/us/blog/living-neurodivergence/202311/the-barriers-to-an-adult-diagnosis-of-autism.

20 Marianna Cerini, 'A Brief History of the Halloween Costume,' CNN (website), October 25, 2020, https://edition.cnn.com/style/article/history-of-halloween-costumes/index.html.

21 Laura Hull, Lily Levy, Meng-Chuan Lai, K. V. Petrides, Simon Baron-Cohen, Carrie Allison, Paula Smith, and Will Mandy. 2021. 'Is Social Camouflaging Associated with Anxiety and Depression in Autistic Adults?' *Molecular Autism* 12(1), 13 (February 2021), https://www.ncbi.nlm.nih.gov/pmc/articles/PMC7885456/.

22 S. A. Cassidy, K. Gould, E. Townsend, M. Pelton, A. E. Robertson, and J. Rodgers, 'Is Camouflaging Autistic Traits Associated with Suicidal Thoughts and Behaviours? Expanding the Interpersonal Psychological Theory of Suicide in an Undergraduate Student Sample,' *Journal of Autism and Developmental Disorders* 50, no. 10 (October 2020), https://pubmed.ncbi.nlm.nih.gov/31820344/; Sarah Cassidy, Eilidh McLaughlin, Ross McGranaghan, Miriam Pelton, Róisín O'Connor, and Jane Rodgers. 2023. 'Is Camouflaging Autistic Traits Associated with Defeat, Entrapment, and Lifetime Suicidal Thoughts? Expanding the Integrated Motivational Volitional Model of Suicide.' *Suicide and Life-Threatening Behavior* 53, no.4 (May 2023): 572–85. https://doi.org/10.1111/sltb.12965.

23 Toni Fitzgerald, 'How Do "The Big Bang Theory" Series Finale Ratings Rank All Time?' *Forbes*, May 17, 2019. https://www.forbes.com/sites/tonifitzgerald/2019/05/17/how-does-the-big-bang-theory-series-finale-ratings-rank-all-time/.

24 H. Obaydi and B. K. Puri, 'Prevalence of Premenstrual Syndrome in Autism: A Prospective Observer-Rated Study,' *Journal of International Medical Research* 36, no. 2 (March 2008): 268–72, https://doi.org/10.1177/147323000803600208

25 Meara Withe, 'Autism and PTSD: Understanding the Link,' *Medical News Today*, February 9, 2024, reviewed by Dannell Roberts, https://www.medicalnewstoday.com/articles/autism-and-ptsd#summary.

26 L. McLellan, T. L. More, and B. Z. Lee, 'Autism Spectrum Disorders and PTSD: Exploring the Co-Occurrence,' *Journal of Intellectual Disabilities* 18, no. 4 (September 2014): 389–399, https://doi.org/10.1080/09687599.2014.949625.

27 Rob Reiner, dir. *The Princess Bride*. Twentieth Century Fox, 1987.

28 Emre Ocak, Rebecca S. Eshraghi, Ali Danesh, et al., 'Central Auditory Processing Disorders in Individuals with Autism Spectrum Disorders,' *Balkan Medical Journal* 35, no. 5 (2018): 367-372, doi:10.4274/balkanmedj.2018.0853

29 'Auditory Processing Disorder,' Cleveland Clinic (website), https://my.clevelandclinic.org/health/diseases/24938-auditory-processing-disorder. Accessed November 20, 2025; Mayo Clinic Staff, 'Auditory Processing Disorder Diagnosis and Treatment.' Mayo Clinic (website), September 30, 2023, https://www.mayoclinic.org/diseases-conditions/auditory-processing-disorder/diagnosis-treatment/drc-20555277. Accessed November 20, 2025.

30 Karen Evans and Katherine Sanchez, 'Let's Give Them Something to Gestalt About: A Review of Gestalt Language Processing,' *The Informed SLP*, February 6, 2022, https://www.theinformedslp.com/review/let-s-give-them-something-to-gestalt-about.

31 Jennifer Gerlach, 'Is It Meltdown, or a Mindstorm?' *Psychology Today*, February 29, 2024, https://www.psychologytoday.com/us/blog/beyond-mental-health/202402/meltdown-or-mindstorm.

32 'All About Autistic Meltdowns: A Guide for Allies,' *Reframing Autism* (website), February 1, 2024, https://reframingautism.org.au/all-about-autistic-meltdowns-a-guide-for-allies/.

33 Justin James Kennedy, 'The Energetic Odyssey of the Brain,' *Psychology Today*, December 3, 2023, https://www.psychologytoday.com/us/blog/brain-reboot/202311/the-energetic-odyssey-of-the-brain?msockid=2a6610cecfc36b5137e206aace4d6a36.

34 Diarmuid Verrier, Stephen Connolly, and Lesley Kimber, 'Autism and Empathy,' *National Autistic Society*, January 17, 2024, https://www.autism.org.uk/advice-and-guidance/professional-practice/autism-and-empathy.

35 Damian Milton, 'The Double Empathy Problem,' *National Autistic Society*, March 2, 2018, https://www.autism.org.uk/advice-and-guidance/professional-practice/double-empathy.

36 Jill Anderson, 'The Effect of Spanking on the Brain,' *Harvard Graduate School of Education* (website), April 13, 2021, https://www.gse.harvard.edu/ideas/usable-knowledge/21/04/effect-spanking-brain.

37 Peg Streep, 'Why Verbal Abuse Can Do So Much Damage,' *Psychology Today*, December 8, 2020, https://www.psychologytoday.com/us/blog/tech-support/202012/why-verbal-abuse-can-do-so-much-damage.

38 Shanta R. Dube, Elizabeth T. Li, Guilherme Fiorini, Caleb Lin, Nikita Singh, Kumayl Khamisa, Jennifer McGowan, Peter Fonagy, 'Childhood Verbal Abuse as a Child Maltreatment Subtype: A Systematic Review of the Current Evidence,' *Child Abuse & Neglect* 144 (October 2023), https://doi.org/10.1016/j.chiabu.2023.106394.

39 Emily Edlynn, 'The Truth About Parents Who Yell at Kids,' *Psychology Today*, January 26, 2024, https://www.psychologytoday.com/us/blog/parenting-is-not-a-fad/202401/the-truth-about-yelling.

40 Tyler J. VanderWeele, 'How Parental Love Impacts Flourishing Later in Life,' *Psychology Today*, June 28 2019, https://www.psychologytoday.com/us/blog/human-flourishing/201906/how-parental-love-impacts-flourishing-later-in-life.

41 Jared Streatfeild, Josiah Hickson, S. Bryn Austin, et al., 'Social and Economic Cost of Eating Disorders in the United States: Evidence to Inform Policy Action,' *The International Journal of Eating Disorders*, 54 no. 5 (March 2021): 851–868, https://doi.org/10.1002/eat.23486.

42 Alina Petre, 'What Do Food Cravings Mean? Facts and Myths, Explained.' *Healthline*, July 20, 2023, reviewed by Amy Richter, https://www.healthline.com/nutrition/craving-meanings.

43 Evelyn Tribole and Elyse Resch, *Intuitive Eating: A Revolutionary Anti-Diet Approach* (New York: St. Martin's Essentials, 2020).

44 R. George and M. A. Stokes, 'Sexual Orientation in Autism Spectrum Disorder,' Autism Research 11, no. 1 (November 2017): 133–41, https://doi.org/10.1002/aur.1892; John F. Strang, Lauren Kenworthy, Aleksandra Dominska, Jennifer Sokoloff, Laura E. Kenealy, Madison Berl, Karin Walsh, et al., 'Increased Gender Variance in Autism Spectrum Disorders and Attention Deficit Hyperactivity Disorder,' Archives of Sexual Behavior 43, no. 8 (March 2014): 1525–33, https://doi.org/10.1007/s10508-014-0285-3.

45 R. George and M. A. Stokes, 'Sexual Orientation in Autism Spectrum Disorder,' Autism Research 11, no. 1 (November 2017): 133–41, https://doi.org/10.1002/aur.1892; John F. Strang, Lauren Kenworthy, Aleksandra Dominska, Jennifer Sokoloff, Laura E. Kenealy, Madison Berl, Karin Walsh, et al., 'Increased Gender Variance in Autism Spectrum Disorders and Attention Deficit Hyperactivity Disorder,' Archives of Sexual Behavior 43, no. 8 (March 2014): 1525–33, https://doi.org/10.1007/s10508-014-0285-3.

ACKNOWLEDGEMENTS

Elora: This book could not have been possible without many people, first and foremost my wonderful coauthor, Cat. She somehow managed to write this book while also parenting a child, which I find astonishing. She even made a second one from scratch, bones and all, during the process. Thank you also to our editors, Drew and Julia, who took a chance on two green writers and showed them the ropes, kindly and patiently. Thank you for believing in us. Thank you to my partner, Ezri, for pulling me back from the brink of insanity time and time again. I am so honoured that this book took up so much of my life, yet you still wanted to be a part of it, despite my constant distraction. Thank you to my family for tolerating my constant outbursts of writer's frustration at inopportune times, and for supporting me emotionally (and financially) when my disability limits my ability to support myself. Thank you to my friends, too many to count, for seeing me as a real, capable, wonderful person, when imposter syndrome sends me spiralling. Thank you to my followers online – you see something worth loving in me, and I will never stop trying to make you see that in yourselves. Thank you to the autism community, for coming together so quickly after thousands of years of autistic isolation. You saved me. I hope that this book is something worthy of such a brave group of people. Thank you to my awful Christian college for forcing me to become a disability rights activist out of sheer necessity. I came for a degree but left with a purpose. Most of all, thank you to God, who made me autistic. I really appreciate it, even if the society around me doesn't. Finally, thank you to me, for checking myself into a psych ward all those years ago instead of killing myself. That was a good call.

Cat: It is often extremely difficult for me to find the good in being autistic when so many people don't. When so much of my greatest traumas come from discrimination or misunderstandings, when the people around me repeatedly tell me I am flawed and 'difficult', and when the tiny handful of people who truly care for me are neurodivergent also. It's hard to say that I'm glad I'm autistic, that I'm grateful for it, or even to admit that I am to people I don't trust. But I cannot change who I am (Lord knows I've tried) and having the chance to write about what's great about being me is an opportunity I never expected to have. The process of writing this – and working with my amazing coauthor, Elora – has helped me to know and love myself, and I hope it goes on to help others do the same. So thank you to Elora, for putting in countless hours of painstaking work, for picking up the slack whenever I lost momentum, and for convincing me to use a gentler way when my natural instinct takes more of a sledgehammer approach. Thank you to our agent, Zeynep Sen, and to the team at Apollo for making it all possible. Thank you to all the magnificent neurodivergent folks who will spread the word about this book and start discussions in our community, and thank you to all the readers who give it a chance. And a special thanks to my family: my parents, who taught me what unconditional love and support looks like; my husband, who is the reason I know I'm autistic, the reason I ever considered it a good thing, and who is more of a role model to me than I think he knows; and to my children, who give me the motivation to build a better world.

This edition published in 2026 by Hardie Grant Books, an imprint of Hardie Grant Publishing
First published in 2026 by Apollo Publishers

Hardie Grant Books (Melbourne)
Wurundjeri Country
Level 11, 36 Wellington Street
Collingwood, Victoria 3066

Hardie Grant North America
2912 Telegraph Ave
Berkeley, California 94705

hardiegrant.com/books

NATIONAL LIBRARY OF AUSTRALIA
A catalogue record for this book is available from the National Library of Australia

The Actually Autistic Guide
ISBN 978 1 76145 281 9

10 9 8 7 6 5 4 3 2 1

Designer: Maeve Norton
Editor: Drew Anderla

Colour reproduction by Splitting Image Colour Studio

Printed in China by Leo Paper Products LTD.

MIX
Paper | Supporting responsible forestry
FSC® C020056
FSC
www.fsc.org

The paper this book is printed on is from FSC®-certified forests and other sources. FSC® promotes environmentally responsible, socially beneficial and economically viable management of the world's forests.